Flying, Fighting & Reflection

Flying, Fighting & Reflection

Peter Jacobs

Foreword by

Air Chief Marshal Sir Michael Graydon, GCB, CBE

Greenhill Books

Flying, Fighting & Reflection

First published in 2018 by
Greenhill Books,
c/o Pen & Sword Books Ltd,
47 Church Street, Barnsley,
S. Yorkshire, s70 2AS

www.greenhillbooks.com
contact@greenhillbooks.com

ISBN: 978–1–78438–390–9

CIP data records for this title are available from the British Library

Designed and typeset by Donald Sommerville

Printed and bound in the UK by TJ International Ltd, Padstow

Typeset in 11.5/15.5 pt Adobe Caslon Pro

Contents

Contents

Illustrations

Unless otherwise indicated, all photographs are reproduced by courtesy of Tom Neil and his family.

Black and White Plates

Neil being debriefed after a sortie.

Neil's parents pictured soon after the First World War.

With his father, on holiday around 1928/29.

On his trusted bicycle, around 1929/30.

Neil with a Tiger Moth at Barton airfield in April 1939.

Neil with course colleagues of No. 8 Service Flying Training School at Montrose, 1939.

Neil's personal Hurricane P3616 GN-F.

Pilots of 249 Squadron relax at Boscombe Down. (*via Pat Wells*)

Neil with Squadron Leader John Grandy and Flight Lieutenant Butch Barton.

Combat report of Neil's first confirmed success.

At readiness in Hurricane V7313, Neil's second personal GN-F.

Neil's log book for the period 2–16 September 1940.

Neil during a visit to the Lancashire cotton industry in early 1941.

Portrait photo of Neil, October 1940.

With Ossie Crossey and Tich Palliser in Malta, summer 1941. (*F. Etchells via Tom Neil*)

Taking a well-earned break on a Maltese beach.

Neil leading his section over Ta Kali. (*F. Etchells via Tom Neil*)

The SS *Sydney Star*, which took Neil on the first leg of his homeward
  journey from Malta. (*IWM*)

Neil's personal Spitfire XII of 41 Squadron, EN237 EB-V.

Rex Poynton, one of 41 Squadron's flight commanders.

Marshal of the Royal Air Force Viscount Trenchard talking
  informally to the pilots of 41 Squadron.

Neil's first P-51B Mustang, which he flew while serving with the
  American 100th Fighter Wing.

Spitfire 3W-K pictured at Rennes in August 1944.

Eileen Hampton, pictured as a flight officer in 1944.

Neil and Eileen on their wedding day, 3 June 1945.

No. 4 (Short) Course at the Empire Test Pilots' School, Cranfield,
  January 1946. (*ETPS*)

The classroom at Cranfield, 1946.

A flypast of four Gloster Meteors at Farnborough during the 'RAF
  Display'. (*Crown Copyright*)

Neil and Hurricane LF363 at Bovingdon, 1951.

Above the Suez Canal Zone in a Meteor FR.9 of 208 Squadron.

Neil's certificate for No. 18 Instrument Weather Course, 1947.

Neil pictured at Abu Sueir.

Visit by the Under Secretary of State for Air to Abu Sueir, 1954.
  (*Crown Copyright*)

Neil at the Abu Sueir tennis club.

The Neil family at Abu Sueir in late 1955.

Neil with 208 Squadron pilots. (*Crown Copyright*)

The Neils enjoying a social function.

Telegram congratulating Neil on the award of the Air Force Cross.

Tom Neil photographed by a colleague.

With HRH Prince Harry in 2015.

Colour Plates

'Pilot Officer Tom Neil' by David Pritchard. (*David Pritchard*)

Pilots of 249 Squadron on 21 September 1940.

A 249 Squadron reunion, September 1990. (*Jonny Cracknell*)

Tom and Sir John Grandy. (*Jonny Cracknell*)

Memorabilia from 41 Squadron. (*Author*)

Tom's medals and log book.

'The First of Four on the Fifteenth', by Geoff Nutkins.
(*Geoff Nutkins*)

Programme for the Farnborough display in 1950. (*Author*)

The author with Tom and other veterans.

Tom and Sir Michael Beetham, at a dinner to mark the sixtieth
anniversary of the Battle of Britain. (*RAF*)

Members of the Battle of Britain Fighter Association, with HRH
Prince Charles and HRH the Duchess of Cornwall. (*Battle of
Britain Fighter Association*)

Former members of 249 Squadron, North Weald, 1990.
(*Jonny Cracknell*)

With former Dambuster Johnny Johnson, Bomber Command
Veterans' Day, 2016. (*Jonny Cracknell*)

Hurricane LF363 of the Battle of Britain Memorial Flight with
Tom's personal markings GN-F. (*Jonny Cracknell*)

Tom and Eileen at a Battle of Britain commemoration.

Tom and Prince Charles at an art exhibition.

Tom and HM the Queen. (*Battle of Britain Memorial Trust*)

Tom and Eileen at their grandson's wedding.

Tom and Eileen.

Tom and his three sons – Ian, Terence, and Patrick.

Tom in the rear cockpit of Spitfire SM520, 2015. (*Boultbee Flight
Academy*)

Over Beachy Head during Tom's flight in SM520. (*Boultbee Flight
Academy*)

Tom signing a painting. (*Jonny Cracknell*)

Signing copies of his book *Acts of Fate*. (*Jonny Cracknell*)

After the award of the Légion d'Honneur in 2016. (*Jonny
Cracknell*)

Illustrations in Text

Foreword

There are just a handful of 'The Few' left. They are a precious few whose gallantry and achievements have given them the status of national treasures. In this the RAF's 100th anniversary year it is fitting to remind ourselves of a time when the future of Western civilisation hung in the balance, and when men like Tom Neil, 'held the whole future of mankind in his two sweating hands. And did not let it go.'*

Tom has written about his wartime exploits in the Battle of Britain, in Malta, and in pre-war flying and flying training. He is a gifted writer and has been much in demand over the years on TV and radio, speaking always in a distinctive and compelling way, much as he writes. So, you might wonder, when for many he is a voice and face of 'The Few', why another book is needed.

Peter Jacobs has written well-received biographies before, but when the chance came to capture the story of Tom's life it was too good to miss; to tell it all, to bring it together with post-war experiences and, most revealingly, reflections from the man himself.

I have known Tom for some twenty-five years; I have known of him for much longer. He is simply one of those characters whose face and bearing sticks in one's mind. Every year at Westminster Abbey, the Royal Air Force celebrates the Battle of Britain on the Sunday closest to 15 September. For all the years I have attended,

---

* From the poem 'Fighter Pilot' by Air Chief Marshal Sir Christopher Foxley-Norris.

the processing down the Abbey of 'The Few' is the intensely moving highlight of the day. And, every year, Tom's presence has graced the occasion.

Every year, too, since 1996 at Capel-le-Ferne where stands the Battle of Britain Memorial, a celebration is held to commemorate the start of that epic struggle. Tom Neil graces that too.

Tom is tall, elegant, and good-looking still. A truly remarkable ninety-eight years. He is not the classic model for a fighter pilot, where stockier build brings benefits to 'g' resistance, and helps avoid back problems, something that afflicted Tom in later life. Yet he was an immensely successful combat pilot, a tribute to a good eye, his situational awareness and constant focus. And, he would say, some luck too.

Peter Jacobs's book is illuminated with Tom's observations and accounts of episodes in his life. That his time in America brought life-long friendships is no surprise. Tom is the sort of man Americans like. His time as a test pilot is equally fascinating. The names he recalls brought back memories of the men a small boy worshipped whose bravery and skill set him on a career in the Royal Air Force. Me!

There are many episodes in this story which caught my eye. But a foreword should not impose too much on the reader, so let me touch on just a couple. RAF combat tactics in the early war days were lamentable in comparison to the Luftwaffe's fluid formations. Tom is rightly critical. There is a lesson here in ensuring that the service remains abreast of what is happening away from home. Tom is critical, too, of 12 Group 'Big Wing' tactics. History has surely supported that view and elevated Keith Park to the man of the match status he deserved.

Tom reminds us of the dangers of test-flying in the late 1940s and early 1950s. The number of pilots killed as the 'Sound Barrier' was challenged and heights and speeds increased is sobering. These were brave men and a time of extraordinary development in aviation. Tom tested a variety of aircraft and many will thank him for this work and for giving us the Chipmunk trainer, which has delighted generations of pilots.

This book is more than just a good read from a skilled pen about a memorable man. It reminds us how human beings can do extraordinary things, survive the horrors of war, the loss of friends and colleagues, the remorseless stress and fear. Perhaps Tom's letters home, and his artistic talents were the necessary outlet, but Tom came through it all to be the father of sons who are immensely proud of him. After reading this book, you will understand why.

Michael Graydon

Acknowledgements

First, and foremost, I would like to thank Tom for making me so welcome in his home and for the many hours he has spent with me talking about his life. It has been a privilege and honour to spend so much time with him. I would also like to thank Tom for giving me unlimited access to his written material, log books, and the many boxes containing documents, letters, cuttings and images, which he has collated over the years, and for his permission to use whatever I had come across. Tom's published works on his experiences during the Second World War have provided a marvellous diary and record of events during those key moments in his life, and without his kindness and generosity this book could not have been written. I am also most grateful for the support of Tom's sons – Terence, Patrick and Ian – without which this book would never have been started.

I must also thank Air Chief Marshal Sir Michael Graydon, GCB, CBE, for kindly agreeing to write the foreword to the book. As a former RAF fighter pilot, Chief of the Air Staff, and President of the Battle of Britain Memorial Trust, I can think of no one better than Sir Michael to do this. So, once again, thank you Sir Michael.

I would also like to thank the staff at the National Archives, the Air Historical Branch (RAF), and the RAF College Cranwell for their help; all have helped me gain access to important historical documents. Many others have helped me with my research too. In particular, I would like to thank Dave Southwood and Ruth Canham at the Empire Test Pilots' School, Bill Morris, Chairman of the Old Bootleians Association, and Amy Shurey of the Boultbee Flight

Academy at Goodwood Aerodrome. I would also like to thank my son, Matthew, for copying Tom's log books, and thank Tom's carers for the endless supply of coffee and biscuits.

Most of the images in the book have come from Tom, but some have kindly been provided by others; these are credited accordingly, but I would particularly like to thank Jonny Cracknell, a good friend of Tom's, and Malcolm Triggs and Barry Duffield of the Battle of Britain Memorial Trust, for providing me with some wonderful images and allowing me to include them in the book. Finally, I would like to thank my editor Donald Sommerville, and my good friend Michael Leventhal at Greenhill Books for giving me the opportunity to tell Tom's story.

Thomas Francis Neil, 1920–2018

⊙

On 11 July 2018, just as this book was going to print, Tom Neil died peacefully, three days short of his ninety-eighth birthday. Everything written before that point has remained unchanged as it is how Tom saw the book at its final stage. *Flying, Fighting & Reflection* is published with the blessing of his family and is a tribute to a most courageous individual and one of the finest men that I have ever had the privilege to know. Thank you, Tom, for sharing your life with us. You will never be forgotten.

Introduction

I first met Tom twenty years ago when I was honoured to be the guest of Pat Wells at the annual dinner of the Battle of Britain Fighter Association, held in the beautiful and historic Georgian mansion at RAF Bentley Priory near Stanmore in north-west London. Pat and Tom had been comrades on 249 Squadron during that hard and decisive summer of 1940, after which they had gone to Malta together. And it was before dinner, in the room that had once been the office of Air Chief Marshal Sir Hugh Dowding, who led Fighter Command during the Battle of Britain, that I first met Tom.

Memories of that wonderful evening at Bentley Priory will always stay with me. I was in the company of the Few. These were the men who had inspired me as a young boy and were the main reason I had chosen to join the RAF. And, having joined the service and finished my flying training, I only ever wanted to fly on fighter squadrons – and I was lucky enough to be able to do so. To follow in the footsteps of the Few was, for me, a boyhood dream come true.

After I first met Tom, our paths did cross again, usually at air shows or events relating to the Battle of Britain where Tom was attending as a guest. But I could never have imagined all those years ago that one day I would be given the honour of writing Tom's life story. When my good friend Michael Leventhal asked me if I would be interested in writing the book, I could never have said no. Meeting Tom again and spending time with him as his guest at his home has been a privilege, and it soon became apparent just how much we have in common, albeit a generation or so apart.

To cover such a long life under one cover has been a challenge. It would have been easy, for example, to fill the book with Tom's memories of the Battle of Britain, or of his time in Malta, or when he was in command of 41 Squadron flying Spitfires over northern France, or about his work as a test pilot after the war, or when commanding a Meteor jet fighter-reconnaissance squadron in Egypt's troubled Canal Zone during the 1950s. I am sure you get the point. There had to be a balance. This also means there is simply not the space to write about who or which unit Tom was engaged with, such as during the Battle of Britain, as these facts can be found elsewhere. Besides, as far as Tom was concerned, they were all the enemy. Whether a Messerschmitt Bf 109 had a yellow nose or a red nose, or any other identifying markings for that matter, was irrelevant. They were all Messerschmitts and they all had to be dealt with. And so, in places, there is no time to dwell and we simply must move on.

Fortunately, though, Tom is an established author. His books *Gun Button to Fire*, *Onward to Malta*, *A Fighter in my Sights*, *Scramble* and *The Silver Spitfire* all cover his experiences during specific parts of the Second World War, and in great detail. They are all wonderfully written and a must-read, whether you are an aviation enthusiast, historian, or simply if you just happen to like good books.

This book goes beyond the Second World War and its title *Flying, Fighting & Reflection*, comes from the three words that best describe the substance of Tom's many interviews and conversations about his wartime experiences and his subsequent life. I refer to him as Tom in the opening chapter, which covers his time as a boy, and I return to the use of Tom in the final chapter when he is looking back on his life as a man nearly ninety-eight years old.

Finally, I consider it a great honour to have been given the chance to tell Tom's story. A nation needs its heroes and the RAF's victory during the Battle of Britain was a decisive moment in our history. The nation will always owe a debt of gratitude to the men later to become known as the Few. Tom Neil is one of those Few.

Peter Jacobs

Chapter One

Early Days

At any other time of his life, looking down on the historic town of Maidstone from 18,000 feet late one fine summer's afternoon would have been a joy for any young pilot. It is an area of outstanding natural beauty with the Kent Downs stretching out to the White Cliffs and the Strait of Dover, and the High Weald leading south to the Sussex coast and English Channel, while behind him he could see the magnificent Thames Estuary and the city of London. But this was no ordinary late summer's day. It was 7 September 1940 and the height of an aerial conflict later to become known as the Battle of Britain. The nation stood alone against Nazi Germany's mighty war machine. Britain was in a desperate fight for survival, and responsibility for its future fell on the shoulders of the young fighter pilots of the Royal Air Force, men later to become known as the Few.

It was the third time twenty-year-old Tom Neil had been scrambled into the air that day; breakfast seemed a long time ago. 'Tallyho' someone cried. Dark bursts of anti-aircraft fire took Neil's eyes onto the black dots appearing in the distance, rapidly increasing in number, and now taking on the appearance of a dark sinister cloud.

The twelve Hawker Hurricanes turned to meet the approaching Luftwaffe armada heading towards London. As they closed from the beam, Neil could now make out the hordes of enemy bombers – Heinkel 111s and Dornier 17s – all protected by an umbrella of fighters – Messerschmitt 109s and 110s – high above. He did not bother trying to count, there was no point. But there must be a hundred of them, maybe more. What possible chance, he thought, did they have against such overwhelming odds?

Quickly putting such a negative thought aside, Neil glanced down to make sure his guns were ready to fire and headed straight towards the pack of bombers. He was soon amongst the Heinkels and was so close that he could now pick out individual aircraft. Selecting one in the leading group, he opened fire. The eight Browning machine guns burst into life, shaking his aircraft in a way that only a fighter pilot can understand. He watched the tracer and smoking rounds tear into the bomber ahead. Then, as he flashed under the pale underbelly of his intended victim, he turned on his back and pulled hard away, falling towards the ground like a stone.

Pulling as hard as he could out of the dive, Neil could see aircraft everywhere but there was not a bomber in sight. Climbing again as quickly as his Hurricane would allow, he soon made out the un-mistakeable shape and markings of the escorting Bf 109s. One was off to his right and seemingly coming towards him. Neil turned hard towards it and opened fire, and then watched in amazement as the 109 turned away in a gentle dive. Wildly excited, he chased after it, firing again and watching his rounds clatter into the enemy fighter. A puff of smoke appeared and then a trail of white, soon thickening and darkening in colour, signalling the start of its demise. Swooping and closing on his prey, Neil fired again. Debris was now dropping from the 109 as it fell away in a trail of smoke in a steepening dive to earth.

Nearly eighty years on, Tom's memories of such telling moments in his long and charmed life are as vivid now as they were back in the summer of 1940. An event such as shooting down his first enemy aircraft during the Battle of Britain is unlikely ever to be forgotten.

Much has changed since then, of course, not only in Tom's personal life but also in the political landscape of an ever-changing world in which he has lived. He is the first to acknowledge that the Britain he now lives in is quite different to the one that he fought for all those years ago.

Sitting quietly at his home in the peaceful rural hamlet of Thwaite St Mary, deep in the south Norfolk countryside where the county borders Suffolk, he is surrounded by memories of the most important things in his life – his days in the RAF, his friends, his love of the countryside, his books and, most importantly of all, his family. He has all the time in the world to reflect on everything that has happened to him since his early days ninety-eight years ago.

Timing is everything in life and no date is more fundamental than the era of one's birth. Thomas Francis Neil was born on 14 July 1920 in Bootle, in the northern suburbs of Liverpool. Had he have been born just a few years later he would have been fortunate to have been just too young for service in the Second World War and would have become part of a secure peacetime Britain soon to be at the epicentre of the swinging sixties. But for Tom and others born in the early 1920s fate was to offer a very different prospect. Their generation was soon to be called upon, quite literally, to save the world in a total war unleashed by Nazi Germany.

Tom was to be an only child. His middle name, Francis, had come from his father's brother, and his birth had come at a time when Britain was just starting out on the long road to recovery following the devastation of the First World War. Both of his parents had been born in the 1890s and so both had played their part during the war. His father, Thomas Gosney Neil, had first served in the London Scottish Regiment and then the Royal Artillery. A precise, punctilious man, and always immaculately turned out, he would go on to forge a good career with the railways. Tom's mother, meanwhile, born Florence Catherine Kelly, was an Irish Catholic. She had been a supervisor in a munitions factory and had a deep but unspoken dread of war, with images of the horrors of trench warfare along the Western Front vividly etched on her mind.

Both parents idolised Tom, they could not have loved him more. The family home was on Downing Road in the Breeze Hill part of Bootle. It was a wonderful place to grow up. The splendid Edwardian houses with large gardens lining streets named after the colleges of Oxford and Cambridge merely emphasised the superior nature of the area. And although he was an only child, Tom was brought up alongside his mother's sister's three daughters; they were a little older than him but all the children were very close.

For a young boy growing up in Liverpool during the 1920s and early 1930s, the docklands, with their busy wharfs, basins and bustling streets, provided a marvellous playground. It was a period marking the pinnacle of Liverpool's economic success when it regarded itself as the 'second city' of the British Empire, and the large Cunard and White Star ocean liners gracing the skyline provided a sight no youngster would ever forget.

The Neil family enjoyed some fine holidays together. With his father working for the London, Midland and Scottish Railway, the holiday season was mostly spent away from home, usually for three weeks or so, at wonderful locations around the country – all thanks to his father's privileges on the railway. Tom was quickly growing up as an adventurous young boy. From a very early age his parents would often refer to him as 'Ginger'. It was a nickname that would reappear later in his life, although Tom has always insisted that his hair was never red!

Tom was first educated at Bootle's School for Boys on Balliol Road, soon to become the Bootle Grammar School for Boys and now the site of the Hugh Baird College. Outside of the school gates, he became a choirboy at the age of ten, at Christ Church at the bottom of Breeze Hill on Oxford Road. He would later describe his group of sixteen choirboys as 'an artful, smirking bunch, brimful of monkey tricks' and whose 'rascality was further masked by faces so angelic that, as a group, we could have raised millions for the starving poor had someone had the nous to recognise our enormous potential'.

For three years Tom endured two services every Sunday and choir practice every Thursday evening, for the handsome sum of one old penny per service, paid to the boys at the end of each quarter, a total of two shillings and tuppence (11p) each.

The church and his faith would remain an important part of Tom's life. Influenced in those early years by his parents, mostly his mother, it would shape his thinking throughout his adult life, particularly during the difficult war years that lay ahead.

It was also in those days as a choirboy that a fellow chorister introduced Tom to the magazine *Popular Flying*. Tom was growing up in the golden age for aviation and the introduction of this new sixty-four-page monthly magazine, edited by the children's author Captain W. E. Johns, in April 1932 included a story by William Earle (a pseudonym for W. E. Johns) titled 'The White Fokker'; the first Biggles story ever published.

For young boys like Tom, stories such as the Biggles series were hugely exciting. Then add to the cocktail real-life events, such as the Schneider Trophy (an international race for seaplanes, which had been won outright by Britain in 1931), and the achievements of Amy Johnson (a legendary English aviatrix who in 1930 became the first woman to fly solo from Britain to Australia) and her husband Jim Mollison (a Scottish pioneer aviator who set many records during the 1930s when flying solo or with his wife), and it can easily be seen how so many young boys of that generation became fascinated and influenced by the world of aviation. The newspapers were rarely without a story involving aviation in some way and so the topic of discussion amongst the choirboys was often more about aircraft than the church.

It was also during 1932 that Tom went to Croydon Aerodrome, then London's main airport, while visiting the capital with his parents. Staring in awe at the huge four-engine Handley Page 42 biplanes, the luxury airliners of Imperial Airways, then Britain's national airline, left Tom with memories he would never forget. But it was not only the size of these mighty machines and intrigue as to how they could possibly get in the air that fascinated him, he was completely taken in by the seductive ambience of aircraft and the aerodrome, the wealth associated with air travel, and the excitement and dangers attached to the world of aviation. These were all things Tom remembers convincing him that this was the world he wanted to be a part of. Flying was the future. It was one of those defining moments in his life.

Tom with his mother during a family holiday.

The harsh reality, though, was that he was still only twelve years old. For now, the excitement of Croydon and the hustle and bustle of London disappeared into distant memory as he returned home to the somewhat quieter routine of Lancashire life where aircraft were rarely seen. But Tom had caught the aviation bug and to compensate for the lack of aircraft near his home he would cycle eighteen miles to Southport so that he could sit and watch the Fox Moths operating pleasure flights from the beach. These small biplanes could carry three of four passengers at a time, but the five-shilling fare was well beyond his financial means. And so, for hours on end, he would just sit there watching them come and go before it was time to make the long journey home.

While cycling thirty-six miles for a day out might be beyond many youngsters today, back in the 1930s it was not such an unusual thing to do. Tom simply loved being out in the countryside. He would often go off alone or with friends in search of fun and adventure, particularly if there was the possibility of seeing aircraft along the way.

It was not long before he saw a military aircraft for the first time. That momentous occasion occurred during a cycling holiday to Wales with his friends, a round-trip of more than sixty miles. Their route took them by paddleboat across the River Mersey and then close to Chester along the marshes of the River Dee, and then adjacent to RAF Sealand, then home to No. 5 Flying Training School. From his vantage point alongside the runway, Tom watched in fascination as the silver and yellow two-seat Avro Tutor biplanes, used by the RAF for initial pilot training, took to the air and then seemingly floated back in to land.

This unplanned opportunity to observe military aircraft from such a close distance confirmed what Tom had been feeling for some time. In his own words he was intoxicated. He wanted nothing other than to be one of those pilots. Being in the RAF was the only thing worth doing. What else could there possibly be in life?

It was also around this time in his life that Tom met someone in RAF uniform for the first time. It was another of those chance meetings, this time during a family visit to friends in Stockport. The young man, still in his late teens, was an aircraft apprentice at RAF Halton. Tom knew nothing of uniforms or rank at that time, but the impression this immaculately turned out young man gave left an ever-lasting memory. The fact that he was not going to fly did not matter at all. In his book *Scramble*, in which Tom writes in much detail about his early life, he records what was another of those defining moments: 'It was the uniform and the overwhelming aura of well-being that influenced me the most. To me, he personified a golden future, a personal Holy Grail. From that moment, my path was charted, irrevocably.'

It had reinforced what Tom wanted to do with his life, but it was still too early for him to do anything about it. Besides, his enthusiasm to pursue a flying career was not shared by his parents. Memories of the horrors of the First World War were still fresh in their minds and they knew nothing about flying. His father's knowledge of aviation extended no further than the one occasion he had been close to a German aircraft that had the misfortune to crash near his gun battery in 1918.

However, the fact that his parents did not share his enthusiasm for the exciting world of flying was never going to deter Tom from following his dream. To broaden his knowledge, he took every opportunity to read about aviation and he learned more about how to join the RAF. He found out about the education and medical requirements of becoming a pilot, and the process that he would be required to go through as soon as he was old enough to apply.

None of what he found out about the entry requirements seemed to be a problem, but one thing he was certain would be an issue as far as his parents would be concerned were the methods of entry. To become a pilot in the RAF either meant joining the regular force as a cadet at the RAF College Cranwell or joining on a short-service commission of four years. But to become a cadet at Cranwell would require a parental financial contribution towards his upkeep of at least £300 a year, a considerable sum of money in the 1930s, and he knew that his parents would be against the idea of him joining the RAF for just four years because he would then face being out of work at the age of twenty-two.

Tom knew that winning his argument to join the RAF would be a formidable challenge. And he was not wrong. Having finally summed up the courage to raise the topic with his parents one evening, he was disappointed, and annoyed, to be told that his parents would not support either option. The reason for them not being able to fund the cadet route was fully understandable, but the reasons his parents had given against the short-service commission were less so. While he had expected them to express their concern that he would, perhaps, be out of work in just four years, their view on short-service commissions was that they were only for those who . . . The sentence was left unfinished, but it had implied all sorts of things. Tom was furious.

For a while Tom was left to cool off, but he was determined not to let go. His next plan was to join the Auxiliary Air Force, the RAF's volunteer reserve element tasked with providing trained personnel in support of the regular force, which he felt would be a compromise. At least he would get the chance to fly.

The AAF was then focused on town-based squadrons using facilities at an aerodrome nearby. Members were generally recruited locally, along similar lines to the Territorial Army, although the Auxiliary squadrons tended to be formed from the wealthier classes. Pilots were required to obtain their licence at their own expense and serve for a minimum period of five years, flying a few hours every year and attending one annual training camp of fifteen days.

After his parents had calmed down, Tom decided to raise the subject of flying once again and suggested he joined the Auxiliaries. This time he was pleasantly surprised. While his parents never fully supported his idea, they did not vehemently object. They could see their son desperately wanted to fly. Besides, in their eyes, being an officer in the Auxiliaries had some respectability at least. And so, they agreed that when he was old enough Tom could apply to join the local Auxiliary unit, 611 (West Lancashire) Squadron, based at nearby Speke on the southern outskirts of Liverpool.

It was marvellous news. And exciting. Speke was a developing airport and the Hawker Harts and Hinds of the Auxiliary squadron had not long moved in. As soon as he was old enough he would apply to join. It was as if a weight had finally been lifted from his young shoulders. But then, out of nowhere, came the biggest bombshell he could imagine, and he had not seen it coming. His father returned home from work one evening to announce he was being elevated to a higher position, and the family was moving to Manchester.

From Tom's point of view, this was disastrous news, not least because it would scupper his plan to join the Auxiliaries at Speke. Furthermore, he had no friends or other family in Manchester. He even tried arguing against the idea. But, of course, he stood no chance. The family was moving and that was that. In what seemed like no time at all, the family had moved to Elm Grove on the edge of Roe Green, a suburban area of Worsley and just a few miles to the west of Manchester.

Although Tom had not been at all keen on the idea of moving, he fully admits that Roe Green, with its lovely village green and rows of silver birches lining the lanes, was a beautiful place to live. With Manchester Grammar School being too far away, he continued the final part of his education in Eccles, where he would later sit and pass the School Certificate.

As far as Tom was concerned, university was never going to be an option. Away from the classroom he thoroughly enjoyed playing sport, mostly football and cricket, particularly cricket as his natural height advantage over the other teenagers made him a good fast bowler and he was soon representing his school in the first eleven. He was also very creative, with a love for writing and drawing, and quite technically minded when it came to making things. He even won a major art prize while at school in Eccles for a project that included the drawing of a biplane.

These skills would never disappear and would later re-emerge at various times of his life, but for now it was the world of aviation Tom was determined to be in. Besides, he was very much aware of the developing situation in Europe. Even to those British politicians who chose to bury their heads in the sand, it was becoming increasingly apparent that the political situation was not as stable as it might be, with Adolf Hitler's Nazi Germany identified as the most likely aggressor.

Although news of Hitler's ranting speeches in Germany was spreading across Europe, war was neither inevitable nor imminent. And so, in the summer of 1937, having just turned seventeen, Tom was one of twelve boys selected from his school to travel to Germany to attend a so-called International Camp held in Wiesbaden, although, in fact, it was just one of many summer camps set up for youths to further the cause of Nazi ideology.

The long journey from Eccles took them by train to Dover, via London, and then by ferry across the English Channel to Ostend, before continuing their train journey through Belgium into Germany. The boys could not help but notice the transformation between Belgium and Germany. It was breathtaking – the people, the way they dressed, their mood, and the infrastructure. When later describing his first impression of Germany at that time, Tom would write: 'Wide-eyed, we all sat in wonderment. Gosh, everywhere seemed to pulsate with an indescribable electricity. It was all most impressive.'

Tom would remember his visit to Germany for the rest of his life, and it is one of the most pleasant memories of his youth. For part of the week they were hosted by boys of a similar age from a school in Koblenz. He later described his constant companion, a boy called Karl-Heinz Moht, as 'gravely formal, disciplined, and courteous, and one of the most agreeable boys I had ever met'.

Moht was a member of the Hitler Youth and he took Tom to one of their evening sports meetings and then to a camp fire where there was much singing, mostly to thumping martial tunes. And then before returning to England, as a final act of courtesy, Tom was taken to meet Moht's family, with everlasting memories of great warmth.

There is no doubt that his brief experience of Germany had thoroughly impressed Tom. There had, of course, been a lot of what he later described as comic-opera stuff, such as the slightly ridiculous sight of what he calls 'Heil-Hitlering' and stiff-armed saluting. But these were clearly people who welcomed discipline and loved playing soldiers. At the same time, there was an obvious toughness about them and an almost tangible atmosphere of dedication. He would later say:

> In retrospect, it would appear I was naïve and superficial in my judgements, particularly in view of what has since been revealed. But, in that bright summer of 1937, the sun shone from a clear blue sky, the air was warm and scented, and I was seventeen years old and full of the joys of spring. I make no apologies; this was pre-war Germany as I saw it.

After returning to England there were several exchanges of letters between the two boys. But they never saw each other again. Tom would forever wonder what happened to Karl-Heinz Moht.

By the spring of 1938, Tom was old enough to apply for a commission in the Auxiliaries. The fact that he now lived in Manchester was not going to stop him from applying for the squadron at Speke. After filling in all the appropriate forms he soon received a letter from the Territorial and Auxiliary Air Force Association Headquarters in Liverpool, inviting him for an interview.

The interview was to be on a Sunday and so not wishing to be late he set off early from Manchester by train. He arrived at the headquarters building in Liverpool in good time, but was somewhat surprised to find it locked, with not a soul in sight. Checking the letter again, and then again, it suddenly occurred to him that he might not be in the right place. And still with no one around, he wondered if he should be at Speke, which was miles away from where he was standing at that point. The letter did not say he should be at Speke, but it was now less than ten minutes to the time of his interview!

Thinking on his feet, Tom found a public telephone box and quickly rang the number on the letter. Fortunately, someone answered the phone, but the voice at the other end was far from sympathetic. As Tom had suspected, he was in the wrong place and he was now told to make his way to the airfield as quickly as he could. But it took him another hour to get to Speke by bus and after making a few rapid enquiries he made his way to 611 Squadron's main office.

It was unfortunate for the young Tom, but hardly surprising, that the whole episode turned out to be something of a disaster. Arriving late was one thing, but the reception he received from the officer on duty was lukewarm at best. And then the interview, conducted by two officers – a squadron leader and a flight lieutenant – did not go at all how Tom would have wished. Their focus seemed more on how he was going to get to Speke from his home in Manchester than anything else. His answer, of course, was by train, the same route that he had travelled that day, but it was an answer that clearly disturbed the two interviewing officers. To be in the Auxiliaries it seemed that one had to own a car, and when Tom admitted to the interviewing officers that he had never even been in an aeroplane, it seemed like the whole world was against him.

In truth, it was. A seventeen-year-old boy who was still at school, who did not own a car and lived over thirty miles away, and who had never flown in an aeroplane before, was not what the Auxiliary officers were used to seeing at interview. Despite Tom's best efforts to convince the two officers that he could make it work, the harsh reality was that he was not going to be given the chance.

Fighting back the tears Tom returned home, in his own words 'crushed, demolished and flattened'. On a more positive note, however, he had been told to consider joining the RAF Volunteer Reserve, which had formed the year before to supplement the AAF and to provide a reserve of aircrew, for all the different branches, in the event of war. But, for now, Tom's boyhood dream of becoming a pilot in the RAF was put on hold.

Within a few months he had left school and was working in a bank in Manchester, courtesy of his father's chance meeting with an old friend who happened to be the general manager of the Manchester and Liverpool District Bank. It was now August 1938 and Tom was promptly despatched to the Urmston branch of the bank, in the south-west part of the city centre, to gain experience in his new profession.

Counting cheques was about as boring a job as Tom could imagine. Furthermore, he had been placed under the watchful eye of the so-called junior, the lowest of the low amongst the bank's staff, making Tom feel utterly worthless. And if that was not demoralising enough, his weekly wage barely covered the cost of him getting to work and no pay rise was due until he passed his exams.

His morale had plunged to a new low, but Tom dutifully carried on at the bank. He even spent three evenings a week attending lectures to boost his knowledge and qualifications, his father meeting the cost of this extra-mural instruction as well as the additional travel involved. But Tom always knew that banking was never going to be for him. He would later admit that he had hated every moment of his service with the bank. He had no intention of staying and when discussions got heated at home, he was quick to remind his parents that it would have been cheaper had they have allowed him to become a Cranwell cadet.

Having now turned eighteen, Tom decided it was time to pursue his idea of joining the RAF Volunteer Reserve. Although he was employed by the bank, war was looking increasingly likely and so major employers did not object to staff applying for voluntary military service. After filling out his application form to join the RAFVR he was invited to an interview at Barton aerodrome just a few miles from his home.

The airfield at Barton had emerged from another of those inter-war ideas to develop a municipal airport. Councils in and around large cities all over the country wanted to be part of the emerging air travel scene and so Barton was one such aerodrome to have been developed during the early 1930s. By the time Tom arrived there in September 1938 the airfield was also home to de Havilland Moth biplanes of No. 17 Elementary & Reserve Flying Training School, one of many flying training schools established across the country to train pilots for the RAFVR.

Having taken the bus to Barton, Tom soon found the RAFVR accommodation behind the airport's hotel. Outside the wooden hut was a Moth, with RAF roundels on the wings and fuselage. His heart leapt with excitement.

This time his whole interview experience was more pleasant, and things went far more smoothly than they had before. He received a warm welcome on arrival and the whole selection procedure was explained clearly to him at the start. The interview, which was conducted by three interviewers – two wearing civilian clothes and a flight lieutenant in uniform – went as well as he could possibly have hoped. He was asked about his academic qualifications, his sporting achievements, his hobbies and other interests, and his reasons for wanting to join the RAFVR. He was also asked why he had not applied for regular service, to which he gave some well-rehearsed replies, but leaving out the bit about what his parents thought of those on short-service commissions!

Inevitably, there were some nervous moments when he was asked questions that he had been unprepared for and had almost caught him out, such as when talking about the prospect of war he was asked if he would be willing to die. For a moment he did not know what to say. He had not expected that question, but he remembers mumbling something along the line of not exactly being willing as such, after which there was silence. He had no idea whether he had said the wrong thing. Notes were then passed between the interviewers, but Tom need not have worried. He had obviously done well. He was then thanked for offering his services and handed a piece of folded paper with the instruction to proceed outside.

The rest of the selection process involved a lengthy medical examination, including some rather comprehensive eye tests. The next thing he remembers is someone talking to him about his expenses and future arrangements. But Tom was struggling to take in what he was being told. All he can remember thinking was that he was in!

Chapter Two

Flying Times

The following month, on 12 October 1938, Tom Neil was attested into the RAFVR with the service number 742234 and the initial rank of leading aircraftman, although he would be promoted to sergeant the following day; such was how the bureaucracy worked at the time. He was then given details of his pay, which simply meant he would be paid for the occasions that he was on duty. And with the formalities over, Neil was told to report to the chief flying instructor at Barton the week after next.

Ten days later, Neil strapped into a Moth and took to the air for the first time. Such moments in life are never forgotten. It was Saturday 22 October, and he had been sat patiently and nervously all day waiting for his name to be called. The school's instructors had been coming and going throughout the day, calling a name for that person to go and fly. But it was always someone else's name that was called. It had become so late, in fact, that Neil had all but given up hope of flying that day. Then, late in the afternoon, his instructor, Mr Sears, called his name. This was his moment. It was finally time for him to go and fly. The occasion is best captured in Neil's own words:

> We taxied out, bouncing and swaying, with bursts of engine and the tail wagging furiously. We seemed to be going jolly fast, with much scraping at the back end and our wingtip almost touching the ground. At the far side of the airfield, we turned into wind and embarked on our take-off run. This was it! My very first flight!

Neil's dream had just come true, but he had not known exactly what to expect. As things were to turn out, the flight lasted just twenty minutes and, somewhat disappointingly, this dream moment in his life, his very first time in an aircraft, turned out to be something of an anti-climax. Neil continues:

> The man in the front was blowing down the speaking tube and shouting something I could not understand. After more shouting, he turned around – insofar as that was possible for a man of his bulk – to mouth something else in my direction, then point. Alas, I could not interpret either his words or his gestures and responded by shrugging my shoulders. After that, we flew around in silence, my instructor no doubt deciding that it was a waste of time trying to communicate with the half-wit he had in the back seat. I sat there miserably, my nose streaming copiously and trussed up like a turkey. I had no idea where we were or which way we were pointing. Mr Sears blocked out my forward view entirely. Also, I was chilled to the marrow. Flying was rather a dreary business, I concluded; not at all the dare-devil, breath-taking affair it was cracked up to be.

As a member of the RAFVR, Neil was required to spend at least two evenings a week, usually at the school's building in Manchester town centre. Lectures included topics such as navigation, meteorology, principles of flight and airmanship. The more technical classes, such as lessons on engines and airframes, were held at the airfield where the instructors could use the aircraft to help teach the pupils. The level of tuition was very good. Neil had joined the RAFVR with three others, and so they were generally taught together as a small group of four.

There were, of course, the inevitable hours of drill, held in a hangar at Barton where there was more space. These sessions were led by their drill instructor, an ex-policeman from Salford known simply as 'Sarge'. While the thought of drill might not have been everyone's cup of tea, Neil found these sessions to be a welcome break from the

The hangar at Barton (*right*) used for drill.

intense ground school lectures and they often provided a source of great amusement.

If there are two things that a young pilot needs at the start of a flying career, then they are good instruction and continuity. But learning to fly during the winter months was never going to be easy. The weather was lousy. Strong winds dominated November and the weather over the Christmas period was bitterly cold with plenty of snow, meaning that continuity was all but impossible. Neil made just twelve flights in his first four months, a total of less than nine hours in the air. And his instructor, Flying Officer Lowe, who Neil remembers as a kind but elderly gentleman, seemed more intent on reminding Neil of the errors he had made the previous month rather than anything else. It was not easy.

Having a gap of several weeks between flights made it difficult for both instructor and pupil. But while his slow progression was beginning to frustrate Neil, he was at least now enjoying the experience of learning to fly. He seemed to be coping with the challenge quite well and there was a further boost when the school converted to the more powerful Tiger Moth.

With the weather having picked up, Neil was considered ready to go solo and that momentous occasion finally arrived on 20 April

1939. The aircraft was a Tiger Moth and the flight lasted just fifteen minutes. He remembers finding his first solo to have been relatively easy with his only difficulty being landing the aircraft.

When reflecting on those early days of learning to fly, Neil remembers initially being rather erratic when it came to land the aircraft, but his technique was soon rectified to the point that his landings became mirror-smooth.

Having successfully completed his first solo, Neil decided to do his fifteen days of continuous training straight away. War was looking increasingly likely and he did not want to be thrown in at the deep end unprepared. However, although the weather had picked up sufficiently for his first solo, it now once again seemed to be against him. Howling gales dominated north-west England at the time, but Neil still managed to fly on average five times a day, amassing forty-five hours airborne during those two weeks. These were crucial hours of flying experience.

Neil was quickly becoming a competent pilot, but with other new arrivals to teach, now arriving in small groups every week, the instructors had very little time for him. Although he had flown plenty of times during his fifteen days of continuous training, there seemed to be very little in the way of learning anything new. His instructors were content to let him go his own way.

While this might not have been a problem, a compliment even, during normal peacetime years, it was now the spring of 1939 and war was not far away. And so, apart from being taught some basic manoeuvres, Neil was left to learn aerobatics and how to handle the aircraft by himself. This involved, he says, 'taking a deep breath and hauling the aircraft around in some extraordinary swoops and tumbles, all purporting to be loops and rolls'.

By the summer of 1939 there were more than sixty pupil pilots at Barton as the country ramped up its effort for war. Neil's handling of the aircraft had gradually improved. He was fast learning how to push the aircraft to its limits and enjoyed exploring the boundaries of flight. Spinning was his speciality, although he described his rolls as 'at best dramatic and at worst a disaster'. Such was his confidence, which was growing every time he took to the air, that he would occasionally perform impromptu aerobatic displays over Worsley Sports Club where his parents were members.

All was going very well, but one day he got a sharp reminder that flying, even in peacetime, could be a hazardous affair. Until that moment he had considered the engine to be something that simply powered the aircraft. As far as its operation was concerned, he clearly knew what to push, pull and switch on and off to make it work, but the principles of its workings were complicated, something of a mystery even. And should his engine ever develop a problem in flight then he was more than likely to be stuck as to what to do.

The reality was that at some time in his flying career, and probably sooner rather than later, he would have an engine problem in flight. And that moment came one afternoon while flying close to the Manchester Ship Canal and several miles from Barton airfield.

The oil pressure gauge was indicating zero. Even with his limited knowledge of the engine, Neil knew this was not good and that the engine was probably about to seize. Thoughts of what to do and what might happen flashed through his mind, but he quickly concluded that he needed to land the aircraft somewhere before the engine came to a grinding halt. The problem was, where could he land?

In a desperate search to find somewhere suitable, Neil closed the throttle and started to glide down. He later recalled:

> I began to search for a suitable field in a minor panic. But there wasn't one, or none that I could see. And the wind! Which way was it blowing? Land downwind and I would float for ever and be through the far hedge like a charging rhino. Smoke, chimneys? Not a sign. Why weren't there some chimneys around here?

By now, Neil had convinced himself the engine was about to seize. He was down to less than 500 feet when suddenly he caught sight of a field. It seemed like it might be all right. It looked green, it seemed to be flat, and was clearly a big enough space, and so he decided to chance it.

Concentrating on getting his approach right, he dropped down closer to the ground, but as he got closer he could see that the field was not as flat as it had first seemed. And then, even worse, obstacles started appearing in the distance ahead. He could see telephone wires, poles, trees, and even a double-decker bus. Neil continues:

> Now totally committed, I gripped the control column as though I were trying to strangle it and pressed ahead. Everything lifted towards me obliquely. Side-slipping. Then a hedge. I was over the top. Holding off, with the ground streaming underneath. At which point my nerve failed. I opened the throttle with a bang and sailed into the air again, the engine sounding as sweet as a nut.

Having climbed back to a safe height he regained his composure before deciding to try again. This time things looked better. He finally floated over the hedge and forced the aircraft down. The ground was hard and bumpy, but at least he was down, and he soon came to a rather untidy stop.

He was naturally delighted to be down in one piece, but there was then the question of what he should do next. Fortunately, common sense kicked in and he decided against the idea of shutting down the engine. To start it again would have required swinging the propeller and he was in the middle of a field, on his own and with no obvious sign of anyone else around. Neil takes up the story:

> So, I sat there, thinking. Feeling utterly spent. Then, another brainwave. I threw off my straps and stood up, lifting myself high enough to look at the instruments in the front cockpit. Oh no! The oil pressure indicator there was registering a very normal 30 lb. What had I done?

Two people could now be seen in the distance. They were heading towards him. Thoughts of the local newspaper headline and the questions he would face back at Barton flashed through his mind before he suddenly concluded that he would have to get airborne again. And as quickly as he possibly could.

The field he was in was big and Neil could see far enough ahead of him to judge that he had just about enough room to get the aircraft off the ground again. He sat down, strapped himself in once more, and opened the throttle. His heart was still pounding as the aircraft limped back into the air and he slowly began climbing away.

As he set course for Barton, his mind was still in a whirl. All sorts of things were going through his mind, not least whether he should tell anyone when he got back or simply leave things to chance in the hope that no one would ever know. What he did think, though, was that the chief instructor would probably go mad at him if he were to find out. On the other hand, however, if he kept quiet and the story later came out through some other source, his days as a pilot would surely be over.

After a most worrying twenty minutes, Neil landed back at Barton. Having then shut the engine down, he got out of the aircraft as quickly as he could to check its underside to see if there were any tell-tale signs of damage or any evidence that he had been in a field. With nothing obvious to his inexperienced eye, he made his way back to dispersal to report the oil pressure gauge in the rear cockpit was unserviceable. He had decided to leave it at that.

For the next hour he kept his head down and avoided everyone before sliding off home early. For weeks it was on his mind but fortunately nothing was ever said. He had been lucky to get away with that incident – and luck was with him again just a few days later when he had a near miss with another aircraft during aerobatics. He still remembers his Tiger Moth jolting viciously as he flew through the turbulence of another Tiger's slipstream.

Although Neil did not think it at the time, he was already leading a charmed life. There had earlier been another lucky escape when attending one of the many Empire Air Days being staged up and down the country. Dressed in his very smart new uniform of the RAFVR, he was at Ringway, then a new airfield and now the site of Manchester Airport, where he was helping to marshal aircraft.

It was a nice bright Saturday and every aircraft possible was on display to the public, who had gathered at Ringway in their thousands. First on the flying programme was a Westland Lysander and, using all his natural charm, Neil had managed to persuade the pilot to let him fly as a passenger in the aircraft. As this meant he had to be properly equipped for the flight, Neil had gone off to try and find a chest parachute and harness. Unfortunately, though, he had been unable to locate the equipment needed in time. The Lysander could not delay its display and so Neil was left to watch in desperate disappointment as it took to the air. After a few routine manoeuvres, the Lysander was then seen to attempt a steep turn to the right, only to fall away and plunge into the ground.

The pilot was rushed to hospital in a critical condition with severe injuries, including a fractured skull. Remarkably, though, he survived. Neil would later learn that the pilot was Hugh Malcolm, whose luck would run out just a few years later while gallantly leading a formation of Bristol Blenheim light bombers during an attack against enemy ground positions in North Africa; this act resulted in Malcolm being posthumously awarded the Victoria Cross.

While Neil's lucky escape at Ringway could be put down to 'what might have been' and his decision to land in a field could be considered part of the learning process, it was the near-miss with another aircraft during aerobatics that played on Neil's mind for some time afterwards. From then on, whenever possible, he would choose to give other aircraft a wide berth rather than run the risk of getting too close.

But, in the telling months that were to come, any idea of being cautious in the air would have to change. Talk had long been of the disturbing developments in Europe. Austria had succumbed to Nazi Germany and the Germans had annexed what remained of Czechoslovakia. The sight of the British Prime Minister, Neville Chamberlain, standing on the steps of the aircraft on his return from meeting Hitler less than a year before, brandishing a piece of paper and proclaiming there would be 'peace for our time', now seemed a lifetime ago.

The RAFVR was providing Neil with all the fun and excitement of learning to fly, but the fact was he was still working in a bank.

At the end of August 1939, he received notification that he was to be transferred to another branch and that he was to report there the following day. Then, on 1 September 1939, just as the bank doors were opening at his new branch, Neil learned that Germany had invaded Poland. War was inevitable and imminent. With war looming, and with the prospect of leaving the bank for ever, Neil found himself working light-heartedly and more diligently than he had ever worked before.

Chapter Three

Preparing for War

The rest of that Friday was full of uncertainty. Germany had invaded Poland, meaning that Britain would surely soon be at war. But it was unclear what Neil should do next. He had no idea when he was likely to be called up, assuming, of course, that he would be called up, and he wondered whether he was expected to show some initiative and report direct to Barton. Or, was he expected to go to the bank the next day as if nothing had happened at all?

The only way to find out was to telephone the headquarters in the town centre, the answer being that he was told to report at 9 a.m. on Sunday the 3rd. His days of banking were gladly over.

The next day his parents helped gather his kit and personal belongings. By now Neil had managed sixty hours in the air but where he would end up and whether he would be any good or not remained to be seen. Nonetheless, it was sixty vital hours of flying experience that he would not have had otherwise, which might one day make the difference between him living or not. Up and down the country similar scenes were being played out. For many young men, boys even, it was the end of university life or civilian employment, or whatever else they happened to be doing at the time. For teenagers like Neil, it was to be the end of boyhood and youth.

On Sunday 3 September, Neil made his way by bus to the town-centre headquarters. Many others were starting to gather there. Some, like him, were sergeants in the RAFVR while others coming from the university air squadrons were commissioned officers. Neil remembers it being the first time any of them seemed to be conscious of rank. He wondered whether he would be required to call them sir and salute them as would normally be the case. 'Surely not! Not with one's chums,' he afterwards said.

Later that morning they all gathered around the wireless to listen to Neville Chamberlain's speech. Britain was now at war with Germany. An officer then appeared and read out four names, instructing the four to report to No. 5 Flying Training School at nearby Sealand. Neil was not one of the names read out, but two of his closer friends – Alan Buck and Robert Shaw – were. Those not on the list were told to go home and wait for further instructions.

For the next eight weeks Neil waited patiently at home. His only connection with the RAF during those early days of war was when he was required to turn up at the town-centre headquarters every couple of weeks to collect his pay. He was now receiving more money than he had ever earned at the bank and with his father having recently bought him a 1936 Morris Ten, for £47 10s, he rejoiced in his newly found affluence and freedom. He later said that he loved his Morris Ten like a brother. It had a sunshine roof, held seven gallons of fuel, and it managed around thirty miles to the gallon. Down a steep hill, with a following wind, it could reach a breathtaking 45 mph.

Apart from enjoying his car, Neil was otherwise left to wait. Nothing much seemed to be happening. It was a period of inactivity, later to be dubbed the Phoney War. Finally, a telegram arrived at his home instructing him to report for posting. At last, for Neil, the war was on.

Having reported to the headquarters, Neil learned that he and around half of his Barton colleagues were off to No. 4 Initial Training Wing at Bexhill-on-Sea, in East Sussex, one of several ITWs being set up at coastal locations to teach new RAF recruits basic service skills and to prepare them for flying training.

He gathered with his colleagues at Manchester's Piccadilly station and it was soon time to board the night train down to London and by noon the following day they were in the ancient seaside town of Bexhill-on-Sea. Although it was late autumn, it was a warm and bright sunny day, later described by Neil as 'An Indian summer, if ever there was one. And no sign of war.'

Neil was on No. 1 Course, the first RAF contingent at Bexhill-on-Sea. Along with 250 others, from all parts of Britain, he was introduced to the RAF and its way of life. Amongst the many buildings used for lectures was the De La Warr Pavilion, an architectural landmark built just a few years before, and still standing and Grade I listed today.

The recruits were accommodated at the Sackville Hotel, wonderfully located on the sea front. With its magnificent public rooms, the once splendid Sackville had been one of the principal hotels along the south-east coast of England and for years had enjoyed a worldwide reputation. Its closure had been enforced following the outbreak of war when it was requisitioned for the RAF. Now, it barely resembled the magnificent establishment that it had once been. All the furniture had been removed and the lift was soon out of order, leaving Neil and his three room-mates to climb the stairs up to the fourth floor several times a day.

The days that followed were full of what might be expected at such a training establishment – kitting out, drill, physical training, aircraft recognition, signals, lectures on identifying rank and other practical subjects – to help the new recruits settle in to the RAF structure that they now belonged to. The days started early but they finished early, too, allowing the men time to explore the town in the evening. They were fed well and with the fresh seaside air it all added up to a wonderful and healthy environment.

Neil very much enjoyed being in the RAF at last and his friends now extended beyond the Barton circle. One was 21-year-old David Gorrie, a pleasant and agreeable young Scotsman from Montrose, while another was Cecil Parkinson from Coventry, some years older than Neil and 'Parky' to his friends, with a quiet and phlegmatic approach to life. And then there was Henry Davidson from Stretford in Manchester, known as ''Appy 'Arry', with his memorable laugh. All three would later fly in the Battle of Britain but sadly none would survive the war.

Neil with Cecil Parkinson (*left*) at No. 4 ITW, late 1939.

There were many more friends, of course, now just distant memories of young fresh faces, full of excitement and optimism. There was plenty of female company, too, with many liaisons formed between course colleagues and young ladies of varying reputation. The De La Warr Pavilion, for example, a lecture theatre during the day, was also home to a small theatrical company that laid on performances during evenings and at weekends, and Neil remembers sitting through endless shows just to get a glimpse of one of the girls. And when the month-long ITW course was complete, the whole company was invited to the end-of-course dance. It was only then, in his own words, that he realised that at close quarters the girls were less enchanting.

Neil's all too brief time at ITW had produced some memorable moments. The beauty of the coastline and the sheer contentment of the situation he was in would remain vividly in his mind. He would often stroll for miles in the glorious sunshine, with the cliffs, the green of the hills and distant Downs, together with the blue-grey sea, all combining to form an unforgettable picture. He later said: 'I have seldom enjoyed myself as much as I did during those first few weeks of the war at Bexhill-on-Sea.'

It was now time to move on and Neil's next stop was No. 8 Service Flying Training School at Montrose. The journey of nearly 600 miles to the east coast of Scotland was made by train, via London, allowing him the chance to spend a few hours in the capital before boarding a train once more for the long journey north. He managed to sleep through most of the night, waking only briefly when the train came to a halt at major cities along the way. Finally, twenty-four hours after leaving Bexhill-on-Sea, the train arrived at the coastal town of Montrose. It was a cold December Sunday morning. There was nothing but silence, and he suddenly felt a million miles from home.

With its history dating back to before the First World War, Montrose is reportedly the oldest airfield in Scotland. Although it had been abandoned during the 1920s, the RAF's expansion programme during the mid–late 1930s had brought life back to the airfield once more. But even then it was barely more than a strip of grass, with nothing but gorse to its north and bounded on its eastern side by sand dunes and the North Sea, while its southern end was immediately adjacent to the golf course just to the north of the town.

The school had been established in 1936, making use of the old First World War wooden buildings and equally old rickety hangars that stood crescent-shaped on the western side of the airfield. Using two-seat Hawker Hart and Hawker Audax biplanes, the school provided *ab initio* flying training for up to forty-eight students with the course lasting up to three months, after which the students were then given a similar period of advanced training prior to joining their operational squadrons. By the time Neil arrived at Montrose, the school was also operating twin-engine Airspeed Oxfords for teaching navigation, radio operating, bombing and gunnery.

With it still retaining the ambience of the good old days of the Royal Flying Corps, Neil immediately warmed to the old airfield of Montrose. The intermediate course, as it was known, operated from the south side of the airfield, while the advanced course flew from the north-west. There had already been talk amongst the students as to whether they would become fighter pilots, bomber pilots or, for that matter, any other type of pilot. They wondered how the decision would be made and whether they would get a say or not. As things were to turn out, it would be simple, and the decision was made on their first day.

After forming up outside the chief flying instructor's office in alphabetical order, the tall and rather impressive-looking black-moustached CFI, accompanied by his entourage, carried out what was described to the forty young hopefuls on Neil's course as their 'singles or twins' interview. Working his way along the line, the CFI asked each student in turn, in a rather abrupt sort of way, whether their choice was singles or twins, then asked them to give the briefest explanation of why. And one by one, the CFI either agreed with their choice or not, telling them it was to be singles or twins, with the adjutant noting the outcome on his clipboard.

Being an 'N' meant that Neil was some way down the line and it soon became apparent that more were destined for twins than singles. Although he had gained some valuable time to prepare his 'speech' as to why he wanted to go singles, that soon turned out to be irrelevant. The impact of the CFI suddenly appearing in front of him was a shock and any words that he might have rehearsed in his own mind instantly disappeared. What happened next, in what was the most crucial moment in deciding Neil's future, is best described in his own words:

> Then, as though in a nightmare, the black moustache was directly in front of me and I heard the question being put. I tried to remain calm. 'I think I'd do much better on fighters, sir,' I faltered. 'Really? Why?' he barked. I swallowed down the golf ball that had stuck in my throat. 'I'm . . . well. I'm just that sort of person. A bit . . . well, pretty mercurial.' 'Mercurial. I see.' And then there was the terrible pause again and two dark eyes boring holes into my skull. Then: 'Singles!' came the verdict and the black moustache moved on. *Eureka!* My relief instant and overwhelming, I could have cried out in happiness.

And so that was how it was decided. Designated No. 15 Course, the students had been split into twenty-five twins and fifteen singles. The fifteen destined for fighters, including Neil, were to be taught on the Hart while those heading for multi-engine types would be

Students of No. 15 Course at Montrose. Neil is extreme right.

taught on the Oxford. But it could so easily have gone the other way and Neil would have faced a future in Bomber Command or Coastal Command. The thought had horrified him.

Designed as a two-seat light bomber, the Hart had first flown in 1928 and proved to be a prominent aircraft in the inter-war period. However, by the time the Second World War broke out, it had become obsolete as a front-line aircraft and had been replaced by newer and more capable monoplane designs. Nonetheless, the Hart was perfectly suitable as a trainer and so several airframes were fitted with dual controls and the Rolls-Royce Kestrel engine de-rated to tone down the performance. The student pilot flew in the front cockpit with the instructor, when present, behind. When flown solo, a large lump of metal was hung on a bar at the rear of the fuselage to compensate for the instructor's weight.

It had been four months since Neil had last flown, and so he was keen to get back into the air. His first flight in the Hart was with the awesome and moustachioed CFI who had put the fear up him only days before. But this time the CFI's manner was far more relaxed, his only comment being on Neil's landing having been a bit fast, adding that had he not have been in the aircraft with Neil then the lack of weight would have resulted in the Hart disappearing off the end of the runway.

Two days later, and after just two hours airborne in the Hart, Neil went solo. He considered it a delightful aircraft to fly, although as he gained more experience on the type he found it to be tiring in its performance and he soon learned of its deficiencies. Nonetheless, it was a thrill to fly, and easy too.

The daily routine was generally split, with half the day in ground school – with endless lessons on topics such as the theory of flight, navigation, meteorology, airframes, engines, maintaining aircraft and armament – and the other half of the day spent flying, with lunch in the sergeants' mess in between. Things were now happening at pace, and by the time Neil made the long journey home to Manchester for Christmas leave he had flown eleven hours on type.

The snow came in mid-January, covering eastern Scotland in a white blanket and producing a scene of different shades and colours. It was winter at its loveliest and a very different landscape to the one Neil had been brought up in. Despite the snow, the airfield was kept open. There was no time to be lost. In peacetime, training might have been suspended for a few weeks but not in war. The students simply had to learn to adapt to operating from a different surface.

Learning to fly in Scotland during the winter months was an absolute delight. The landscape was one of a barren wasteland of frozen white. On his navigation exercises, Neil would venture into the Grampians. He recalls flying down the valleys along frozen streams, with the mountain tops towering above him, and then skipping over the brow of hills, describing it all as 'an unforgettable joy'.

Although he occasionally caught a glimpse of other aircraft types, the war seemed to be an event going on elsewhere. But the arrival at Montrose of a detachment of Supermarine Spitfires from 603 Squadron, based at Prestwick, to counter any enemy intruders that might suddenly appear along Scotland's east coast, provided a timely reminder that the nation was still at war.

Away from flying, Neil would often venture into the countryside and walk for miles in the snow. On one occasion he went off with two colleagues in search of David Gorrie's farm. After ITW, Gorrie had gone on to further training elsewhere, but he had told Neil that he would always be welcome should he ever visit the family's farm. He was right. Having found the farm, Neil was welcomed in by Gorrie's sister, Ina. It was the start of a friendship that would last more than sixty years.

Three more of Gorrie's friends were already at the farm that day and one of Neil's new acquaintances was twenty-year-old John Lenahan, a pre-war regular also going through pilot training at Montrose. Lenahan was then recovering from his injuries after crashing an Audax just a few miles to the north. He had spent fifteen hours in the wreckage before the mountain rescue team finally reached the site and pulled him out. It was another of those stark reminders of the hazards of flying training. But while Lenahan had been lucky on that occasion, his life would be cut short just a few months later; he was another young victim of the Battle of Britain. David Gorrie, too, would not survive the war. He got through the Battle of Britain but was killed in 1941.

The Spitfires of 603 Squadron were often airborne from Montrose and when they were in the air they always had priority over the training aircraft. It was on one such occasion that Neil had another of his lucky escapes. Several Spitfires were in the circuit to land and the queue of training aircraft waiting to take off had started to grow. Neil was second in line, solo in his Hart, and was lined up behind an Oxford.

Neil watched the lead Spitfire make its curved approach to land, but then noticed it was about to undershoot, with its nose raised too high. It then dawned on him that the Spit was heading in his direction and he realised its pilot would be unable to see the aircraft on the ground waiting to take off. Before he or anyone else could react, the Spitfire rammed into the Oxford at the front of the queue. There was a catastrophic bang and an explosion. Bits of aircraft flew in all directions. Neil could only watch the horror unfolding in front of his eyes. Fire engines, ambulances and rescuers were soon on the scene. The Spitfire pilot was fortunate to walk away limping and bleeding. The Oxford, however, had disintegrated. Its two occupants were later recovered from the wreckage and taken off on stretchers.

It is not surprising that an accident such as the one Neil had witnessed at Montrose would play on his mind for many years to come. Fortunately, however, he had been second in line that day and not at the front of the queue. But there was no time to dwell on what might have been or the 'what ifs' in life. After that, though, he would never be fully comfortable while waiting on the ground in the path of a landing aircraft.

There were other issues, too, with operating small detachments of fighters at remote training airfields. One major problem at Montrose was that its communications set-up was not linked to the main Fighter Command operations system. This meant that to intercept any enemy intruders along the east coast of Scotland essentially relied on visual observations, and it was during one dual sortie to the south of Stonehaven one day that Neil saw an enemy aircraft for the first time.

At first it was not obvious to him what he had seen. He could see a large aircraft off to his right, flying parallel and at the same height, but he did not know what it was. However, no sooner had he seen it than his world was suddenly turned upside down. Neil vividly remembers the instructor yanking the controls and taking the Hart into a steep dive as fast as it would go back towards the cliffs, shouting, 'It's a Hun, a Heinkel!'

Confirmation that it was, indeed, an enemy intruder was given by the sight of three Spitfires rushing past them towards the area where the unidentified aircraft had been seen. But nothing much happened after that. Neil later described his first encounter with an enemy aircraft as a 'non-event', although it had clearly been far more of a drama for his instructor, and he later admitted that the whole episode had 'more interested than frightened' him. The fact that the enemy aircraft might have shot them down never even entered his head.

For those destined for fighters, learning to fly in the dark was not a priority. Although the fighter squadrons supposedly had the capability to intercept enemy aircraft at night, the reality was that the basic technology fitted to RAF fighters at that time meant this could only be considered, at best, a secondary role. Nonetheless, night flying was part of the training and so periods of flying in the dark were squeezed into the rest of the course. But even then, Neil only flew five hours at night in the following three months, less than two hours being solo, which merely reinforced the lack of priority placed on night flying for those destined to go to singles.

From Neil's point of view that was fine. It was an eerie sensation operating from the airfield into complete darkness – and not without its dangers. For a start, no radios were fitted to the aircraft and so there was no way of communicating with the ground. And with a blackout in force across the country, leaving the airfield's flare path always produced a feeling of being completely alone.

Neil was neither anxious nor enthusiastic about flying in the dark. It was simply something that had to be done. But while night flying was not as bad overall as he had expected, his brief experience of it at Montrose was not without incident. During one dual sortie at night, while about to take off, he managed to taxi into another Hart, and on one of his solos he managed to touch down short.

The first incident resulted in the two Harts being badly damaged and so Neil found himself centre-stage at a court of inquiry. The incident had occurred during his second period of night flying, which took place several weeks after the first. The students were operating that night from the school's satellite airfield at Edzell, just a few miles to the north-west of Montrose. It was the first time Neil had been to Edzell and he would later describe the airfield as little more than a football field with the most basic of lighting to say the least.

The plan for the evening was a brief period of dual flying followed by a night solo. Several aircraft were operating from Edzell that night and, after completing his first dual sortie, Neil was on the ground and in position for his next. The green blink of the Aldis lamp signalled the all-clear for take-off. He could see nothing in front other than darkness, and so he opened the throttle. The aircraft started to roll forward, but then came to a sudden halt. Neil tried to move forward again but there was no response. All he could hear was the most unpleasant 'thwacking' noise from somewhere ahead. And then came the swearing from his instructor behind.

After switching off the engine, Neil climbed out to see what the problem was. Feeling his way in the dark, he worked his way round to the front of his aircraft only to find bits of broken propeller on the ground. He then noticed the rather chewed up wing of another Hart and looking up into the darkness he could see the face of his course colleague, Alex Osmand, staring back at him from the cockpit.

The inquiry determined that both student pilots had seen the green light, and both assumed it had been for them. But being the Hart behind, the spotlight fell on Neil's aircraft, although being dual meant that his instructor took most of the blame. And so, as far as Neil was concerned, that was the end of the matter.

With the school now two aircraft down Neil's dual instruction was cut short. He was, however, soon sent off on another night solo and it was on that sortie that he landed short. Everything seemed to be going well during his final approach when suddenly he noticed the ground rush up to meet him. Fortunately, the aircraft literally bounced back into the air and, clinging on tightly to the control column, Neil held the aircraft straight for just long enough until it came back down to earth. He later learned that his first touch-down had been in the field short of the runway but this time he was fortunate to get away with his error.

The intermediate course finished in early March after which Neil was granted three days' leave. He was now considered fully trained and so was permitted to wear the coveted pilot wings. But there was no formal presentation or ceremony as such, not even a certificate or special entry in his flying log book. Nothing! He was told that he could either draw his wings from stores or instead go in to Montrose and purchase a padded pair of wings, which looked far better, from the local shop. And so he and his colleagues went off into town.

The advanced course was about preparing the students for the procedures employed by the operational fighter squadrons – such as formation flying, air gunnery and bombing – while there were additional navigation exercises as well. Rather worryingly, though, was the rumour that few of the sergeants on the previous outgoing singles course had been posted to a fighter squadron. The others, it appeared, were being posted elsewhere, such as to torpedo-bombers or target-towing aircraft.

There was a far more relaxed atmosphere about the advanced course than there had been previously. Training was now carried out on the Hawker Audax, a modified variant of the Hart designed for army co-operation. Essentially, there was no difference in performance between the two aircraft, but the main change as far as the student was concerned was there was no provision for a second pilot and so an observer was carried instead, or the aircraft flown solo. For weapons training the Audax was fitted with racks for four small bombs and each crew member had a 0.303-inch machine gun, the pilot's being forward-firing and synchronised, while the observer's Lewis gun was mounted on a Scarff ring, although it could be replaced by a camera gun for cine training.

The course required each student to fly as observer for another student pilot on one long-range cross-country navigation exercise, and it was during his turn as observer that Neil was almost unwell in an aircraft for the first time. In fact, the whole experience was rather strange. For a start, the small fold-away seat, harness, and parachute arrangement in the rear cockpit were all quite different from the front because the observer was required to stand up to fire the gun.

For this one-off experience, Neil's pilot was Alex Osmand, his taxiing accident colleague. Whether Osmand wanted to impress the young Neil in the rear cockpit or whether he always took off that way is unclear, but as the aircraft lunged into the air Neil's navigational instruments, maps, and pencils all ended up on the floor and then disappeared into the fuselage behind him. He had no choice but to get down on his hands and knees to recover his belongings but being so tall meant he struggled to crawl around on the floor, never mind turn around. It was impossible and so Neil was of no assistance to his colleague for the rest of the exercise. He simply sat on his seat facing backwards, thoroughly bored. But he also found that facing backwards in a manoeuvring aircraft was not at all comfortable and the only way he could prevent himself from being unwell was to turn around, face the front and persuade himself that he was flying the aircraft. It was not a pleasant flight.

Neil spent the Easter weekend as duty pilot, but not because he had done anything wrong; it was simply his turn. As the duty pilot he was required to sleep in the watch office. The weather that weekend was particularly bad. Heavy mist and rain were coming in and there was much activity over the North Sea. With Montrose being a diversion airfield for operational aircraft in the area, it had to be kept open around the clock and so it turned out to be the busiest of weekends, as Neil explained in a letter to his parents: 'In the bank, I was never allowed to stamp an envelope without supervision. Here, seven months later, I appear to be running the entire Air Force single-handed!'

The fantasy of youth maybe, but it is true that Neil was a prolific letter writer during the war. His parents' devotion to him was un-questionable, and understandable given he was their only child. His mother wrote to him five times every week, wherever he happened to be at the time, while his father supplemented her letters with one of his own, written every Sunday. Neil always responded as dutifully as he could at the time, but never less than twice a week.

Apart from the occasional duty, weekends were generally free. One of the more popular places to visit was Dundee to the south, a bus ride away, which usually involved the Saturday night being spent at the Royal British Hotel before returning to Montrose the following day.

Memories of one notable weekend in Dundee stand out. Neil had met a girl and they had spent a most pleasant time together on the Sunday before it was time for him to make his way back to Montrose. But instead of getting back to the airfield in good time, as he really should have done, he first decided to escort his companion home. That would have been fine except that Montrose was to the north and the girl lived in a village called Wormit to the south, on the other side of the River Tay.

The girl told him that she lived just a matter of yards from the village railway station, and so he was sure there was enough time to get her home before catching the last train back across the Tay Bridge to Dundee. But, as it turned out, she lived further from the station than she had led him to believe. Nonetheless, there was still enough time to catch the last train, providing he ran.

He was still a hundred yards or so from the station when he heard the whistle of the train and the sound of it puffing northwards into the distance. When he arrived at the platform, a man carrying a lantern confirmed it was the last train to Dundee and that it had left a few minutes early because there was no one at Wormit to board the train.

Neil sat on the platform in total darkness contemplating what he should do next. He simply had to get back. As a young boy he had often walked along railway tracks with his father, and so he decided that was his best option now. But, unbeknown to him, the Tay Bridge was guarded. It was wartime after all and, having walked into the rather startled sentry's position, Neil was firmly told that he was not going to cross the bridge on foot. His only option now was to wait until morning and catch the first train.

The sentries did, however, offer him the use of their sentry hut and, after a night of little or no sleep, Neil finally boarded the first train back to Dundee. From there he jumped on the first bus to Montrose, eventually arriving back at the airfield just in time for parade. It had been an extremely close-run thing!

Another popular place to visit was the city of Aberdeen, a train journey of some forty miles up the coast. And it was in Aberdeen that, in Neil's own words, he was 'introduced to hard drinking for the first time and to girls, but not quite for the first time!'

Neil also took what opportunities he could to return home. After working the Easter weekend, he was given three days off *in lieu* and so returned to Manchester before making the long return trip north for the final weeks of his course.

He came back to Montrose to find that training had moved on to gunnery. Those destined to be successful in air combat would soon learn that it was not all about dashing around the sky as fast as possible taking on anyone and everyone. While pure flying skill would help a pilot learn how to master his aircraft in the sky, it was not the only important factor. To be a good fighter pilot required a combination of flying and personal qualities: excellent aircraft handling skills; a good understanding of his own aircraft's performance and that of his opponent; quick reactions; good eyesight; anticipation; patience; courage; and self-control to name but a few. And, of course, a fighter pilot would also need to be a good shot.

The easiest way to shoot down another aircraft is from line astern, where there is little or no deflection and where closing speed can be more easily managed to give the attacker maximum time to fire at his opponent. Also, the closer the attacker can get then the easier it becomes to hit the opponent, whereas firing at excessive range means the bullets are subjected to the effects of ballistics, such as gravity drop. But opportunities to get into a close position line astern are rare, and a manoeuvring target is much harder to hit because of the amount of lead required in the aim. And when attacking a manoeuvring aircraft there are several other factors to consider, such as speed and the rate of turn. The faster the attacking aircraft then the greater its radius of turn, and the less its rate of turn in degrees per second. Any hard manoeuvring also reduces the attacking aircraft's speed, but speed can be maintained by losing height. But then height is also very important to the fighter pilot. And so it goes on.

Neil readily admits that he found the air-to-air gunnery phase of his course far more difficult than he had ever imagined. The course focused on 'quarter attacks' with so much to take in. Operating in pairs and curving towards each other in turn, the students were first taught how to attack another aircraft using camera guns, pressing the trigger on the spade grip at the appropriate moment to record their attack on film. They practised again, and again – and then again, with gradually improving results. Neil later recalled: 'The trick lay in gauging the distance, judging accurately the curve of pursuit, and firing within range.'

Next came the air-to-ground gunnery phase, which involved firing at targets in Lunan Bay to the south of Montrose. The next piece of the armament jigsaw was dive bombing, which took place in the Montrose basin with the targets sited in the mud flats. Diving towards earth from 5,000 feet, with the speed building rapidly and the ground rushing up before finally releasing the practice smoke bomb, and then pulling hard out of the dive, was all such a thrilling exercise. But Neil was given a sharp reminder of the dangers of such manoeuvres on his first solo dive-bombing exercise when his bomb failed to release. He kept tugging at the bomb release lever but still nothing happened. And all the time the ground was rushing up at him. Hauling as hard as he could on the control column he finally pulled out of the dive just in time.

Climbing back up to height he set himself up again. Four times he tried to get a practice bomb away, but he only managed it twice. Frustrated, he returned to the airfield and explained what had happened to the ground crew. The bomb release was working perfectly well on the ground, but he was relieved to learn that it was a known problem when diving in the Audax at high speed. The stresses on the airframe were known to cause the wire from the bomb-release mechanism to tighten to the point where it became impossible for the bomb-release lever to be moved correctly.

It was often the case that a student pilot only found something out when he experienced it for the first time. The problem with this example, though, is that flying at high speed towards the ground is not the time to find something out.

Neil has some wonderful memories of his days at Montrose, with smiling faces and lots of fun. Like one lunchtime when a waiter came through the door to the kitchen and tripped, dispatching the contents of his tray, soup as it happened, over the back of one of Neil's colleagues. The broken crockery and soup on the floor were soon cleared. But if that incident alone was not funny enough, the roars of laughter inside the dining room rose to another level when the same waiter reappeared with another tray moments later only to slip on the soup from the first tray, again dispatching the contents over the same student! It was slap-stick comedy at its best.

The course was now approaching its end. Talk of some being commissioned started to spread. Neil was one of those in the frame. In addition to him doing well in training, his age, educational background, sporting prowess and overall presence all helped make him a strong candidate for a commission. But then, others were suitable too, and in the end thirteen were identified to have the potential to be an officer.

The selection process involved an initial interview with the chief ground instructor, during which Neil seemed to have all the right answers. This was followed by a further interview with the officer commanding the advanced squadron, Squadron Leader Eric Verdon-Roe, son of the British aviation pioneer Alliott Verdon-Roe, which also went well.

Neil was then put in front of the commissioning board. In addition to the chief ground instructor and Verdon-Roe, the board included the commanding officer, Group Captain John Sadler. Again, the interview seemed to go well and fortunately for Neil there was no mention of the taxiing accident earlier in the course. There then followed several days of waiting for news of how he had done before Neil was called for a medical, which he sailed through without a hitch, followed by more days of silence.

Meanwhile, the course entered its final phase of training, which involved formation take-offs, battle climbs up to 15,000 feet (the highest they were permitted to fly without oxygen), more air-to-air attacks, this time against a drogue (something that Neil started to excel at), and low-level bombing, which Neil could also do very well.

The final two weeks were to be spent at the armament training camp at West Freugh on the west coast of Scotland to fire live ammunition. It was the end of April and Neil flew one of the ten aircraft detached. It was the first time he had flown in such a large formation and was an exhilarating experience. On landing at West Freugh, Neil was amazed to see so many different aircraft types. It was a beautiful day and he felt part of what he described as 'the old, peacetime Air Force, with war a distant planet away'.

Apart from a couple of days of poor weather, the rest of the flying programme went as planned. The air-to-air gunnery exercises against drogues, towed by Hawker Henleys as tugs, were both demanding and exciting. Neil loved the noise, vibration and smell of firing live ammunition. And when he was not flying, walking in the surrounding hills was an absolute delight.

It was while he was at West Freugh during the early days of May that Neil was told he was to go to Cranwell for an interview with the Air Officer Commanding-in-Chief Training Command as the final part of the commissioning selection process. This meant leaving the armament camp and making the long journey across Scotland and down to Lincolnshire by train. Also going to Cranwell for an interview was Alex Osmand, and so they travelled down together.

Of all the interviews in the commissioning process, Neil remembers finding the final one at Cranwell to have been the most relaxing and easiest. To him, the AOC-in-C came across as a most pleasant and smiling man. And with the final interview over, he and Osmand returned to West Freugh, although they had to complete the last eight miles on foot. Their train had arrived in Stranraer during the early hours of the morning and with no obvious way of getting back to the airfield until later in the day, they decided to walk.

Five days later, Neil and Osmand were summoned to the flight commander's office to be given the good news that both were to be commissioned. The official date promulgated for their promotion to the rank of pilot officer was 12 May 1940, by which time they had returned to Montrose; the transit back was Neil's final flight on the course.

Sadly, Alex Osmand was another of Neil's course colleagues not to survive the war; he was killed in the Far East during 1943. And there were to be many more sad tales of his friends not making it through the war, or for that matter, the next few months. One was Alan Buck, a friend of Neil's from their early flying days together at Barton. Buck had been one of the lucky four to go straight to Sealand on the opening day of the war. Neil bumped into him at Montrose just as he was finishing his training, when Buck landed at the airfield in a Hurricane. The two friends talked of old times and of current times as well. Buck was soon to go south with his squadron to Tangmere, although he did not know what had happened to Robert Shaw after they had finished their training at Sealand, but he believed Shaw had gone across the Channel to France.

This was all incredibly exciting news. Two of his erstwhile mates had successfully passed through pilot training and were now on operational fighter squadrons. There could be nothing better than that. If Neil was lucky enough, he might get the chance to do the same.

The two men parted in the highest of spirits. But it was the last time Neil and Buck would see each other. As with all the sad tales of his friends that have gone before, Alan Buck would be killed just weeks later. Robert Shaw, too, would be killed just a few weeks after Buck, another victim of the Battle of Britain. It was all very sad, very sad indeed.

Chapter Four

249 Squadron

Less than twenty-four hours after Neil had returned to Montrose from West Freugh, German Panzers were rolling into northern France, Belgium and Holland. It was 10 May 1940. The Phoney War was over, and the air battles fought over France and the Low Countries during the next twelve days would be fast, furious and deadly. Only the month before, Hitler had launched his offensive against Norway and Denmark, and so his latest move was not entirely unexpected.

Neil's course had already been dispersed. His sergeant friends had left Montrose for their next destination, but because he was to be commissioned he had to get his new uniform from Edinburgh and so he was one of a handful still left on camp. He wrote to his parents:

> Today, I received the last bits of uniform and am transferring to the officers' mess. Everything is mucked up completely by events on the Continent. Apparently, I was posted to a place called Sutton Bridge in Lincolnshire but owing to the proximity of Belgium and Holland and the war news, it has been cancelled. Now, I don't know what is happening, except that I shall probably be home in a day or so.

He was disappointed not to have had the chance to say goodbye to many of his friends. None of them could possibly have known how things were going to turn out in the future, but memories of their names and smiling faces would remain with Neil for ever. Life had been something of an adventure so far – learning to fly, good friends, and lots of fun. Sadly, though, the harsh reality of war meant that within a year there would only be a handful of his friends left.

Now that he was an officer, Neil was eligible to travel first class and his long train journey home was spent thinking of family and friends, rather than the war. He suddenly felt coldly miserable and quite alone. When he arrived back in Manchester, he still had no idea of what was to happen to him next. But he did not have to wait long to find out. Just twenty-four hours after he arrived home, a telegram appeared. He was posted to 249 Squadron, based at Church Fenton in Yorkshire.

Located fifteen miles to the east of Leeds and a similar distance to the south-west of York, the ancient village of Church Fenton lies in the Selby district of North Yorkshire. Just outside the village on the York side is the airfield. It is now the site of Leeds East Airport, but back in 1940 Church Fenton was one of the RAF's main operational stations in No. 13 Group Fighter Command, tasked with defending northern England and Scotland.

Being so far north, and some 200 miles from the Luftwaffe's main offensive, Church Fenton was an ideal location for uninterrupted training and for the working up of a new operational squadron. Its newest resident, 249 Squadron, was one of several fighter squadrons to be reborn following losses in France. It had only briefly existed before, at the very end of the First World War when based in Scotland for coastal patrol duties.

In command of 249 was 27-year-old Squadron Leader John Grandy, a pre-war pilot from Middlesex. His most recent flying experience had been as an instructor with the London University Air Squadron and subsequently as the chief flying instructor at a flying training school in Scotland. He had then briefly commanded a Blenheim squadron at Catterick prior to being told that he was to form 249 Squadron.

Grandy had arrived at Church Fenton with the simple task of getting 249 Squadron formed and trained up to operational standard in the shortest time possible. To help him set up his new squadron, he had as his adjutant the very capable Flying Officer Ewart Lohmeyer, a veteran of the First World War during which he had flown as an observer and had been awarded the Distinguished Flying Cross. He would be of tremendous support to Grandy, not only during 249's early days but throughout their time together on the squadron.

Amongst the first pilots to arrive at Church Fenton was thirty-year-old Flight Lieutenant Ron Kellett, known as 'Boozy', a former stockbroker from Tadcaster and a pre-war Auxiliary pilot. He arrived from 616 Squadron to become one of 249's flight commanders. Another early arrival was Flying Officer John Young, or 'Dobbin' as he was known, a graduate from Cambridge and former Auxiliary squadron qualified flying instructor. Young arrived from 603 Squadron and he would assist with the work-up of 249's new pilots once they arrived. Kellett would be the oldest pilot to join the squadron, but most of those posted to 249 were far less experienced than him or Young, having been posted to the squadron direct from a flying training school, like Neil.

After receiving the signal instructing him to report to Church Fenton, Neil travelled to Yorkshire by train the following day. He noticed the signal had used his new service number – 79168. It was the first he knew of it. The signal also stated that he was posted to 249(H) Squadron and so he very much hoped the (H) stood for Hurricanes. During his journey he bumped into a couple of his former course colleagues from Montrose, both sergeants. One, Pether, was also on his way to join 249 while the other, Ivor Arber, was going elsewhere.

It was a quiet Sunday afternoon when Neil arrived at Church Fenton. There seemed to be hardly anyone around, and so he made his way to the ante room for afternoon tea. A handful of officers were sitting in silence and when he asked if anyone was from 249 no one knew anything about the squadron. It must be new they said. Other than that, there was very little conversation to be had at all.

Neil began to wonder if he was in the right place, but then an older man in uniform approached him. He was wearing the rank of a flying officer, an observer brevet and medal ribbons denoting the Distinguished Flying Cross and service in the First World War. He introduced himself with a warm and pleasant smile. It was Lohmeyer.

During the conversation that followed it became clear to Neil that 249 Squadron was still in the process of forming. Gradually, a few more pilots started to arrive. Some already had squadron experience, such as 23-year-old Canadian Robert 'Butch' Barton from 41 Squadron on promotion to flight lieutenant, who was to become 249's other flight commander, and Flying Officer James Nicolson, another pre-war pilot, who arrived from 72 Squadron. And then there was 21-year-old Pilot Officer Bryan Meaker, an Irishman slight in stature but always smiling, from 46 Squadron, and the rather quiet Sergeant John Beard from Sussex, also aged twenty-one, who came from 609 Squadron. Others, however, like Neil, had come straight from the flying training schools and, although he would quickly get to know the officers, it would take him longer to meet the sergeants; such was the nature of having two separate messes dividing what were, essentially, good squadron chums.

Neil had arrived at Church Fenton amid rumours and uncertainty. What was certain was that the squadron had yet to receive any aircraft. But then came two surprising pieces of news. Firstly, the squadron was to move immediately to Leconfield, some thirty miles away in the East Riding of Yorkshire, and, secondly, 249 was to be equipped with Spitfires and not Hurricanes as had been believed.

It was a short drive to the former bomber airfield of Leconfield, just to the north of Beverley. Now part of Fighter Command, it was a large, rolling area of grass, and home to the Spitfires of 616 Squadron. While 249 Squadron continued to build its numbers, 616 moved south to Rochford to exchange places with 74 Squadron, although the two squadrons would soon change places once again, such was the moving around of squadrons at the time.

Grandy's knowledge of the university air squadrons and the calibre of the undergraduate pilots they produced was instrumental in his setting up of 249 Squadron. He knew that many of them were undergoing training at Cranwell and so one of the first things he did was to go to Lincolnshire to secure some of them for his own squadron. This, he believed, would make his operational training task that much easier and quicker to achieve.

One to fall into this category, 23-year-old Pilot Officer John Beazley, the son of a High Court judge and who had studied at Pembroke College, Oxford, had already joined 249. He would soon be followed by four more straight from Cranwell. Pat Wells, also aged 23, had mostly been raised in South Africa but was originally from an affluent Midlands brewing family. He had studied mining engineering at London University and was a former member of the university air squadron. Another South African was 22-year-old Percy Burton, the son of a prominent government minister, who was older than he looked and had studied at Christ Church College, Oxford, before the intervention of war. George Barclay was just twenty. He was a tall, dark and handsome clergyman's son from Surrey and a graduate of Trinity College, Cambridge. And the last was twenty-year-old Robert Fleming, a small, gentle, and unfailingly polite undergraduate of London University and another former member of the university air squadron.

The squadron was initially allocated eight Spitfires and, with more pilots arriving, the squadron's two flights were formed. Neil was allocated to 'A' Flight, with Boozy Kellett as his flight commander. Neil would later describe Kellett as 'the antithesis of the popular image of the dashing young fighter pilot'. He also owned a vintage Rolls-Royce, which he made available to all as a general run-around car on the station, but having never seen him laugh, or even raise a smile, Neil summarises Kellett as simply 'different' and a man who gave the impression of disliking someone on sight. Neil never felt comfortable enough to call him Boozy like others did, and he always felt that Kellett considered him to be of rather ordinary stuff and that he might not meet the standard.

This could not have been an easy start for Neil. As one of the pilots previously trained on biplanes, he was required to be introduced to flying a low-wing monoplane and so, two days after arriving at Leconfield, he flew his familiarisation sortie in a Miles Master advanced trainer with Kellett as his instructor. In his book *Gun Button to Fire*, which records in detail his time on 249 Squadron during 1940, Neil describes the flight:

My first efforts in the Master were not impressive. Surrounded by a mass of new-fangled systems, gadgets, and instruments, I was almost overcome with the novelty of it all. After take-off, which was shatteringly impressive after a biplane, I would be fiddling with the airscrew pitch when I should have been raising the wheels, and in the excitement of pulling up or lowering the flaps, would ignore every known speed limitation. And so on, if not these, then other elementary errors. Time after time.

After three short trips in the Master, Neil was considered safe and ready for the Spitfire. But before he was given the opportunity to get airborne in one, he first spent hours in the hangar sitting in the cockpit to familiarise himself with its layout, mentally going through numerous start-ups, take-offs and landings.

Then, during the late afternoon on 21 May, Neil was to fly the Spitfire for the first time. With only eight aircraft on strength, he had to wait his turn and while waiting for his aircraft to be refuelled, he was talked through just about everything by James Nicolson. Known as Nick to his friends, Nicolson was three years older than Neil and had already flown Spitfires with his previous squadron. Although he and Neil had only known each other for a short time, they got on very well. But the more Nicolson explained about flying the Spitfire, the harder it all suddenly started to sound.

It was then Neil's turn to go. Having finally started up and taxied across the grass to the far end of the airfield, it was time to take off. Neil suddenly experienced a stomach-clenching moment of black apprehension before opening the throttle slowly but firmly. He recalls: 'There were no half measures about that aircraft. With the howl of a Dervish, the Spitfire set off across the grass like an electric hare, the acceleration alarming.'

In what seemed like no time at all he was airborne, the airfield falling away below and now left some way behind. He continues:

I flew around, my confidence growing by the minute. What a wonderful aircraft! Such a sense of power, agility, and

P9506, Neil's first Spitfire, May 1940.

strength. Intoxicated by the sheer joy of it all, I suddenly became aware of time. Fifteen minutes was all I had been allowed, and I had already been up almost twenty. I dropped the nose and began to search for the aerodrome.

After a slight bounce he landed safely and taxied in. An hour later he was airborne again, and by the end of May he had flown the Spitfire thirty-six times, totalling thirty-two hours in the air. He was very quickly gaining experience on type.

Neil was now experiencing his life's ambition. He would later describe this period of his life as 'wonderful and just perfect'. He had never been so happy.

Meanwhile, across the Channel, things were not going well for the Allies, although Neil was never more than mildly concerned at the time. To him, the war was still something happening elsewhere. Working up to operational readiness in Yorkshire seemed a long way from what was going on down south. Besides, no one on his squadron really felt that Britain might be on the brink of defeat. Morale, in fact, had positively soared. They were hearing great stories of Hurricane pilots enjoying overwhelming success over their Luftwaffe counterparts, and with Spitfires they were certain they could do even better. Propaganda was clearly playing its part, but then came news of Dunkirk. If the importance of getting 249 operational as soon as possible had not been made clear enough to all before, then its significance was certainly evident now.

While 249 continued its work-up – with formation flying, developing its tactics, air-to-air and air-to-ground gunnery training, as well as refuelling and re-arming exercises on the ground – 74 Squadron moved south to cover the evacuation at Dunkirk. To learn from their experience, a senior pilot of 74 was invited to brief those on 249 of his squadron's involvement during the evacuation.

The briefing turned out to be very graphic and was followed by a talk by one of Leconfield's medical officers who explained to the pilots how to use the first aid kit provided in each aircraft, amongst other things. Things were now getting serious and one piece of advice given by the medical officer was to remain with Neil throughout his flying career, that being the importance of rest and sleep during times of stress, such as in between operational sorties.

249's work-up to operational status was going very well but, on 10 June, and seemingly out of nowhere, a signal arrived from group headquarters. The squadron's Spitfires were being withdrawn to be replaced by Hurricanes. There were always rumours circulating in the squadron, but nothing like this.

The reason given was because the Spitfires were needed in the hard-pressed south of England, but the news brought a mixed reaction amongst the pilots. Neil, however, was not bothered one bit. Everything he had heard about the Hurricane had been good. His only disappointment was that he was to lose his own personal aircraft, in the squadron code of GN-D.

The first of the squadron's sixteen Hurricanes arrived the following day. The rest would appear in the coming days and the number would eventually reach twenty. Not only was there a change of aircraft but there were some changes of personnel as well. Those not considered to be at the operational standard required were moved elsewhere; one was Pether, Neil's former course colleague at Montrose who had joined 249 the same day, who went off to an operational training unit.

While Neil had been disappointed to lose his personal Spitfire, he was boosted by the news that he was to be allocated his own brand-new Hurricane, registered P3616 and coded GN-F. It was like having a new car. He immediately felt at home in the cockpit. The Hurricane was, after all, a single-wing development of the Hart and so the cockpit layout was similar to what he had been used to before, albeit with more instruments. His only complaint was the throttle design, which he described as 'a flimsy little lever and very insignificant'.

In the air Neil found the Hurricane to be very steady. He found the ailerons to be lighter than the Spit, markedly so at speed, but the elevator was much less sensitive and the controls, if anything, better balanced than those of the Spitfire. Although he had expected the Hurricane to be noticeably slower, he was pleasantly surprised. However, it did not have the legs of a Spit, nor its sprightly acceleration in a dive. Moreover, although the Hurricane could climb more steeply, it did so at a slower speed. And there was no rudder bias, an irritating omission he felt, meaning that climbing at full throttle required a heavy right boot on the rudder, and an even heavier left boot when descending. But, overall, he was delighted. The Hurricane possessed an obvious ruggedness and strength.

Because of time, there was to be no conversion to the Hurricane as such. From the outset Neil flew four times a day. And then there was night flying. On one night, 18/19 June, during the squadron's designated period of night flying, a lone Heinkel dropped its bombs on the airfield. It was probably a straggler from a larger force attacking targets in the Midlands, and with there being flying from the airfield that night, the flare path, and the many other associated lights, would have made the airfield an inviting target. Fortunately, only one bomb fell within the airfield's boundary, just a hundred yards or so from the watch office where Neil was on duty at the time. The rest fell harmlessly outside. Thankfully, no one was injured and damage to the airfield was negligible.

There followed a few nights of enemy activity in the area. Much of the Luftwaffe's effort over England during June was at night, mostly against targets in the eastern part of the country. Neil found these night raids to be more of an interest to him rather than frightening. Nonetheless, the threat they posed meant that 'A' Flight, including Neil, detached further north to Prestwick in Scotland for a few days to complete their night flying work-up without further interruption.

June fairly flew by and, on the 29th, 249 Squadron was declared operational. During that last month alone, the squadron had flown a thousand hours. This extraordinary effort was put into perspective in a letter to Grandy from Air Vice-Marshal Richard Saul, the Air Officer Commanding No. 13 Group, congratulating the squadron on becoming operational. The AOC wrote: 'I do not remember a case where a squadron has ever passed the 1,000-hour mark in a month, and this intensive effort to become operational at the earliest moment reflects the greatest credit on all concerned.'

Much of that day was spent at Church Fenton being formally inspected by Air Commodore Charles Nicholas, the group's senior air staff officer, after which there was a practice scramble and demonstration of refuelling and re-arming. At the end of the day the squadron returned to Leconfield. Everyone went into Hull to celebrate. It was a great day and an even better evening. There was much drinking of beer before Neil decided imprudently to go on to the whisky. He was still only nineteen years old and not such a hardened drinker as others. Fortunately, though, he had a guardian angel with the old and extremely wise Lohmeyer sinking some of the many drinks lined up for Neil. It was the first of many times Loh would come to Neil's rescue in the coming months.

249 Squadron did not have to wait long for its first operational action. It came during the afternoon of 4 July and Neil was one of those involved. There had already been a few scrambles during the morning, but they had led to nothing. Then, during the late afternoon, Neil was flying one of three Hurricanes, led by Dobbin Young, that were scrambled to intercept a lone enemy aircraft approaching the

east coast. It was Neil's first scramble and the chance to go into battle had come rather sooner than he had expected.

The three Hurricanes climbed out towards Flamborough Head. It was nearly 5 p.m. There was a fair amount of broken cloud but soon after coasting out to the south of Bridlington, Neil spotted the enemy aircraft. He recalls:

> I saw the bogey immediately, about three miles away, a slim, dark shape cruising as calm as you like between scattered white dumplings of cloud. On a converging course, too, and several thousand feet beneath. I could scarcely believe my eyes. A German! A Dornier Flying Pencil, in fact, the distinctive outline obvious.

The enemy aircraft he had spotted was a twin-engine Dornier Do 17. Neil pulled level with Young and waggled his wings furiously, while pointing to the aircraft below. Young ordered the Hurricanes into line astern for what was known as a 'No. 1 attack' as he considered it to be the best way of intercepting the Dornier while avoiding the risk of collisions between his own formation.

The German crew must have spotted the Hurricanes at about the same time but rather than turn away and run the Dornier turned into the attackers and went into a dive. It was a brave and calculated move. Neil continues:

> Going through the nonsensical No. 1 attack routine, we reared up like startled pheasant chicks, dropped into line astern, then plummeted down on the Dornier, which was now making to fly between our legs. I found myself behind Dobbin, almost over the vertical, jumping around with excitement and willing him to get out of the way. The Hun was at that point about 2,000 yards ahead, going hard for a cloud. Overtaking him rapidly and almost screaming with frustration, I saw that he would just beat us to it. And he did. He was in, then out. Then in again. A dark shape, twisting and turning in slow motion.

The Hurricanes shot into the cloud after the Dornier and then out the other side. For several minutes they raced up and down in and out of cloud in search of their prey. They even zoomed up to 20,000 feet to get a better view from above. But they saw nothing. The Dornier had disappeared. After fifteen minutes of hanging around, they turned for home. Neil was disappointed. They had let the Hun get away.

Neil was scrambled several times during the next few days, even at night, but nothing was ever seen. While his spirits had started to drop, the squadron was given a huge lift on 8 July when a section of 'B' Flight claimed a Junkers Ju 88 near Scarborough. It was 249's first success.

The squadron moved back to Church Fenton the following day. It had only been a matter of weeks since 249 had left and so very little had changed with the exception that another Hurricane unit, 73 Squadron, was in residence, having returned from France in a depleted state, and was now working back up to strength.

The fall of France had been inevitable, and the French surrender on 22 June had meant that Britain stood alone. The Nazi war leaders knew that the RAF would have to be defeated before an invasion of southern England could take place. Understandably, there was an air of confidence amongst the German hierarchy. During the aerial exchanges that had taken place so far, it was often the case that the Luftwaffe had employed the better tactics. The RAF was still using rigid pre-war techniques based on a typical squadron-size formation, whereas the Luftwaffe's fighter groups flew in fluid and flexible formations with breadth, depth and variations in altitude, tactics that had been tried and tested during the years before.

Little time had been allocated to training the RAF's new young fighter pilots like Neil, and they would have to learn fast as better tactics evolved. But, equally, the Luftwaffe was about to become involved in a quite different air war to what it had encountered before, when it had flown in support of a ground offensive. It was now all about gaining air superiority. And while the German fighter pilot would often have the advantage – with greater numbers and height, and with just one responsibility to engage the RAF fighters or, at least, prevent them from getting amongst the bombers – he would not have everything his own way. It was unnerving to cross the Channel in a single-engine fighter and any technical malfunction could result in disastrous consequences. He would also have to maintain awareness as to where he was and how much fuel he had, never easy during combat, and so he would have to scan the fuel gauge in his cockpit continually to see when the low-level warning light started to flash.

The stage was now set, and the players were in place. The RAF had to be defeated, or at least reduced to a level where it could not mount any serious opposition to Hitler's planned invasion of Britain. And so, in early July, the Luftwaffe launched its next major offensive with a vast armada of bombers and a fighter force superior in numbers.

According to historians, the Battle of Britain officially began on Wednesday 10 July 1940, not that this date was in any way significant to the young men of Fighter Command at the time. But, for historical purposes, the battle has to start somewhere, although it is true to say that some of the days leading up to its start were as busy as its historical first day. Nonetheless, the Luftwaffe's attack against a British convoy in the English Channel during the early afternoon of 10 July has since marked the opening of the greatest air battle in history.

The disposition of Fighter Command at that time meant that 249 was one of twelve operational squadrons allocated to No. 13 Group. These squadrons were located at ten airfields, controlled by six established sector stations, of which Church Fenton was the southernmost, with the Hurricanes of 249 Squadron and Spitfires of 616 Squadron at Leconfield under its control.

249 Squadron suffered its first fatality on the night of 15/16 July. Neil was on duty that night having been loaned to 'B' Flight because of its shortage of night-qualified operational pilots. The pilots had been warned of possible raids on targets in Yorkshire that night, and as midnight approached the telephone rang. Unidentified aircraft had been detected in the area, their target believed to be Leeds, and so the first Hurricanes were ordered off.

Neil was down the batting order in fifth and so it would be a while before he was likely to be sent up. He went outside to watch the others get airborne. The third to go was Bryan Meaker. It was now just after midnight, but as Meaker started his take-off run, the airfield suddenly plunged into darkness and he was left to roar off unseen into the night.

The silence that followed was soon broken by the sound of an aircraft overhead. It turned out to be Meaker. He had hit an obstacle while taking off in the dark and the damage suffered meant he could not lower his undercarriage. The airfield lights were now on, and then off. And then on again, and the next thing Neil heard was the sound of the Hurricane belly-landing in the distance. Meaker had been fortunate and, although his aircraft was badly damaged, he managed to walk away unhurt.

Next off was Sergeant 'Masher' Main. His aircraft was heard roaring off into the distance. There followed another period of silence until the familiar drone of enemy bombers could be heard overhead. Suddenly, a bright flash ahead was spotted in the distance, a mile or two away, before it died to a stuttering glow. It looked like incendiary bombs, someone said.

Neil made his way back inside the dispersal hut to await his turn to be scrambled. Then it came. He was told to patrol the area between Gilberdyke and Pickering at 15,000 feet. He ran out into the darkness, but his trusted mount GN-F proved to be unserviceable with a coolant leak. Having eventually got airborne in a spare aircraft, Neil spent the entire sortie wandering around all over southern Yorkshire in the dark and in total silence, wondering where he was thanks to what he believed to be a faulty radio. With thoughts of finding the enemy all but gone, his priority now was to find his way back to the airfield. Any airfield, in fact, would do.

Suddenly, his words of prayer were followed by a moment of divine inspiration. Feeling around in the dark he realised the generator was switched off. He had it permanently wired on in his own aircraft, but it was left in the off position in this aircraft. It was a huge relief. With the radio eventually coming to life, he re-established contact with the ground only to find out that he was over the Wash, miles away to the south. Heading back northwards, he was soon able to find Hull and then Leeds, and finally Church Fenton.

Once he was safely back in the crew room, there were many tales being told about the night. But then Grandy appeared, his face solemn with concern. The bright flash and glow they had seen beyond the airfield only an hour or so before had been 22-year-old Masher Main crashing to his death. His engine had failed after take-off and he had come down in Copmanthorpe Wood, a few miles to the north of Church Fenton. Grandy then turned to Neil, who best describes what happened next:

> Then he turned and, noticing me, brightened. 'Ginger!' – my newly acquired nickname and a foul slur, in my opinion – 'Glad to see you back. In the Ops room you disappeared off the table altogether and we thought you'd gone for good.' Gone for good! I made some off-hand remark, trying to look and sound imperturbable. If only he knew!

For Neil, it was a defining moment during his time with 249 Squadron. Until that moment, he was convinced that Grandy did not particularly like him.

However, apart from occasional incidents such as these, Neil was starting to find life in Yorkshire rather dull. During periods of night duty, the squadron would disperse its Hurricanes to the nearby airfield of Sherburn-in-Elmet in the early evening from where they would operate until returning to Church Fenton the following morning. Life was starting to become somewhat routine and there was now more flying at night than there was by day, and Neil had become rather bored with flying in the dark.

There had also been some changes in personnel. Boozy Kellett, for example, Neil's flight commander, was promoted to squadron leader and moved south to form and command 303 Squadron. To replace Kellett, James Nicolson was promoted to flight lieutenant and appointed flight commander in his place. Neil, for one, was more than happy with this change. Although his relationship with

Kellett had improved over time, there were no tears shed on Neil's part when Kellett moved on.

August came. The weather was good, and many hours were spent sitting on readiness. At any other time of his life, things would be perfect. But this was a time of war and Neil wanted to get on with it. News of much aerial activity over southern England merely added to his frustration. Even the squadron diarist noted:

> There seems to be very little activity in the north now, but things are boiling up in the south of England and attacks are being carried out by large numbers of enemy aircraft on convoys and south coast ports. We are all hoping to get a move south.

However, the frustrations of not being centre-stage in the air battle being fought down south were soon tempered by the news that one by one Neil's friends from his course at Montrose were being shot down and killed. He later wrote:

> Killed! It was difficult to comprehend. Fellows I had known so well only weeks before. The Huns were really concentrating on big raids in the south; unlike us, the chaps down there were really getting it.

An organisational change within Fighter Command meant that Church Fenton was now transferred to No. 12 Group. For 249's pilots this administrative change made little difference, although they would now be operating further south to protect the area from Harwich to the Humber. The change did, however, mean they had to suffer the inconvenience of two visits by senior officers in consecutive days; the first by their former AOC and the second by their new one, Air Vice-Marshal Trafford Leigh-Mallory.

As things were to turn out, though, 249's time with No. 12 Group would last just four days. It was while on duty in the dispersal hut at Sherburn-in-Elmet during the early morning of 14 August that Neil first heard the squadron was being moved south. He had been woken by the sound of the telephone and the squadron commander answering. There had been a rumour of a move the previous day after Grandy had been informed that 249 would probably soon be transferring to Boscombe Down. Now it was on. The squadron was to depart immediately.

There was much excitement and no time to waste. Word was that it was to be a short, temporary move of maybe some seven days or so to support the hard-pressed squadrons in the south. By lunchtime the squadron was ready. Wives, girlfriends and sweethearts had all gathered to watch them go. Neil climbed into his aircraft and then, at midday, the twenty Hurricanes took off and headed south, leaving belongings and ground crew to follow on behind. At last, Neil thought, 249 were off to the real fighting. This was it, although he had never heard of Boscombe Down.

Chapter Five

Into Battle

The airfield of Boscombe Down can be found just a mile to the south-east of Amesbury in Wiltshire. Its origins date back to the First World War, when it was first used as a training airfield, but Boscombe Down has long since been associated with testing and evaluating aircraft for Britain's armed forces. Back in August 1940 it was home to the Aeroplane and Armament Experimental Establishment, but Boscombe Down was also used as a fighter airfield as part of No. 10 Group in the Middle Wallop Sector, Sector Y, with its main responsibility being the defence of the key ports and docklands of Southampton and Portsmouth.

It was the early afternoon of 14 August when 249 Squadron landed at Boscombe Down. Apart from a little cloud around in the south it was a warm and sunny day. The cloud and rain of the previous week had long disappeared, and southern England was now enjoying a spell of sunshine and clear blue sky.

With its lack of hardened runways, Neil would later describe Boscombe Down as a 'rolling chunk of Salisbury Plain'. As he taxied in to where the Hurricanes were to be parked, he was fascinated to see so many aircraft types, many of which were obsolete and seemingly now abandoned in the long grass around the airfield boundary. The squadron took up its new home in a hurriedly prepared dispersal area in the quiet grassy south-west corner of the airfield. Neil recalls there being some tents, a five-bar wooden fence, which was mostly used for somewhere to sit, two iron-roofed Nissen huts and a telephone, but very little else.

After the relatively easy-going atmosphere at Church Fenton, the resonant tension of Boscombe Down was immediately apparent. It was clear that life was going to be very different to what it had been like in Yorkshire before.

There to greet them was the station commander, Group Captain Ralph Sorley, a highly decorated veteran of the First World War. Sorley would later receive much credit for the RAF's success in the Battle of Britain, not just for his leadership of a fighter station but because of his work several years earlier while serving at the Air Ministry. It had been at his instigation that the next generation of RAF fighters were fitted with eight machine guns, rather than the standard two at that time, and this was ultimately included as part of the specification leading to the Spitfire and Hurricane.

Sorley explained to Grandy that 249 Squadron had arrived at Boscombe Down during a period of intense enemy activity over southern England. Only the day before, the Luftwaffe had launched the second phase of its offensive intended to annihilate Fighter Command, with the Luftwaffe's bombers attacking the RAF's ground organisation – specifically the airfields and radar sites – as well as Britain's aircraft industry. Intelligence sources estimated that as many as 2,000 German aircraft had carried out operations during the previous day, forcing Fighter Command to disperse its squadrons across southern England, while still maintaining an element of control. And so Boscombe Down was now a satellite airfield for Middle Wallop with a further relief landing ground soon to become available at Chilbolton, to the south of Andover, to accommodate another Hurricane squadron. How much of this was known by German intelligence is unclear, but it would be Fighter Command's main sector airfields, such as Middle Wallop, that would receive the brunt of the attacks.

Although there was a distinct atmosphere of confusion, uncertainty and apprehension at Boscombe Down, 249 Squadron was soon getting organised. The squadron was required to operate from dawn to dusk, and provide an available section at night, although this section would only be called upon in an emergency. Tents were erected for the ground crew, communications were established with the sector operations centre at Middle Wallop, and rosters were drawn up to take it in turn as operations officer.

The sense of urgency about the station was reinforced during the late afternoon when the distant drone of enemy bombers could be heard, with the occasional sight of small groups of aircraft heading off in different directions. An operation was building in the central Channel with the Luftwaffe's main objective being the fighter airfields in the south-west. In response the group's controller had scrambled sections of fighters into the air, while just a few miles away to the east, Middle Wallop was being attacked for the second time in consecutive days.

The attack on Middle Wallop that afternoon resulted in six station personnel killed and several Spitfires and Blenheims destroyed on the ground. 249's first day at Boscombe Down was at an end. The squadron was now at readiness. Some of the pilots remained at the dispersal overnight, while others, including Neil, made their way to the comforts of the officers' mess. There had been little time to prepare for what was to come, but the squadron was now ready. Everyone felt sure the following day would see the squadron go into action, and they would be right.

The following morning Neil made his way down to the dispersal. It was already warm, and all the indications were that it was going to be another hot sunny day. Apart from the occasional noise of an aircraft overhead, there was hardly a sound. As far as the war was concerned, it was a quiet start to the day. Something of a pattern had started to emerge. The calm of the night continued for some time after dawn while the Luftwaffe conducted its reconnaissance sorties in preparation for major raids throughout the day. But, for the pilots of 249 Squadron, most of their first full day at Boscombe Down was spent sitting around. Those who were not on readiness could do much as they pleased while those who were could do nothing but wait. This was how things were going to be.

And then it happened. Around 5 p.m. radar stations along the south coast reported two large enemy formations approaching the

Isle of Wight and Portland further to the west. Those RAF fighters already scrambled tore into them over Southampton and the Solent, but the mass of bombers pushed inland, half making for the airfield at Worthy Down while the others headed for the airfields at Odiham and Middle Wallop.

It was now 249's turn to go into action. The squadron was scrambled in two separate flights, six Hurricanes in each. What happened next is best captured in Neil's own words:

> I found myself with John Grandy, Nicolson and three others, and we climbed hard to 15,000 feet into the bluest of skies towards Warmwell in Dorset, and beyond. We were vectored hither and thither but saw nothing. And yet there were obviously Huns about, I could sense it from what little information we were given. If so, why on earth weren't we seeing them? With unlimited visibility and south-west England spread out before us like a map, it seemed incredible that even a single aircraft could escape our notice.

After wandering around the sky for what seemed like endless periods, with silence from control, they returned disappointed and frustrated to Boscombe Down, only to learn that 'B' Flight had been more successful. Neil joined the circle that had gathered around the 'B' Flight pilots to hear their stories. Overhead Middle Wallop they had encountered eleven Junkers Ju 88s escorted by an estimated fifty Messerschmitt Me 110s, claiming three of the 110s shot down. Neil was green with envy. His flight had achieved nothing.

Neil was scrambled for a second time later that day, but again nothing was seen. He was then on duty overnight and came off readiness at 8 a.m. And since he had been on duty overnight, Nicolson would not let him fly that day, and so Neil reluctantly gave up GN-F to Pilot Officer Martyn King, telling the young King to make sure that he looked after his aeroplane.

The rest of the morning of the 16th was spent standing around frustrated. It was a hot, sunny Friday, with a cloudless sky and slight haze. As usual, nothing seemed to be happening at that time of day and so Neil went off to the mess for lunch. But, no sooner had he arrived than he heard the squadron taking off. He rushed back to the dispersal to find out what was going on.

The twelve Hurricanes, led by Butch Barton, had been scrambled to patrol a line between Poole and Southampton. Another section was urgently required to patrol overhead Boscombe Down and so Neil quickly got airborne with John Grandy, Pat Wells and George Barclay. But, again, as far as Neil's section was concerned, nothing was seen.

After forty minutes of stooging around, Neil landed to find the original formation had returned. He immediately sensed tension in the air. Two of the Hurricanes were missing, one being GN-F. A group had gathered, and Neil rushed to join them. Eric 'Whizzy' King, a supernumerary squadron leader soon to take command of his own squadron, was flying with 249 as Red Three that day and was the only one from his section to make it back to Boscombe Down. His aircraft had been damaged, but he was unhurt. And now he was hurrying about, garrulous, and in a highly emotional state.

Gradually the facts started to emerge. It became apparent that an enemy formation had been spotted on the far side of the Solent. Red Section, led by Nicolson, had been sent to investigate but as they got closer Nicolson could see Spitfires already engaging them. Then, as they were climbing back to re-join the squadron, Red Section was bounced from above and astern. Nicolson's aircraft was hit and set on fire, but he had been seen to bale out. Martyn King's aircraft had also been hit and he, too, had baled out. Now all the squadron could do was to wait and see if they both turned up.

News filtered through that Nicolson was in hospital in a serious condition, having sustained extensive third-degree burns to his hands and body. It later emerged that his aircraft had been hit by cannon shells, wounding him, and setting fire to the gravity petrol tank. As the flames took hold, Nicolson prepared to abandon his burning aircraft but as he did so, he noticed a Messerschmitt 110 diving at approximately the same angle and on a converging heading. At about

James Nicolson, Fighter Command's only recipient of the Victoria Cross.

200 yards Nicolson opened fire and he kept firing until he could bear the heat inside the cockpit no more. Only then did he decide to bale out, but he had already sustained serious burns to his hands, face, neck and legs. Finally, he freed himself and jumped. Even then, his troubles were not over. When he was about to hit the ground, an enthusiastic member of the newly formed Home Guard, thinking that he was a German, loosed off both barrels of his 12-bore into his buttocks!

It would take more than a year for Nicolson to recover from his injuries, and so he never returned to the squadron. It would later be announced that he was to be awarded the Victoria Cross, Britain's highest award for gallantry. It would prove to be the only VC awarded to a member of Fighter Command, a somewhat surprising fact.

As for young Martyn King flying GN-F that day, he had managed to bale out but sadly did not survive. His parachute got caught around the chimney stack of a house, but his straps had been damaged and they snapped, leaving King to fall to the ground where he died from his injuries. He is buried in All Saints' churchyard at Fawley, near Southampton, and, although his headstone has him aged a year older, it appears that Martyn King was just eighteen years old, in which case he is probably the youngest pilot to have fought in the Battle of Britain. It is one of many truly sad tales of war.

Whether the two Hurricanes were shot down by 110s or 109s was not clear – both types were operating in the area at the time – but they were 249 Squadron's first battle casualties. Neil did not write to his parents that night. Even when he did write next, a couple or so days later, he did not mention the losses, or even the engagement. As he says, 'There was no sense in worrying them.' Many years later, he recalled:

> Poor Nick. And young King. But, in a way it was almost funny. Nick, who had been telling us for weeks how to do pretty well everything, shot down on his first operational engagement! Not so funny was the loss of my aeroplane. Dear old GN-F. Still, I was jolly glad not to have been in it.

From that moment on, there would be a constant rotation of pilots occupying the beds in the accommodation huts. A once familiar face would be quickly replaced by another smiling young face. But men would not return to the huts for all kinds of reasons. There was little time to become close to anyone, and there was certainly little time for grief.

With Nicolson gone, Denis Parnall, fortunate to escape the campaign in Norway prior to joining 249, was promoted to acting flight lieutenant to become Neil's third flight commander in three months. Neil had first met him at Barton before the war when Parnall was personal assistant to a visiting air marshal. He was a member of the affluent family that had formed the aircraft manufacturer Parnall Aircraft, had studied engineering at Cambridge University, and might well have gone on to great things had the war not intervened.

The hectic events of 16 August were followed by a lull in the air fighting over southern England. It was a quiet day, the quietest in fact for two weeks.

The following days were frustrating for Neil. The squadron now had eighteen Hurricanes, of which twelve were at readiness at any one time during the day. These were allocated in four sections of three, leaving two spares for the day and time for the others to be serviced or repaired. However, the squadron had nearly twice as many pilots as it had Hurricanes at readiness, which meant that roughly every other day was spent on the ground. And when Neil was in the air, although the weather was generally very good and there was clearly plenty of enemy activity around, it all seemed to be happening well away to the south-east, and so he did not see a thing. Patrolling the beautiful south coastline, with the Solent and Isle of Wight spread out before him in a glorious, if hazy, panoramic view was wonderful, but sight-seeing was not what he was there to do.

In the five days since arriving at Boscombe Down, 249 Squadron had flown eighty-six operational sorties for just two engagements; 'B' Flight's on the day after the squadron had arrived and 'A' Flight's on the 16th that had resulted in the loss of Nicolson and King. But it was not as if there was no activity at all for the squadrons of No. 10

Group, it was just happening elsewhere. During the same five days, the squadrons of No. 11 Group, which were protecting London and the south-east, had flown more than 1,500 operational sorties with nearly a hundred separate engagements. While this might well have been a frustrating period for Neil, and understandably so, it simply shows where the Luftwaffe's concentration of effort was at that time.

The rest of August followed a similar pattern. There was just one success, during the afternoon of the 24th, when 'B' Flight had a brief encounter with some 109s over the Isle of Wight. For Neil, though, it was still all very frustrating. He started to doubt the quality of the directing and strategy of the group's controllers. And when a large force of more than 200 aircraft had been detected forming up over the French coast during the afternoon of the 25th, which then went on to approach Weymouth before splitting into three groups to attack airfields and targets in the south-west, including the sector's forward operating airfield at Warmwell, near Dorchester, Neil was so annoyed that he later wrote:

> It had us spitting. What on earth was going on? With no controlling at all, by the law of averages, we could reason-ably expect to intercept enemy forces of that size simply by running into them! As it was, I had been 'controlled' on ten scrambles and completed more than ten hours of full-throttle climbing and flying against some of the biggest raids ever experienced and had not seen a thing. We were wasting our time at Boscombe Down, that was crystal clear.

These were strong words and there was further frustration the following day. Having climbed to 25,000 feet over the Isle of Wight, and now hopping about in anticipation of a fight, his formation was told that the enemy had turned back when just twenty miles off the south coast of England. He simply could not believe it: 'Turned back! Did major raids come all that way across the Channel just to turn back? It was hard to believe.'

Neil's feelings were not in isolation. Even the squadron records comment on the 'many patrols being flown but the enemy nearly always appear to approach the coast then turn south'. It was very annoying. There was even time to host a royal visit when HRH the Duke of Kent visited Boscombe Down. Neil was also given the opportunity to return home for a few days of leave. A Hurricane needed to return to Church Fenton, and so he flew it back to Yorkshire. Then, having collected his car, which he had left at the airfield, he set off across the Pennines.

He was not due back at Boscombe Down until 2 September, which was a Monday, and so he decided to drive back south in his car, accompanied by his parents so that he could spend the weekend in London with them, after which they planned to make the return journey north by train.

While Neil was in London, and quite by chance, he happened to bump into a squadron colleague, the South African 'Ossie' Crossey, who was staying at the same hotel. Crossey's nickname Ossie had come about because he habitually wore a black, roll-necked jersey beneath his flying overalls in the manner of Sir Oswald Mosley, leader of the British Union of Fascists. But what Crossey had to tell him came as a complete surprise – 249 was being moved to North Weald and he was now on his way to join up with the rest of the squadron.

Neil offered to take Crossey with him in his car and by the time they set off for North Weald the following morning, still accompanied by Neil's parents, 249 Squadron had already been released from its operational state to allow the transfer of aircraft and personnel.

Led by Grandy, fourteen Hurricanes eventually took off from Boscombe Down and headed eastwards for North Weald. There to greet them was the station commanding officer, 36-year-old Wing Commander Victor Beamish, an Irishman and one of three brothers in the RAF. There as well to welcome 249 was the sector operations officer, Squadron Leader John Cherry, who happened to be Grandy's brother-in-law, who briefed the new arrivals on the sector's operating procedures.

North Weald is north of London and about three miles to the south-east of Harlow in Essex, on the edge of Epping Forest. It was then the sector station for No. 11 Group's Sector E, and in terms of its facilities was one of the most advanced airfields in Fighter Command. Its 400 acres had been developed to include an extension to the northern boundary and the construction of two hardened runways to add to the already established grass runways, with an asphalt perimeter track on the western side to ease movement around the airfield. The aircraft hangars, operations block and officers' mess were all situated in the south-east corner of the airfield.

The North Weald sector covered the area to the north-east of London and had three airfields; the other two being its satellite airfield at nearby Stapleford Tawney, just to the south, and Martlesham Heath, to the east of Ipswich in Suffolk. The sector was bounded to the north by the Debden sector and its southern boundary, to the east of London, was with the Hornchurch sector. Within the North Weald sector there was a line of radar stations covering the eastern approach to London and the south-east coast of East Anglia, a large anti-aircraft battery near Harwich and an Observer Corps centre near Colchester.

Much had happened at North Weald in the week prior to the arrival of 249. The airfield had been attacked twice and both Hurricane squadrons based there at the time – 56 and 151 – had been severely depleted, including the loss of their commanding officers, to the point that both were being moved elsewhere. And so 249 Squadron was to relieve 56 Squadron while the Blenheims of 25 Squadron, a squadron that flew mostly in the night-fighter role, returned from Martlesham Heath for their second stint at the airfield.

The move to North Weald was a most welcome one for 249's pilots. No. 11 Group was, after all, getting most of the action. Grandy was told they could expect to be there for just a week and so decisions had to be made as to what to take and what to leave at Boscombe Down. The temporary move also meant 249's ground crew had to stay behind. Once 249's pilots had arrived at North Weald they would use the Hurricanes and ground crew already there, while

56's pilots would return to Boscombe Down in 249's Hurricanes, the reason being they were fitted with the old TR9 HF radio, which was not compatible for No. 11 Group operations, whereas the Hurricanes at North Weald were fitted with a VHF radio.

Although Grandy had been told to expect to stay at North Weald for a week, 249 Squadron would, in fact, be there for nearly nine months. The squadron occupied the north-west corner of the airfield in what was a collection of wooden huts, hard-standings and blast pens. Until their inherited Hurricanes could be repainted, the squadron would operate in the 'US' markings of 56 Squadron rather than its own squadron code of 'GN'.

It soon became apparent that 249's stay at North Weald was to be longer than expected and so it meant inheriting 56's ground crew on a permanent basis. Having been through so much of the battle together, the ground crew had been sad to see their pilots go and had not necessarily been keen to see a new bunch arrive. Some of the ground crew were even critical of 249's pilots during their early days at North Weald, one even describing their attitude as 'nonchalant' and seemingly unaware of the critical need for urgency when ordered to scramble. This attitude between ground crew from one established squadron and a new bunch of pilots arriving from another would not entirely have been unexpected, but within days the prejudices were forgotten, and an efficient team spirit was soon established.

By dawn on 2 September, 249 Squadron had been brought back up to operational readiness and did not have to wait long to go into action from its new home. At 7.20 a.m. ten Hurricanes were scrambled to intercept a large formation of Do 17s, escorted by Messerschmitt 110s and Bf 109s, crossing the Kent coast; their target being Fighter Command's airfields in the south-east. One of six squadrons scrambled to meet the raid, 249 was ordered to patrol Rochester at 15,000 feet to cover the airfields of Rochford and Eastchurch.

The enemy bombers were sighted soon after and so Grandy led the attack. The melee that followed resulted in 249 claiming one Do 17 and one Me 110 for certain, and another two Do 17s and two 110s as probably destroyed or at least damaged. But it had not all gone

249's way. Percy Burton, John Beazley and Dicky Wynn were shot down, but all escaped with their lives: Burton crash-landed wheels-up in a field at Meopham and was unhurt, Wynn managed to crash-land near Chartham but was badly wounded in the neck, and Beazley baled out near Gillingham and escaped unhurt.

Neil arrived at North Weald around lunch time. He had first dropped his parents at Epping station, so they could catch a train back to London and then continue their journey north, after which he had made his way to the airfield to join up with the squadron. It had been an emotional farewell for his parents, reducing them both to tears. They had seen the Hurricanes roaring off into the distance. His father was so affected by the sight that he had completely disintegrated with grief and, in a state of collapse, could not be consoled. It was as if they were both convinced that they would never see their only child again.

The Luftwaffe's bombers returned in the afternoon and again 249 was scrambled to meet them, with the squadron claiming two more Me 110s destroyed and another damaged, without loss. 249's first operational day at North Weald had turned out to be a very busy one but, overall, it had been a good day.

Having been away from the squadron for several days, Neil felt rather lost. Everyone, it seemed, had been at North Weald longer than him, even though it was only just a day. He was also saddened to hear of the death of 151 Squadron's CO, Squadron Leader 'Whizzy' King, who had only left 249 a short while before to take up his command. King had been killed just three days before Neil arrived.

Neil quickly set about familiarising himself with his new surroundings. When not required for immediate duty, the junior pilots had rooms adjacent to the officers' mess. These were in huts and each room was fitted with a primitive coal stove that looked good but would not be enough to stop the room becoming desperately cold in winter. Neil could never understand why the ground branch officers enjoyed the luxuries of the officers' mess. He would end up spending nearly nine months at North Weald and even though he asked for a room in the main building on numerous occasions, he was never granted one. Instead, he would tend to spend most of his time at the squadron dispersal, which included a hut constituting the crew room, half occupied by beds. This would be where he would spend eighteen, sometimes twenty-four hours a day. He would eat there, rest there, sleep there, and, of course, be scrambled into the air from there.

Neil was at readiness the day after he arrived at North Weald. It was 3 September. The country had now been at war for a year. The squadron had quickly settled in to a routine, which meant being at readiness from half an hour before dawn until half an hour after dusk, a total of eighteen hours a day in September. The day started with the Hurricanes being run-up by the ground crew well before dawn, making it all but impossible for the pilots already at dispersal to sleep past 4 a.m. Each pilot had his own routine but essentially it involved getting up and donning flying clothing before clambering back onto his bed once more. Breakfast arrived in boxes around 8 a.m. Neil remembers it always being the same: bacon, hard-yolk eggs, and squares of fried bread. They would line up like sleep-walkers to take their share. Those who could stomach it would eat. And then there was the dreaded wait. This was how the days were going to be spent.

At 9 a.m. the whole squadron was ordered to patrol a line between Chelmsford and Eastchurch. Neil was in the lead section of three with the CO and Percy Burton. But nothing was seen.

Having returned to North Weald, the Hurricanes were still being refuelled when the air raid siren wailed. The squadron was ordered to scramble again and to patrol base, with a large raid detected and approaching from the east. The Hurricanes, some fully refuelled, others only partially replenished, scrambled back into the air with Grandy again leading. Climbing as fast as they could, they had reached 12,000 feet when puffs of ack-ack fire could be seen above and to the left. Neil recalls what he saw next:

> Everything in slow motion. Then, aircraft! In the middle of all the puffs, Huns! Oh, God! Masses of them! 'Tallyho!' My eyes glued to them. Fascinated. Growing closer. Clearer

now. Large ones in the front and in the middle. Others like flies, stepped up and behind. Thousands, it seemed. And there were only twelve of us.

From 20,000 feet on a fine bright morning, and with the sun behind them, it would have been easy for the thirty Do 17 crews, protected by their escort of fifty Me 110s, to see the mouth of the River Thames and Canvey Island. As they began their descent to 15,000 feet for the attack, the armada then turned northwards across Essex to find North Weald.

Although they had been climbing as steeply as they could, 249's Hurricanes were still well below and to the south. Even with more warning time they would have struggled to gain enough height to intercept an enemy raid as far north as the Thames. As they got closer Neil could make out the distinctive shapes of the bombers and their escorts, but he could see they were not closing on the bombers fast enough. There was nothing he or the others could do other than to watch in horror as the Dorniers started to bomb North Weald. Their own airfield. Having finally arrived overhead North Weald, Neil looked down but the whole airfield was hidden beneath what he described as 'a huge, spreading grey-brown pall of smoke and dust'.

George Barclay was not on state that day and so he had taken cover in one of the air-aid shelters. He kept a diary during his time at North Weald, in which he described the unbelievable and utterly terrifying noise of the bombs and felt certain that his shelter would be hit by at least one. And when the raid was over he emerged from the shelter to see the airfield covered in a vast cloud of smoke and dust, with the hangars on fire and the sound of ammunition exploding.

More than 200 bombs fell on North Weald during the raid, cratering the southern part of the airfield and destroying several buildings, as well as vehicles, two unserviceable Hurricanes and a Blenheim. Two hangars had been hit, so had the operations block, the water mains were out, and two personnel were left dead with

A carefully composed, classic image of the Battle of Britain:
the young fighter pilot looks skywards as he is debriefed after a sortie. Tom Neil
with 249 Squadron's Intelligence Officer, Flying Officer 'Shirley' Woolmer.

Thomas Gosney Neil and his wife Florence pictured soon after the First World War, before the arrival of the young Tom.

With his father, pictured, he thinks, while on holiday around 1928/29.

On his trusted bicycle, probably in Southport around 1929/30. He would cycle for miles just to watch the de Havilland Fox Moths operate pleasure flights from the beach.

Neil with a Tiger Moth at Barton airfield in April 1939 soon after joining the RAF Volunteer Reserve.

Neil (*second left*) pictured in late 1939 with course colleagues, all sergeant pilots, of No. 8 Service Flying Training School at Montrose. Cecil Parkinson (*far left*) and Leslie Pidd (*far right*) were later killed during the Battle of Britain, while Harry Newton (*centre*) was shot down and wounded. The fifth member of the group is Ivor Arber who survived the war but died soon after.

A poor quality but important photograph of Neil's personal Hurricane P3616, in his personal markings GN-F. This aircraft was lost to enemy action on 16 August 1940 while being flown by eighteen-year-old Pilot Officer Martyn King. Sadly, King was killed.

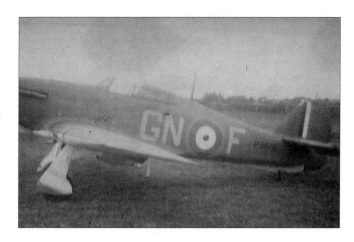

Pilots of 249 Squadron relax at Boscombe Down with 'pipes various', August 1940. *From left:* George Barclay, Percy Burton, Pat Wells, and Bryan Meaker. Only Wells would survive the war.

Neil flanked by his CO, Squadron Leader John Grandy (*right*) and the Canadian Flight Lieutenant Butch Barton. After Grandy was shot down and wounded in early September 1940, Barton took temporary command of 249 Squadron until his appointment was made official later that year.

Neil's combat report of his first confirmed success, a Messerschmitt 109 shot down near Maidstone during the afternoon of 7 September 1940, the day the Luftwaffe turned on London. Note that the Heinkel bomber also claimed as damaged was deleted by an over-zealous intelligence officer.

COMBAT REPORT

Sector Serial No.	(A)	——
Serial No. of Order detailing Flight or Squadron to Patrol	(B)	——
Date	(C)	7 Sept. 1940
Flight, Squadron	(D)	Flight: A Sqdn. 249
Number of Enemy Aircraft	(E)	30 Bombers 100 plus fighters
Type of Enemy Aircraft	(F)	He111s Do17 or 215s Me109s Me110
Time Attack was delivered	(G)	1715 approx.
Place Attack was delivered	(H)	Vicinity of Maidstone
Height of Enemy	(J)	18000 feet
Enemy Casualties	(K)	1 Me109 destroyed
Our Casualties Aircraft	(L)	4
Personnel	(M)	1 killed, 1 missing, 2 wounded
GENERAL REPORT	(R)	

P/O T. F. NEIL   Yellow 2

Attacked formation of about 30 enemy bombers, from beam & fired a 4 sec burst into foremost vic of Heinkels. Broke away sharply & did not observe effect. Range was very close & E.A. were so packed that fire was bound to have effect. Encountered Me109 flying in opposite direction. I pulled up sharply and gave him short burst full deflection. Turned sharply & got on tail of E.A. firing short bursts. Large pieces flew off E.A. which turned over slowly & went down smoking. Fired at other E.A. with no effect. Later joined another Squadron (either JN or JZ) & attacked formation of bombers from above & in front. Fired 2 second burst & continued my dive with others of the Squadron to 2000 feet. E.A. were firing at us from rear. No result was observed.
I claim 1 Me109 destroyed & ~~1 bomber damaged.~~

Signature	Thos Neil
	Section Yellow
O.C.	Flight A
	Squadron 249 Squadron No.

At readiness in Hurricane V7313, Neil's second personal GN-F, at the height of the Battle of Britain. It was in this aircraft that he shot down his first enemy aircraft on 7 September 1940. Eight days later he was an ace, all achieved while flying V7313.

Neil's log book showing the period 2–16 September 1940. His combat successes are clearly shown and include the four he shot down on the 15th, later to be remembered as Battle of Britain Day.

As a twice-decorated fighter ace of the Battle of Britain, Neil was suddenly propelled into the public eye. He is shown here during a visit to the Lancashire cotton industry in early 1941. As a local boy who had done exceptionally well, he was required to meet and talk to the workers to boost the war effort.

October 1940, after the award of Neil's first Distinguished Flying Cross.

With Ossie Crossey (*left*) and Tich Palliser (*centre*) in Malta, summer 1941, outside the newly erected pilots' dispersal at Ta Kali.

Taking a well-earned break from the air fighting. Neil shown relaxing on the beach with Patricia Pullicino, the daughter of a Malta judge, Sir Philip Pullicino.

Neil leading his section overhead Ta Kali while practising for a planned attack against an enemy airfield in Sicily.

Left: The SS *Sydney Star*, which took Neil to Port Said, on the first leg of his homeward journey from Malta. The passage through the eastern Mediterranean was anything but peaceful.

Below: Neil's personal Spitfire Mark XII of 41 Squadron, EN237 EB-V, pictured at Hawkinge in April 1943.

South African Rex Poynton, one of 41 Squadron's flight commanders, described by Neil as a brilliant leader, is shown here with the squadron's mascot Perkin.

MRAF Viscount Trenchard (sat facing camera wearing a hat) talking informally to the pilots of 41 Squadron during a visit to Hawkinge. Neil is sat next to him.

Neil's first P-51B Mustang, which he flew while serving as an RAF liaison officer to the American 100th Fighter Wing. The picture was taken at the advanced landing ground at Staplehurst in Kent just weeks before the Allied landings in Normandy.

Spitfire 3W-K pictured at Rennes in August 1944. After it was left abandoned in France, without any apparent owner, Neil commandeered the aircraft as his own. Having erased any evidence of its provenance and stripped the aircraft down to its bare metal, he flew it for the rest of his time with the Americans; the episode later formed the basis of his book *The Silver Spitfire*.

Eileen Hampton, pictured as a flight officer in 1944. Neil met Eileen while she was serving at Biggin Hill.

Neil and Eileen on their wedding day, 3 June 1945.

No. 4 (Short) Course at the Empire Test Pilots' School, Cranfield, January 1946. Neil is in the back row, fifth from the left. Flight Lieutenant Neville Duke, who would go on to achieve the world air speed record, is also in the back row, sixth from the right.

The classroom at Cranfield, 1946. Neil is in the third row and seen peeking at the camera (above the head of the student seated at the left of the front row).

A flypast of four Gloster Meteors at Farnborough during the 1950 'RAF Display'.

Neil pictured in front of Hurricane LF363 at Bovingdon, Hertfordshire, prior to flying the aircraft, 28 September 1951. LF363 is believed to have been the last Hurricane to enter service with the RAF and is now part of the Battle of Britain Memorial Flight.

Above the Suez Canal Zone in a Meteor FR.9 of 208 Squadron.

Neil's Empire Central Flying School certificate for No. 18 Instrument Weather Course.

Neil at Abu Sueir, Egypt. Neil commanded 208 Squadron at Abu Sueir during 1953–5.

Hosting one of the many important visitors to Egypt. On this occasion it is a visit by George Ward, MP, Under Secretary of State for Air, 14 January 1954.

Recreational facilities at Abu Sueir were very good and so Neil tried to find time whenever possible to go to the tennis club.

Neil (*far left*) and Eileen (*second from right*) with their three children at Abu Sueir in late 1955 not long before they returned to the UK. They are all pictured with the station commander, Group Captain Pat Hanafin, and his wife Nora.

Above: Neil *(kneeling centre)* pictured in front of his personal white-nosed Meteor with his 208 Squadron aerobatic display team.

Right: The Neils enjoying a social function. It was only when married accommodation became available at Abu Sueir for the last year of his tour in Egypt that Eileen and the children could join him.

Right: Telegram from the C-in-C Middle East Air Force, Air Marshal Sir Claude Pelly, congratulating Neil on the award of the Air Force Cross.

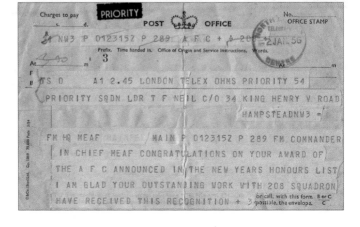

This very professional looking image of Neil was, in fact, taken *c.* 1955 by one of his colleagues practising to be a photographer.

A picture to mark a most wonderful occasion. In the rear cockpit of a two-seat Spitfire after his memorable flight on 15 September 2015, Battle of Britain Day in the seventy-fifth anniversary year, with HRH Prince Harry alongside.

many more injured. Remarkably, though, despite the damage, and despite the fact there were still unexploded bombs lying around, the airfield remained operational.

By the time the Hurricanes were back in the circuit, much of the smoke and dust had disappeared. It was then a case of trying to find an area to land. In the end, the best place was to touch down across the concrete runway on the grass. Although Neil was glad to get down, he was left feeling very annoyed. Their own airfield had been bombed and he had not even fired a round in its defence.

After several uneventful patrols, 249 was back in action during the afternoon of 5 September. Once again, the Hurricanes were struggling to gain enough height to intercept the approaching enemy bombers reported to be high above the Thames Estuary at 20,000 feet. And so, again, the Hurricanes had no option but to carry out a beam attack while climbing, making it all but impossible to get amongst the bombers. Besides, Neil had to keep an eye on the escorting fighters high above. It was the first time he had seen Messerschmitt Bf 109s at close quarters.

Using Bf 109s as close escorts had come about because of increasing bomber losses, after the Me 110s had proved unable to protect either the bombers or themselves from marauding RAF fighters. But it had been a hugely unpopular decision amongst the 109 pilots as it reduced their effectiveness by tying them to the route, heights and timings of the bombers. Furthermore, the limited range and endurance of the 109 was now proving to be a critical factor, a situation not helped by having first to join up in a large formation before crossing the Channel. Even when crossing at the narrowest point, the 109s had only about twenty minutes of combat time over southern England before having to head back home. This combat time was reduced further still when escorting bombers as far as London, in which case their combat endurance was often as low as ten minutes.

Neil had heard so much about the Bf 109, but what he had heard more fascinated him than worried him. Suddenly, though, the 109s swooped down:

The 109s, being several thousand feet above us, had the advantage. Never having seen one close-to, I suddenly had several within yards of me. One, in fact, overtook me almost within touching distance to my right so that I could plainly see all the details of the fuselage with its coloured nose and black cross, and the spinner of the propeller, which had some sort of spiral emblem on it, rotating. I was fascinated. It looked so pretty, slim, and waspish. And fast, my goodness! It fairly scooted past me and, no doubt thinking I might be intending to turn on it, put its nose down with a jerk and dropped away like a stone.

Suddenly, there were others all around, passing above and below, diagonally and in various attitudes. Aircraft, friend and foe, flashed around his head like flies. In those next few panic-stricken moments, he did not know which way to turn.

Aware that he had been 'ball-watching', Neil galvanised himself into action, pushing and pulling, intent only on escaping, waiting all the time for the dreaded sound and smell of cannon shells clattering into his aircraft. His vision started to grey due to the excessive g-force. He was fighting for survival. But suddenly there was nothing. He was all on his own.

Quickly taking in what was going on around him, Neil could see he was still over the Thames and could now see some Hurricanes in the distance. They were seemingly heading in different directions. He formed up on one, then a third joined formation and eventually there were a handful. They were now over Gravesend and chasing the fleeing bombers, but they were never going to catch them. Looking below and across to the north side of the river he could see thick black smoke. The Germans had hit something and, again, he had not fired a shot. He felt almost ashamed.

What Neil had seen burning in the distance were the oil tanks at Thameshaven. He eventually landed back at North Weald, in his own words, 'limp with emotion and irritated by my own performance'. Some of 249's pilots made claims, but nothing could be confirmed.

One Hurricane was missing, that of Butch Barton who had been shot down by a Bf 109 but he had managed to bale out unhurt.

Overall, 249 Squadron had been lucky. They had been desperately climbing to intercept the enemy bombers when they had been bounced by the 109s, which enjoyed a considerable advantage over the Hurricanes. That night Neil lay quietly on his bed in dispersal, reflecting on the events that day. He later wrote: 'I was not very good, was I? I just couldn't go on reacting; I had to do something positive.'

But Neil knew that to do something positive was easier said than done. He would have to concentrate on one aircraft at a time, but the 109s had darted about like minnows and seemed to hunt in pairs. If only they would keep still, just for a moment.

That night he listened to the drone of bombers in the distance, nothing unusual there, until he drifted off to sleep, unhappy and completely exhausted.

Chapter Six

The Hardest Month

Much had already happened in Neil's short life, particularly in the past year since leaving home to go off to war. He had not long celebrated his twentieth birthday, but he was having to grow up oh so quickly and 7 September was to be another of those defining days in his life.

Not that the day started differently to any other during that hard summer of 1940. Southern England was enjoying the most perfect of Indian summers. It was misty at first, but already promising to be another bright and sunny day, a Saturday as it happened, not that it made any difference. 249's CO, John Grandy, had been shot down the previous morning. It had been the usual story of the Bf 109s having the advantage and then swooping down on the Hurricanes as they were tackling the bombers. Grandy had been caught by a 109, baled out slightly wounded, and was now in hospital, leaving Butch Barton to lead the squadron.

Neil was scrambled twice during the morning of the 7th, but nothing was seen. It was unusual given the pattern of recent days. Other than enjoy the panoramic view of the English landscape stretched out before him, there had been little else for him to do. Back on the ground, there was a strong feeling around those in dispersal that something was up. But no one was quite sure what that might be. Talk naturally focused on the long-anticipated German invasion, but was this the start? No one knew. There was nothing during the early afternoon either, not even a scramble. Neil even had time to grab some sleep.

For a while now, Fighter Command had been feeling the effect of the Luftwaffe's continuous attacks on its airfields. Meanwhile, across the Channel, German intelligence had assured the head of the Luftwaffe, Reichsmarschall Hermann Göring, that Fighter Command had lost nearly 600 aircraft since the beginning of July. The RAF was, they said, down to its last 300 fighters, of which 200 were in the south-east of England. German intelligence was convinced that the RAF was virtually beaten and on its knees. The reality was, in fact, quite different but, satisfied that the battle was almost won, Göring unleashed his bombers against London during the afternoon of 7 September. It was a decision that would prove to be the turning point of the campaign.

The Luftwaffe had gone to considerable lengths to conceal the direction of attack and the intended target. At radar sites along the south-east coast of England, several groups of aircraft had been detected forming up across the Channel, before it finally became apparent that the enemy was about to attack on a wide front, with a huge armada of 350 bombers protected by more than 600 fighters.

It was around 4.30 p.m. when the order came to scramble 249 Squadron with the instruction to patrol Maidstone at 15,000 feet. And within half an hour, Fighter Command had scrambled all twenty-one squadrons based within seventy miles of London, with most patrolling the airfields in response to what had gone on before.

As usual, a dozen Hurricanes of 249 Squadron got airborne with Neil flying as Yellow Two in V7313, his new GN-F, in the third section. Overhead Maidstone he could see one large group approaching, a wedge of He 111s, then Do 17s, all beneath a cloud of fighters, Bf 109s and Me 110s. It was twelve against a hundred.

Approaching from the beam, he watched the Heinkels grow in his gunsight as he closed. In no time at all he was amongst them and he could now pick out individual aircraft. Choosing one in the leading pack he opened fire. His eight Browning machine guns burst to life. Neil watched the tracer and smoking rounds tear into the bomber ahead. Then, as he flashed under the pale underbelly of his intended victim, he turned on his back and plunged away, falling towards the ground like a stone.

Pulling sharply out of the dive Neil could see aircraft everywhere, but not a bomber in sight. Climbing again as quickly as his Hurricane would allow, he could soon make out the distinctive shape and markings of the escorting 109s. One, off to his right, was coming towards him. Neil turned hard into it and opened fire. He then watched in amazement as the 109 curled away in a gentle dive.

Wildly excited, he chased after it, firing again and watching his rounds clatter into the enemy fighter as a puff of smoke and then a trail of white, soon thickening and darkening in colour, signalled the start of its demise. Swooping and closing on his prey, Neil fired again until debris was seen falling from the 109 as it dropped in a trail of smoke and a steepening dive to earth. Neil best sums up what he saw in his own words: 'It was dying. The aircraft was dying. Like an animal, mortally wounded. Not the pilot or a man, but an aircraft. It fell away. Sadly. The angle steepening, the trail thickening. I let it go. To its death. Watching.'

The action had taken place over Ashford and, having been drawn in to the one-on-one that had just taken place, Neil suddenly came to. He looked around. He was down below 10,000 feet and his squadron had disappeared. He was, in his own words, 'committing the cardinal error of being alone'.

Climbing again as quickly as he could, he spotted what looked like Hurricanes in the distance and closed on them. They were indeed Hurricanes but not from his squadron. But at least they were friendly aircraft, and it gave him a strong feeling of security. He stayed with them, but could not talk to them, as they were not on the same radio frequency, and he did not recognise the squadron code on the side of the fuselage. They seemed to be off somewhere in a hurry, though, and so all he could do was stick with them.

Then he saw the 109s, more of them, yellow-nosed this time, turning in on them. But the Hurricane leader, whoever he was, ignored them and took his section into a dive at a gaggle of Dorniers below. Neil later recalled:

Neil in the cockpit of his Hurricane, V7313.

It was to be a madly exciting twenty seconds, a cavalry charge of the wildest kind with all weapons bared. I found myself going down in a thirty-degree dive towards the starboard front quarter of the bomber formation. One of a solid wedge of Hurricanes. Firing!

The Dorniers were rapidly growing in his sight. Thin streamers of white from the bombers' air gunners were curling in his direction, but they were ignored. And just as a collision seemed inevitable, the Hurricanes were through and out the other side, and below.

Neil straightened out. He was now over the Thames and below 3,000 feet, and all but out of ammunition. There was no point in hanging about any longer. He made his way home and landed alone, having spent an hour and twenty-five minutes in the air. He taxied in, shut down and climbed out. But there were very few Hurricanes to be seen. Only five others in fact.

No sooner had he landed than the air-raid siren sounded again. But there was nothing he could do. His aircraft was out of fuel and out of ammunition. He could only stand and watch his five colleagues launch back into the air. It was not long, though, before his aircraft was ready again. There were still enemy aircraft about, some were even seen overhead the airfield, and so he took off for the fourth time that day.

As he climbed as steeply as he could, it was clear the raid was over, and the enemy bombers were now disappearing way in the distance. He did see a parachute coming down and wondered whose it might be, and he also got close to a straggling Dornier, but it was high above and too far ahead. Nonetheless, as a final forlorn gesture, he raised the nose and fired off a burst. He had at least had a go. Of more concern was the ack-ack going off around him. He turned for home, in his own words 'totally spent'. He had already been in the air for nearly four hours that day.

There was an anxious feel about the place when Neil walked into dispersal. In the absence of Grandy, it was left to Victor Beamish, a frequent and welcome visitor to the squadron, to maintain morale. But the reality was 249 Squadron had been decimated. Six Hurricanes were missing.

From the reports later pieced together it appears that 'Boost' Fleming had been the first to be shot down. He had fallen to 109s over Maidstone as soon as the action had started. Fleming was seen to bale out on fire but died later of his horrific injuries. Sergeant Richard Smithson, one of the original members of 249, had been hit by the same group of 109s; he was wounded but managed to crash-land at Eastchurch, although it would be a while before Smithson would return to the squadron. Just a few minutes later, the friendly and diligent Sergeant Fred Killingback, another original member of the squadron, was shot down by 109s and baled out wounded. George Barclay, who Neil describes as being rather noisy but in a frightfully decent way, and a thoroughly enthusiastic fighter pilot, had been hit by return fire while attacking the Heinkels. Deciding to stay with his aircraft rather than bale out, Barclay did not quite make it back to North Weald and crash-landed wheels-up in a field near the village of Potter Street; he was unhurt. Fifth to fall was Pat Wells, some fifteen minutes after Barclay. Wells had also been hit by return fire from the bombers and baled out wounded. It would be some time before the

Victor Beamish, the fearless Irishman who commanded North Weald
during the Battle of Britain.

squadron received news of Wells, but it turned out he was in hospital.
The last of 249 to be shot down that day was John Beard. He was
hit around 6 p.m., possibly by friendly anti-aircraft fire, although he
managed to bale out unhurt.

It had, indeed, been an incredibly hard day, not only for 249
Squadron but across Fighter Command. Twenty-eight RAF fighters
were destroyed and a further sixteen damaged, with twelve pilots
killed and five seriously wounded. The Luftwaffe had lost more
than forty aircraft, including the 109 shot down by Neil, which was
confirmed as destroyed. It was his first success, or kill, depending on
how such an event is viewed. Nonetheless, the Luftwaffe had struck
its first heavy blow against London.

The main weight of the attack had fallen on the capital either side of 6 p.m. Vast areas of docklands were devastated, and several hundred Londoners had been killed or injured. The German bombers had reached the city in broad daylight and had bombed it successfully, due in the main to the high degree of fighter protection given to them. There followed the largest concentrated night attack launched by the Luftwaffe thus far, and one which proved to be the beginning of a night offensive against London that would last for many months.

At North Weald, the dispersal hut seemed rather empty that night. All Neil could do was reflect on what had been a very hard day, a day that he would never forget. It was a day full of emotions. He was exhausted.

After so much activity on the 7th, things were quieter for 249 during the following few days. It was just as well. 'A' Flight was down to two serviceable Hurricanes and pilots, while 'B' Flight was faring little better with five. But nine replacement aircraft soon arrived. Neil remembers there never being a problem with 249 getting spare aircraft or, indeed, new pilots. Also, Grandy had returned, although he was not yet fit enough to fly; the injuries to his right leg prevented him from working the rudder, and so Barton continued to lead the squadron.

Fighter Command's squadrons would from now on operate in pairs, or as a wing of three, with 249 teamed up with the Hurricanes of 46 Squadron, operating from nearby Stapleford Tawney, and 504 Squadron based at Hendon.

Talk was still very much about the possibility of a German invasion, not that it worried Neil at all. He was, however, saddened at the recent losses. It was their job to get at the bombers and in that role the Hurricane was performing well. However, having to concentrate on the enemy bombers often meant they were sitting ducks for the marauding escorts. And when it came to fighter versus fighter combat with the Bf 109s, that was a different matter altogether. Not that Neil was overly concerned. He was more irritated at not having the performance to catch the 109s or to gain a favourable position, which was as much down to the tactical situation encountered as anything else. The 109s had all the time in the world to gain a height advantage before crossing the English coast.

There was, however, a mounting fear amongst the pilots of being badly burned. It was no longer something that happened elsewhere, it was now happening to their friends. Nicolson, Fleming and Wells had all gone down in flames, others too. They were all good men. Apart from the apprehension of sitting nervously in dispersal waiting to be scrambled, which, incidentally, was a feeling that would never go away, or ever get any easier, Neil recalls only two fears at the time, one of which was being burned in his aircraft, while his other fear was drowning. And so the days of flying in shirt-sleeves with the hood open were over as every effort was now being made to minimise the risk of fire and horrific burns.

Neil flew just once in the three days following the dramatic events of the 7th but by the afternoon of 11 September the squadron was back up to strength. Shortly before 3 p.m. the radar sites again detected a large build-up of hostile aircraft in the Calais area. One large formation, soon to be identified as He 111s, was heading for the Thames Estuary and London. 249 was one of six squadrons scrambled to meet them with the order to patrol overhead the docks in east London at 17,000 feet. 249 Squadron arrived on the scene to see a thick line of bombers, flying at a similar height, with their fighter escort of 109s some 10,000 feet above. Exactly how many there were did not matter. There were still too many of them.

Barton led the attack as 249 tore into the bombers head on. Neil was flying as Blue Two, again in his GN-F, his guns ripping and shuddering as he watched lines of sparks and smoke streaking and curving ahead. Four Heinkels were seen to break formation, seemingly in a bad way. But suddenly Neil noticed the wing of another Hurricane wobbling crazily by his left ear, forcing him to pull away earthwards. Having composed himself, he fortuitously came across another group of He 111s, slightly below and flying in a loose and irregular formation, and without any escorts in sight.

Never had he enjoyed such a position of advantage, and so he decided to attack the bomber furthest right in the formation from beneath. But as he did so the Heinkel's rear gunner started firing back at him. Neil could see the tracer, a twisting streamer of white curling lazily towards him. He veered away for a second or two before turning back, pulling up and then firing again, his rounds rippling into the bomber. With no enemy fighters anywhere in sight, he even had time to drop back a little before closing in and firing again. He describes what he saw next:

> A greasy trail began to stream from the starboard engine, not smoke exactly but a darkening stain. I saw that the Heinkel was losing ground and falling away from the formation. Encouraged, I fired again. And again. I followed the Heinkel down as it gradually lost height. A long way, through patches of cloud until, eventually and still under control, it crash-landed in a field alongside a railway line some way south of London. I circled it several times at about 500 feet and saw one, then two, figures emerge from the wreckage. They didn't wave. But then, I could hardly have expected them to.

Neil was elated. It was his second success. Another Heinkel was confirmed to have been shot down by 249 and another listed as a probable, for the loss of one Hurricane, although the forever smiling Sergeant Bill Davis baled out. But there was hardly time to draw breath. The squadron was soon off again. This time they saw the yellow-nosed 109s again, whoever they were, but the Hurricanes were lower than them and so 249 avoided any combat. It would not have been an encounter fought on even terms.

There followed a couple of days of cloud, wind and rain, keeping the Luftwaffe at bay. Neil spent much of the time reading, sleeping, writing letters home, and playing endless games of 'L'Attaque' or 'Totopoly' with his squadron colleagues, as well as getting beaten at snooker by Ossie Crossey.

Then came Sunday 15 September, a day later to be for ever remembered as Battle of Britain Day. It was a day that witnessed the largest ever German formations over London and the south-east, in two big raids, that were met head-on by twenty-four squadrons of Fighter Command. It was the greatest air battle to date and resulted in an undisputed day of victory for the RAF.

As usual, the day had started quietly for 249. It was misty at first, but all the signs were there that it would clear up to be a fine day. And it did, although medium-level cloud started to form over southeast England during the late morning, and would progressively get thicker during the day.

The first of the major raids crossed the English coast between Dover and Ramsgate late in the morning, by which time seventeen RAF squadrons were already airborne to meet them. It was one of those rare occasions when the defending forces were overwhelmingly stronger than those of the enemy.

Soon came the order to scramble 249, and its twelve Hurricanes, led by Denis Parnall, joined up with 46 Squadron before being vectored onto a large formation of Do 17s to the south of London. 249 arrived to find the bombers slightly above and heading in the opposite direction. Still climbing and turning hard towards them, the Hurricanes soon became spread out. Neil latched on to one of the Dorniers, closing and firing as he went. There were now aircraft everywhere, of all types and from both sides, including 109s. At one stage he even had a Spitfire on his tail. It was chaotic. Neil returned to North Weald disappointed. He would not be troubling the intelligence officer as he had no claims to make. While others filled out combat reports at dispersal, he had lunch and then went to sleep.

Once refuelled and re-armed, the squadron was ordered back into the air again. It was just before 2 p.m. Neil had only just got to sleep and had been woken by the sound of the telephone followed by shouts of 'Scramble!'

A large enemy force was building in the Calais–Boulogne area and just as 249 was being scrambled, three large enemy bomber formations, around 150 aircraft, began crossing the Channel. Fifteen minutes later, five smaller formations, another hundred aircraft, followed behind. And for every German bomber there were an estimated two escorting fighters.

The three lead formations advanced over a narrow front of less than thirty miles, and by 2.15 p.m. every available RAF fighter squadron was in the air to meet them. There were none in reserve.

After joining up with 504 Squadron over Hornchurch at 15,000 feet, 249 was ordered to patrol to the south of London. The broken medium-level cloud provided a wonderful backcloth for aerial fighting, with the bombers starkly revealed against a carpet of white, and about the same height as the Hurricanes.

It was the most northerly group of bombers, Do 17s followed by He 111s, that 249 Squadron attacked. Curving towards the nearest group of seven or eight Dorniers flying in a broad vic formation, Neil concentrated on the furthest right rather than risk flying into the centre of the formation. The last thing he wanted was to be met by cross-fire from three very angry rear gunners.

Now closing fast and line astern, Neil opened fire, catching the entire port side of the bomber with devastating accuracy. He recalls:

> The effect was instantaneous; there was a splash of some-thing, like water being struck with the back of a spoon. Beside myself with excitement, I fired again, a longish burst, and finding that I was too close, fell back a little but kept my position. Then, astonishingly, before I was ready to renew my assault, two large objects detached themselves from the fuselage and came in my direction, so quickly, in fact, that I had no time to evade. Comprehension barely keeping pace with events, I suddenly recognised spread-eagled arms and legs as two bodies flew past my head.

Neil was shocked by what he had just seen. The crew were baling out, but he had no time to dwell on the matter as he was immediately engulfed by 109s, which swept overhead and then turned towards him venomously, clearly intent on revenge. Neil pushed and pulled in a desperate bid for survival, firing at the 109s whenever he got the chance. And then there was nothing. They had gone. And as he had now experienced all too many times before, he was suddenly alone.

A few moments later he started to see other aircraft around. One was a lone Dornier. He chased after it, cutting it off from its intended path as it headed straight for a large cloud. Neil then noticed another aircraft about 200 yards on his left, a Spitfire, heading for the same bomber.

The Dornier was now about half a mile ahead, running as fast as it could, as the two fighters closed in on their prey. Then it disappeared into the cloud. For a moment it looked like the bomber had escaped but Neil was relieved to see it come out of the cloud once again. The Dornier crew must have been distraught. Having made the safety of cloud they must have prayed that it stretched as far as the French coast. But it did not. No sooner had it entered cloud than it was out again, with the two fighters still in pursuit.

The Dornier now went into a shallow dive in a final attempt to gather speed and make its escape. But, the reality was that it stood no chance. Thereafter, it was an easy kill:

> Without interference, we took turns in carrying out astern attacks and were gratified to see a translucent stain of dark smoke emerge from one, then both engines. Meanwhile, the Dornier continued to descend, flying eastwards down the estuary and out towards the sea, gradually losing height and speed.

The bomber's rear gunner had long been inactive, but time was running out. Realising that he was almost out of ammunition, Neil carried out one final, and very precise, attack from dead astern, during which all but one of his guns fell silent. He then tried firing again, just to make sure. After a quick noise there was nothing. He pulled off to one side and watched the Spitfire close in to finish the Dornier off.

Remarkably, though, the Dornier kept flying on. It was still descending, barely missing the masts of a convoy of ships off Shoeburyness, until it was just twenty feet above the waves and heading out over the North Sea. Neil noticed its tail dropping and nose rising. The Dornier then lurched forward and crashed into the sea in an enormous flurry of white spray. Initially it sat on the surface waterlogged but then slowly and gradually it sank. The two fighters circled the area a couple of times before heading back together. There was nothing left where the Dornier had gone down, although records confirm that two of its crew somehow managed to survive the ditching and were later picked up.

Back at North Weald, Neil joined the queue to brief the intelligence officer of his successes. Everyone was in high spirits. They had all enjoyed a fantastic fight. No one was missing and there was a mounting tally of Huns. Neil was credited with shooting down the first Do 17; it had come down in the Thames Estuary. The second Dornier was officially shared with the Spitfire pilot. So, one and a half kills in fighter speak.

The excitement was still in full flow when the order came to scramble again. It was just after 5 p.m. This time, though, there was nothing to be found and after an hour and twenty minutes of stooging around at 20,000 feet, getting colder by the minute, they turned for home.

249 Squadron was credited with seven and a half enemy aircraft destroyed that day with several more listed as probable or damaged, without 249 having suffered any casualties. Just one of its Hurricanes had come down, that flown by Flying Officer Keith Lofts, who had only joined 249 a few days before. Lofts managed to crash-land at West Malling without injury.

The radio broadcast that evening announced 180 enemy aircraft had been shot down during the day. The true figure was, in fact, a third of that but nonetheless it had been a costly day for the Luftwaffe, for the loss of twenty-six RAF fighters. There was a party in the mess that night and Neil later wrote: 'This was the day, apparently; if the Huns had pulled it off today, the invasion was on.'

A day of intense air activity had ended. Words of congratulations praising the squadron's efforts came from all over.

Bad weather during the next couple of days provided another welcome rest, albeit a brief one, although there was an increase in nocturnal activity as London remained the priority target. Neil and Ossie Crossey decided to go into the capital, but what should have been a wonderful evening of celebration turned out to be quite a disappointment. London had been heavily bombed in places and people were understandably on edge. Many theatres and cinemas closed early, and his fond earlier memories of the Regent Palace Hotel were now blotted out by the sight of what he later described as 'small, fat, crinkly-haired gentlemen who never somehow managed to get into the war'. He would later write that half the country's population 'appeared to be onlookers on the war, some even using it to their own advantage'. Neil was scrambled four times on the 18th and during the second sortie was credited with damaging a He 111 in a head-on attack near Southend. Back at dispersal there were confused reports. Everyone agreed that the Heinkels had been hit but none had been seen to go down.

In Neil's view these head-on attacks were hopeless. And dangerous too! Not only had 249 been unsuccessful during the encounter, but the popular Denis Parnall had failed to return. He had first come back to North Weald alone with a gun-firing problem and then got airborne again in another Hurricane, after which nothing more had been heard.

It was hoped that Parnall would turn up later. It was no longer considered unusual for an aircraft to put down elsewhere and then return to North Weald subsequently. Either that or word would filter through that he was still alive. In the case of Pat Wells's loss earlier in the month, for example, it had taken five days for the good news that Wells was alive to reach the squadron. And so there was hope.

Parnall's bed in the dispersal hut was next to Neil's. It would remain empty that night and, sadly, there was to be no good news. For several days there was no word of Parnall until fragments of his aircraft were found in a field near the village of Margaretting, just a few miles to the east of North Weald. His Hurricane had totally disintegrated on impact having clearly gone into the ground at high speed.

For years the circumstances behind Parnall's death remained a mystery. The action involving 249 that day had taken place many miles away and 109s seldom ventured north of the Thames. But long after the war was over, a man, who had been a youth living in the village at the time, told his account of the day when he had witnessed an aerial battle being fought above him in which a Hurricane had been shot down by German fighters.

Taking off alone was not the way to go and Parnall's loss had been another hard lesson learned. Neil had done the same thing only a matter of days before but got away with it.

The day after Parnall's loss, two intelligence officers arrived at the squadron to speak to Neil. Having first confirmed that he was the Hurricane pilot involved in bringing down the Do 17 over the sea on the 15th, they went on to inform him that the Spitfire pilot he had shared its destruction with, named as Pilot Officer Eric Lock of 41 Squadron, had also seen Neil's courageous encounter with the 109s moments before, during which Lock had witnessed Neil shooting down two of the 109s.

Neil would retrospectively be credited with the two 109s, but the intelligence officers were there to hear his account of the shared destruction of the Dornier with Lock. The idea was to bring the two pilots together at some point for publicity value and so, like any fighter pilot, Neil happily gave his version of what had happened.

Sure enough, one evening the following week Neil and Lock were brought together at Hornchurch to prepare a script for a broadcast that would later go out on the BBC. The same age as Neil, 'Sawn-Off' Lock, as he was known, had already achieved considerable success during the summer of 1940 with thirteen confirmed victories in the month prior to the encounter with the Dornier. The whole story of their shared destruction of the German bomber was repeated many times over several beers. They made an interesting pair, Lock being just 5 feet 4 inches and Neil being a foot taller. It was quite a night.

Having now been credited with shooting down five enemy aircraft, Neil was officially an 'ace' and he had quickly become one of 249's leading fighter pilots. Grandy made him a section leader while the station commander, Victor Beamish, was full of praise for the young man he now knew as 'Ginger'. This was great news for Neil. Not only would he rather lead in combat than be led, he was clearly going up in the world. Beamish, for one, a man who knew no fear, and whose aggressive fighting spirit was an example to all, reserved his praise only for the bravest and the best. And it was Beamish who informed Neil that he was to be awarded the Distinguished Flying Cross. Neil was stunned, breathless and absurdly happy.

Along with Bryan Meaker, also awarded the DFC, Neil was therefore one of 249 Squadron's first decorated pilots. Neil was particularly pleased for the quiet and unobtrusive Meaker, an Irishman and a little older than himself, who had been credited with shooting down at least seven enemy aircraft and had been involved in every major engagement from the start.

The nightly blitz against London continued, but there followed a lull in the day fighting, initially due to poor weather and then because the Luftwaffe focused its efforts elsewhere. Such periods of inactivity gave Neil and his squadron colleagues the chance to read Fighter Command's intelligence summaries and to reflect on how the overall air battle was going as far as the senior commanders were concerned. What was becoming increasingly apparent, particularly during the large raids, was the failure of No. 12 Group to provide No. 11 Group's squadrons with adequate reinforcements in time. No. 12 Group's so-called 'Big Wing' tactic was simply not working. It was taking far too long for large numbers of fighters to join up and then transit south to where the action was taking place, and this was now causing a difference of opinion between the group commanders.

At just twenty years old, Neil did not take much of an interest in the politics of command, and neither he nor his colleagues would ever come close to the point of criticising those at the top. But when there was no fighting to be done, the young pilots did talk, and rumours did spread. Whether the group commanders ever fell out or not was not for them to decide but they had witnessed first-hand what the intelligence summaries were concluding. Reinforcements were not getting to the battle area in time. Neil would later write:

> All too frequently, when returning to North Weald in a semi-exhausted condition, all we saw of 12 Group's contribution to the engagement, was a vast formation of

Hurricanes in neat vics of three, streaming comfortably over our heads in pursuit of an enemy who had long disappeared in the direction of France. Our reactions on such occasions, though mostly of resigned amusement at first, grew to be more harshly critical later on.

The recent lull in daytime activity ended on 27 September with the Luftwaffe launching another major daylight assault on London. At North Weald, the order to scramble came just before 9 a.m. After climbing through some light cloud to join up with 46 Squadron, the Hurricanes were told to patrol Maidstone where dozens of enemy fighters, both Bf 109s and Me 110s, had been reported roaming over the Kent countryside.

Using 109s and 110s in this way was a tactic employed by the Luftwaffe to tempt the RAF's fighters into the sky so that they would use up their fuel tackling the Messerschmitts. This would then give the bombers following on behind the opportunity to reach their targets unopposed while the RAF fighters were back on the ground refuelling.

The Hurricanes had reached 18,000 feet when the familiar 109s were spotted way above, before a group of twenty 110s were spotted over Redhill flying in a defensive circle at the same height as the Hurricanes. Whether the 109s were not interested in the Hurricanes, or they had simply not seen them, is unclear. But it made no difference. Barton led the attack against the 110s.

Neil, now proudly wearing the ribbon of his DFC, tore into one of the 110s, rushing straight at it. The squadron soon became scattered and there seemed to be aircraft everywhere. Having broken away and reversed direction to follow the circular flow of the 110s, Neil latched on to the same one as before, which was now just 400 yards away.

The 110 was still in a steep defensive turn, making it easier for Neil to reduce the range. As he continued to close, tracer from the rear gunner appeared, passing above and to his right. But still he closed, expecting to be hit at any moment, until he was just fifty yards behind. He opened fired again and could clearly see sparks and twinkling flashes everywhere as his rounds hit home. Finally, the 110 dropped away in a gentle turn. Resistance from the rear gunner had gone.

Making sure that his own tail was clear, Neil fired again. A bubble of red appeared and then a stream of black smoke. He later recalled: 'I'd got him! He was going! Diving hard. Straight. Now steepening. The 110 disappearing into haze and still diving steeply. Streaming. A goner! It must be! Finished!'

Neil pulled away and climbed back up northwards to re-join the others. At 14,000 feet he spotted another 110 with a Hurricane already in pursuit; it later turned out to be John Beazley, not that Neil knew it at the time. As Neil also closed in, the 110 went into a dive in a desperate bid to escape.

Diving down after it, the two Hurricanes took it in turns to attack. Once again, tracer from the rear gunner flashed around Neil's head. The 110 was now hugging the earth's contours at full speed, rising only occasionally to avoid hitting obstacles on the ground. Still the rear gunner returned fire and then the other Hurricane pulled up and disappeared.

Neil was now alone and closing on another kill. But then he noticed oil on his windscreen, darker in colour and far more than would normally be expected from a leaking oil seal behind the propeller. Oil was soon spraying all over his cockpit and the top of the fuselage. Either he had been hit or there was a severe leak somewhere.

He was now so close to the 110, only about 200 yards or so, and did not want it to get away. It was now or never. Taking as careful an aim as possible, he opened fire again. Still the rear gunner fired back. Neil admired his courage, that was for sure, but it was a final act of desperation. The 110 turned slowly to the right and began to lose speed. As he got closer Neil fired again, observing more twinkling strikes. But then silence. He was finally out of ammunition.

Needing somewhere to land, and soon, all Neil could do was watch the 110, with a growing trail of smoke and a line of white coolant streaming from its starboard engine, disappear out over the sea. He left it and the crew to their fate.

Neil managed to touch down safely at Detling, near Maidstone, but he had landed in the middle of an air-raid alert. With everyone taking cover there was no one around. Another Hurricane soon landed. Neil could see it was one of his own squadron and was even more delighted when he saw it was his good chum 'Appy 'Arry Davidson, his long-time colleague from their days together at ITW who had followed in Neil's footsteps by joining 249.

After the all-clear Neil was told by the ground crew that the oil splattering was the result of a routine oil leak rather than because of any battle damage. Having been refuelled and re-armed, and with his oil tank replenished, Neil took off with Davidson and the pair were soon back at North Weald. They were greeted by a much relieved Lohmeyer. It was only then that the outcome of the squadron's action became apparent. Eight of the 110s were claimed as shot down but four of 249's Hurricanes had been missing. With Neil's pair now back from Detling and having also determined that Butch Barton had landed at Gatwick after his Hurricane had been damaged during the encounter, that left Percy Burton, one of the squadron's young South Africans, still missing.

It would later emerge that Burton was killed when he collided with one of the fleeing 110s at tree-top height while over Hailsham in East Sussex. Witnesses on the ground suggested that Burton, who had by then run out of ammunition, had deliberately rammed into the 110 to stop it getting away. Burton's heroic demise led to his name being put forward for a Victoria Cross, but nothing came of it, much to the disgust of those serving with 249 at the time. Burton was instead posthumously awarded a mention in despatches. Neil would later say that it was a shameful official misinterpretation of protocol that denied a gallant young man his rightful place in history.

John Beazley, too, was out of action. He was on his way to hospital having been wounded by the rear gunner's return fire while chasing the 110 at low level with Neil.

The ground crew, meanwhile, quickly set to work on Neil's Hurricane, having a more in-depth look at the reason for the oil leak. Neil would later write:

I had never failed to be impressed by the enthusiasm and devotion of our riggers, fitters and other tradesmen. In particular the senior non-commissioned officers, who provided the expertise and the disciplined organisation which helped so much to keep our Hurricanes in the air. Theirs was not an exciting or highly rewarding war; just one of graft and dogged hard work at all hours of the day and night. The salt of the earth, without a doubt.

By mid-afternoon 249 Squadron was back in the air and patrolling the Guildford area at 18,000 feet. This time it was Ju 88s spotted over South London, accompanied by the usual large formation of enemy fighters, again a mix of 109s and 110s. Ignoring the enemy fighters as best they could, the Hurricanes went straight for the Ju 88s. Neil counted at least ten in the group they attacked first, but much to his annoyance it was another beam attack.

More twisting lines of tracer came back at them from the rear gunners and almost immediately he noticed a Hurricane to his left fall away. Having then swept over the bombers, he turned sharply to find the 88s immediately below but going very fast. He describes what happened when he swooped down on one:

> Wallowing in the slipstream of an 88 I fired a long burst from slightly underneath and had the satisfaction of seeing a succession of vivid strikes on the rudder and starboard wing. I was about to fire again when there was a minor explosion on the right-hand side of the 88 and a shower of debris which produced a thin blade of flame and a developing stream of smoke. As if mortally wounded, the aircraft immediately began to fall away to its right. I watched it slowly drop its nose and drift over onto its side and beyond as though totally uncontrolled. The sight was almost unnerving. What on earth had happened? Had I done that?

Neil followed the Ju 88 down but not for long. Aircraft were all around him. Spotting a group of Hurricanes ahead of him, he latched on to one that he recognised as belonging to the squadron's new Australian, Pilot Officer Bill Millington, who was already closing on another Ju 88.

Ju 88s were always difficult customers. The Dorniers were fine, but the Ju 88 was fast and seemingly able to absorb unlimited punishment. As Neil took it in turns with Millington to fire, the 88's starboard engine was soon set alight. Neil best describes what he witnessed next: 'The fire was a raging, violent, bubbling red, as angry a conflagration as ever I had seen in the air, almost frightening in its intensity and spewing out a rolling cloud of greasy black smoke in its wake.' But the Ju 88 continued onwards, flying flat out as fast as it could. It was hard for the Hurricanes to keep up. The fire was still raging like a blowtorch and then gradually the Ju 88 began to lose height. Now out of ammunition, Neil and Millington followed it down and out to sea off Shoreham where they finally watched it crash in a plume of spray and steam.

Back at North Weald, Neil's feeling of joy and more success was quickly dampened by the news that Bryan Meaker had been killed during the action. The gallant young Meaker, who had just been awarded the DFC with Neil, had been shot down by return fire from a Ju 88. It was terrible news. Neil had liked Meaker and got to know him well during their time together. He later said of him: 'Although he had shown no early signs that he might soon develop into a most determined and capable fighter pilot, he was a very courageous man and I always enjoyed flying with him.'

From the bits and pieces put together by the pilots at the end of the day, it appears that the Hurricane Neil had seen fall away during the initial attack on the Ju 88s had been that of Meaker. Others had also seen the Hurricane fall back during the attack, after which a parachute was seen to develop but it had instantly become entangled with the tail of the pilot's own aircraft, dragging him downwards and presumably to a horrible death. It was a tragic way for such a brave young man to die.

There were now more empty beds in the dispersal hut. Neil and others went to the cinema, but it was just an ordinary evening: 'I was

Bryan Meaker (*left*) and Percy Burton, both of whom were killed within hours of each other on 27 September 1940.

unhappy about our losses, of course but, if the truth were told, not really distressed. How impervious we were becoming to injury and death.'

Friday 27 September was another defining day of the battle. The Luftwaffe had again suffered badly with the loss of fifty-five aircraft, many to the guns of 249 Squadron. In return, twenty-eight RAF fighters were lost, including those of Percy Burton and Bryan Meaker. But they had not been 249's only losses that day. John Beazley had been wounded, while Butch Barton and George Barclay had both been shot down. Other Hurricanes had been damaged during the day as well, leaving 249 once again decimated.

Neil was now one of the few survivors of the original squadron from the Yorkshire days. He had watched friends and colleagues be killed, wounded, or simply disappear for all kinds of reasons, with an indifference that almost frightened him. But never at any point did he expect to become a casualty. He saw no reason whatsoever why he should not continue to survive, despite statistical evidence to the contrary. Even so, it didn't escape his mind that it would be a shattering blow to his parents were some evil stroke of luck to result in his death. Hardly a day passed when they did not form part of his more reflective moments.

As always, losses were soon replaced. There were more young faces and new names to get used to, with more introductions to the Thatched House or the Cock in Epping. When it came to nights out, the squadron's unofficial rule was that the officers tended to use the Thatch while the sergeant pilots used the Cock, although there were many occasions when they all ended up in the same place. And it always seemed to be the reliable and dependable Lohmeyer who stopped Neil from going under, helping him work through the copious pints that always seemed to be lined up.

Alcohol had long been considered an essential part of an evening's entertainment and there were occasional wild parties, both in and beyond the officers' mess, which Neil describes as including a blend of genteel formality and irresponsible chaos. But such outbursts of outlandish behaviour were only the occasional foible of an otherwise normal and well-mannered group of young men whose average age was just twenty-two, and who otherwise had very little opportunity for personal expression.

The working day of flying, sleeping and eating, for anything up to eighteen hours a day during the hectic summer of 1940, left little time for anything else. But the thought of being defeated never entered their heads:

> Such thoughts were never in my adolescent mind in 1940, as I was always confident that Britain and the RAF were indestructible. Moreover, never once in 249 Squadron, even when under the greatest stress, did I ever hear the word *defeat* ever mentioned.

The end of September brought an end to the major daylight raids on London. Although the nightly blitz against London would continue for some considerable time, the Luftwaffe's latest losses meant that the German high command could no longer sustain daylight massed formation attacks against the capital, and so the planned invasion of southern England was put on hold. The brave young men of Fighter Command had won a decisive battle.

Chapter Seven

On the Offensive

The beginning of October 1940 marked a new phase in the air battle being fought over Britain. The Luftwaffe was now using its main bomber force almost entirely under the cover of darkness, while attacks were carried out during daylight hours by lone intruders or small numbers of fast Ju 88s and bomb-carrying Messerschmitts, protected by fighters above. While tactically this might have been difficult for Fighter Command to deal with, strategically it proved to be of little benefit to the Germans.

The month started relatively quietly for 249, helped by the poor weather, as news filtered through of more awards to the squadron's pilots. There were well-earned DFCs for Butch Barton and Keith Lofts, while Gerald Lewis, a tall, good-looking South African with an unforgettable mop of flaxen hair and energetic grin, and a relative newcomer to the squadron, was awarded a Bar to the DFC he had earned with his previous squadron. And for the ever-reliable John Beard there was a Distinguished Flying Medal.

The weather was again awful on the 6th, but Neil was scrambled with Crossey. They were vectored onto a lone aircraft detected to the north-east of the airfield. Neil soon spotted the intruder, a Do 17, flying in and out of cloud. As it dived for the cloud below, the closest he could get was around 200 yards but, nonetheless, he opened fire just as it disappeared. And that was the last he saw of it.

Back on the ground, an irate George Barclay confronted Neil. A Hampden had been reported shot down in the same area. Neil knew what a Do 17 looked like but for a while there were concerns

Neil (*in cockpit*) with Pat Wells and Wilfred the duck.

that he might have shot down a friendly aircraft. Fortunately for Neil – not that he had ever been in any doubt – Grandy later confirmed that a damaged Do 17 had been encountered by Hurricanes of 17 Squadron based at nearby Debden. They had come across the Dornier at around the same time and in the same area where Neil and Crossey had been, after which they had finished off the stricken bomber. The result was that Neil was credited with a third of a kill.

A couple of days later, Neil went home to Manchester for a week of well-earned leave. He had had very little time off since joining 249 back in May. On returning to North Weald he found that much had happened in the short time he had been away. Sadly, the squadron had lost another pilot, Sergeant Ed Bayley. There were other changes as well. Firstly, the Blenheims of 25 Squadron had been replaced by another Hurricane unit, 257 Squadron. Secondly, his second beloved GN-F had been lost to enemy action while he had been away. And thirdly, 249 had acquired a new mascot, Wilfred the duck, introduced by Bill Millington, to add to their little black and white terrier called Pipsqueak and several kittens.

There followed several more days of poor weather and uneventful sorties, which now even included boring convoy patrols, with only the occasional engagement here and there. After the excitement of August and September, October was proving to be a mournful, miserable month.

There was, however, the BBC broadcast in London with Sawn-Off Lock when the two re-enacted their shared destruction of the Dornier the previous month, although that incident already seemed like years ago. The two hardened fighter pilots were reduced to bags of nerves when they found out the radio audience was to be around forty million. But, after several rehearsals, the broadcast apparently went well, not that Neil found anyone back at North Weald who admitted to having listened to it!

Although it had been a relatively quiet month so far, the enemy had not exactly disappeared. Shortly before midday on 25 October, Neil was flying as Yellow One to the south-east of London at 25,000 feet when the squadron encountered a formation of Bf 109s, crossing ahead and a little lower. As the Hurricanes approached, the 109s turned and made off in a dive towards the Sussex coast. But, as they did so, more 109s swooped on the rear section of Hurricanes, instantly shooting down two.

From his position out front, Neil had seen nothing of the 109s coming in from above. He was chasing one of the fleeing 109s and quickly got into position to attack, delivering a two-second burst. He then watched as a large piece of the aircraft broke away before him as the 109 turned on its back and went vertically down. Neil followed him. He could see that he was to the north of Hastings, but the 109 was getting away and the distraction of more enemy aircraft and the presence of cloud prevented him witnessing what finally happened to the 109.

Not for the first time Neil found himself in the rather uncomfortable position of being alone, and so he cautiously made his way north back towards North Weald. He had hardly been on the ground long when he was scrambled back into the air, again leading Yellow Section. This time, though, it was his own section that was jumped.

The first Neil knew of the danger was when Ossie Crossey, flying on his left, upended his aircraft and vanished. Crossey was fine, but the next thing Neil saw was a 109 flashing through. It had clearly got in unseen from behind and had just overshot. Now it was nose-down and disappearing fast. Neil went after it, firing more in hope than anything else. He was never going to catch it, although he did see a part of the 109 break away from its starboard side. He fired again. It was now smoking but, equally, it could have just been the exhaust as it disappeared in the distance.

The fact that his section had been bounced unseen was of concern to Neil. That only happened to others and not to him. It played on his mind. For the first time he had been caught out. Had the 109 not been so erratic, his number might well have been up. It was very worrying indeed.

Neil was again scrambled during the early morning of the 27th. A lone Do 17 was spotted above North Weald at no more than 1,000 feet and was dropping bombs on the airfield. After completing its attack, the Dornier turned to make its escape. Neil chased after it, going in and out of cloud, before he finally managed to catch up as it approached the Thames Estuary. Knowing there would be little opportunity to get it because of the covering cloud, he got in as many bursts as he could before the Dornier disappeared into cloud for the last time with smoke pouring from both its engines.

Fighter Command flew a thousand sorties that day, giving a clear indication of its strength at the time. Plenty of cloud and rain the following day then reduced enemy activity over southern England and made hunting difficult. Neil was again leading Yellow Section and by mid-morning was already on his second patrol. This time they were over East Sussex when a Do 17 was spotted well below and heading for home. As they screamed down after it, the Dornier dropped down into cloud to make its escape, much to Neil's annoyance. He was now going so fast and was nearly vertical in the dive, but he was determined not to let the Dornier get away and so he shot into the cloud after it.

Flying in cloud in such a nose-down attitude, particularly when fast running out of height, is not a safe place to be. Neil had to interpret his instruments quickly and safely recover the aircraft before he smashed into the ground. Pulling hard and then climbing away, he was relieved to come out on top of the cloud and into bright sunshine once more. He then spotted another Hurricane in the distance, that of Bill Millington who had been leading Blue Section, and so he decided to catch it up.

While Neil might have been disappointed to have lost out on his Dornier, he did not have to wait long before he spotted a Ju 88 just half a mile or so ahead. Chasing after it, he was the first to reach the 88 and he opened fire with a sustained burst. He could clearly see brilliant flashes as his rounds clattered into the area of the rear cockpit, but he then had to pull away because he was closing so fast. He then attacked it again, this time from slightly above. But still the Ju 88 flew on.

Millington then had a go, but they were just about to cross the coast and were now running out of time. Neil could clearly see the 88 was in a mess, but it just kept going. As he had witnessed before, the Ju 88 could absorb almost unlimited punishment. However, it was time for the Hurricanes to head for home. Neil later admitted that he had felt almost sorry for the Ju 88 crew, even though they had shown every sign of escaping, but it later emerged that the crippled 88 had been finished off by others in their sections. It would be a quarter of a kill for Neil.

The following afternoon 'A' Flight was stood down and so Neil was back in his room relaxing when the sound of approaching aircraft could be heard. There was nothing unusual with that until it became obvious the sound was quite different to what he had heard before. He went to his window to see what they were, just in time to see a stream of 109s flashing overhead. He threw himself to the floor. The 109s were attacking the airfield. It seemed to go on for ages. Then, after all had been silent for a while, he went out to observe the scene before hurriedly making his way down to the dispersal with the others.

What Neil had witnessed was a dozen bomb-carrying 109s dive-bombing the airfield just as 'B' Flight and 257 Squadron were being scrambled. Although a couple of 249's aircraft had been hit by debris as they were taking off, the pilots escaped unhurt. But one of 257's pilots, 22-year-old Sergeant Alex Girdwood, was not so fortunate. His Hurricane was caught fully by the blast of one of the bombs and burst into flames just short of 249's dispersal hut. Neil later wrote about the sad sight:

> A Hurricane sat outside our dispersal hut, on its belly and on fire. I peered through the smoke and flames. Where was the pilot? A nod. Inside! It was like a funeral pyre. As the flames took hold, we watched a blackened and unrecognisable ball that was a human head sink lower and lower into the well of the cockpit until, mercifully, it disappeared.

Nineteen were killed during the raid and forty-two injured. Neil went to bed that night more than a little concerned that he had treated the cremation of the 257 Squadron pilot so lightly. He later wrote: 'What on earth was coming over me? I had watched a colleague burnt to a cinder and had felt . . . well . . . almost nothing. Not like me at all. Downright worrying in fact.'

There was more bad news the following day with the loss of Bill Millington. He was last seen chasing a Bf 109 out across the Channel. Millington was the eighth pilot from the squadron to be killed during the Battle of Britain, a battle that for the record officially ended on 31 October 1940. Countless more, at least twenty, had been wounded or injured, not that the war had started in July or ended in October.

The first week of November was marred by more bad weather. 257 Squadron left for Martlesham Heath to make way for 46 Squadron from Stapleford Tawney from where, as an all-grass airfield, it would be impossible to sustain operational flying during the winter months. Otherwise, life was much the same at North Weald except for the cooler temperature and shorter days marking the onset of winter.

The 7th brought a welcome change in the weather and during the early afternoon Neil was leading Yellow Section over the Thames

249 Squadron, North Weald, late 1940. Neil is second from right.

Estuary at 15,000 feet. They were then ordered to head out over the sea where a convoy was coming under attack by Junkers Ju 87 Stukas. Descending fast, Neil burst through some cloud. He could make out the faint outlines of ships way below and then an aircraft appeared in front of him. It took him a moment to recognise what it was: 'A Ju 87! As large as life! The first I had ever seen, close-to. It was turning and climbing slightly, an upright aircraft with cranked wings and, in actuality, rather bigger than I had imagined.'

Closing too fast, Neil did everything he could to slow down but he quickly flew through and lost sight of the Stuka now behind him. Then, hauling his aircraft around and up again, he caught sight of another turning hard away. He followed it round but again flew through with too much speed.

Now pulling like a madman, Neil attacked again. There was no doubt in his mind that the Stuka pilot knew what he was doing. This time Neil was greeted by the familiar curl of tracer from the rear gunner, but he closed in and opened fire with devastating accuracy.

The Stuka started to fall away and then almost in slow motion toppled over. Neil followed it down. He was, once again, alone, and just at the point the Stuka was about to fly into the sea, he noticed three aircraft slightly above and to his right. They were 109s.

With attack so often being the best form of defence, Neil decided to fly straight at them, firing as he went. The 109s broke formation and either lost sight of him or became distracted by something else. Determined not to let them get away, Neil went after them. He seemed to close in unobserved; either that or the 109s had no fuel left to stay and fight. It made no difference. He fired on one and then turned his attention to a second. Still they did not react, intent only on flying out to sea. Neil continued to chase after them and then fired on one again. He watched as a thin trail of white coolant emerged from under the fuselage. The white changed to black smoke, and then he spotted flames coming from the cockpit. The 109 was not manoeuvring, but instead was diving towards the sea.

Finally, the other two 109s reacted to Neil, seeking revenge, but one presented itself on the beam and so Neil fired a long burst as he closed in a quarter attack. The 109 turned over and fell into the sea. Neil had now lost sight of the remaining 109. Besides, he had run out of ammunition and was heading further out to sea. He turned for home: 'They'd had it, by God! Two of them! Quite, quite unbelievable! This couldn't be happening to me.'

But the day was far from over for Neil. Later that afternoon he was again leading Yellow Section, this time over Maidstone at 15,000 feet, when suddenly, and without any warning, Victor Beamish, flying as Red Four, broke formation to investigate something he had seen.

Neil was just yards behind and remembers there being nothing particularly unusual in this. Beamish would often go off on his own. But then, several minutes later, came what Neil can only describe as 'a cataclysmic, grinding bang' from somewhere behind him. In an instant, his Hurricane pitched up vertically before flopping over onto its back and then went into a spin. Neil was struggling to regain control, trying everything he could to recover the aircraft. At first, he thought he might have been hit, but he could not work out from where, and for the next 10,000 feet of downwards confusion he stayed with the aircraft. But whatever had happened, it made no difference now. He had gone into cloud and was down low, somewhere in the region of 5,000 feet. He had to get out. What happened next is best described in Neil's own words:

> The decision to bale out was not an easy one to make. Thereafter, much relieved in my mind, my actions were surprisingly methodical. I opened the hood and, deciding to keep on my helmet, undid my straps, rose to my feet, with difficulty, and pushed myself over one side. Immediately I was catapulted forward by the lurching of the aircraft and out over the windscreen, for several horrifying seconds being restrained by my long oxygen tube which, still connected, was stretching like a piece of elastic, and also by my toes which were hooked over the edges of the windscreen frame. Lying along the top of the reserve fuel tank, I was aware of the very unsettling presence of the propeller whirling like a circular saw within several feet of my head.

Neil was then suddenly free, just in time, his head catching the top of the starboard wing as he fell towards earth before finally pulling his rip-cord. And then there was a brief silence before he suffered the uncomfortable feeling of crashing through some branches before he hit the ground. And then nothing. He eventually came to, to the sound of voices. A small crowd had gathered. People were trying to work out whether he was 'one of ours or one of theirs'.

Neil had come down near Maidstone, his aircraft having crashed just half a mile away from where he had landed. Given the short time he had spent in his parachute and the close proximity of the crash site, he had probably only been about a thousand feet or so above the ground when he got out. It had been a lucky escape.

After a while, two army officers took him away by car to their anti-aircraft battery where they offered him tea in the mess, although it took until later that evening for Neil to contact North Weald by telephone to let the squadron know that he was safe, albeit he had damaged his leg getting out of the aircraft. The news came as a most welcome surprise. His Hurricane had last been seen entering cloud in a spin. It was almost as if they had all given up on him.

Neil eventually arrived back at North Weald to be greeted by a very apologetic Beamish, who explained that he had gone off south in search of the enemy but after a fruitless excursion he had tried to regain his position in the squadron formation, with a disastrous result. He had hit Neil's aircraft and, having lost the propeller from his own aircraft, Beamish had crash-landed near Detling.

The injury to Neil's leg was worse than he had first realised, and so he was sent home for a few days of leave to recover. He returned the following week to find out that he was to be awarded a Bar to his DFC. It was Beamish who delivered the good news. Neil was delighted, of course, and many letters of congratulation arrived over the next few days.

Neil had long hardened to air combat and was seldom shocked by what he saw in war, but one act that he witnessed on 14 November enraged him beyond words. The squadron had been scrambled during the afternoon to investigate an enemy fighter sweep over the Kent coast. It turned out to be a diversionary tactic. Nonetheless, two 109s were picked on by the Hurricanes, with one 109 soon in trouble.

The encounter had happened out over the sea. Trailing a now familiar white line of engine coolant, the 109 was never going to make it across the Channel to France and so its pilot decided to turn back towards the Kent coastline, resigned to landing in enemy territory. Delighted at the thought of the squadron capturing a fully intact 109, Neil was in formation with it and about thirty yards on its left, close enough to see every detail. He watched it coast in near Margate, heading towards the airfield at Manston. The pilot was clearly having to work hard to get the crippled fighter back safely on the ground. Neil even remembers willing the German on. As a fellow aviator he was on his side. He wanted the German to survive, hoping the engine would not seize.

Satisfied that the German was going to make it safely to the ground, Neil turned away. But then, when the 109 was less than a mile from the airfield and at just 150 feet, he watched in disbelief as a Hurricane took up a position line astern and then opened fire. The 109 tipped forward and nose-dived into a wood, killing its pilot. Shocked and enraged, Neil is best left to describe his feelings in his own words:

> In five seconds some bloody fool had undone all our good work besides wantonly murdering a man and destroying what was patently a helpless and surrendering enemy aircraft. I whirled about. Who was it? I would kill the bastard! Even one of my own side.

The villain was later identified. He was a new and inexperienced pilot who had clearly been carried away by combat fervour during what had been his first engagement. Formally reprimanded, and roundly abused by the rest of the squadron, the pilot was posted elsewhere within days. The incident had so upset Neil that he wrote of it in passionate terms to his parents that night. It was a moment he would never forget, and he would spend the rest of his life contemplating how the incident fitted into the rest of the war's darkest moments.

The following day came news of James Nicolson's Victoria Cross for his encounter over the Solent back in August. Everyone at North Weald was stunned. No one had known what Nicolson had been through. Neil even remembers feeling a sense of pride. 'Good old Nick, damn good show!' he would later write.

As winter crept in there was so much rain at North Weald that the airfield soon became nothing short of a quagmire. There was little flying. And even when there was flying to be had, there were endless hours of fruitless haring around in poor weather. Although the occasional enemy aircraft was seen, there were no engagements for several days.

It was all quite different from only a couple of months before. But just as it was beginning to look like the main action might be over for the year, Pat Wells was shot down in flames, suffering horrendous burns and injuries, while George Barclay was shot down and wounded the following day. It would be a few months before either of these stalwarts returned to the squadron.

There was little flying during the first days of December as winter started to take hold, but as the year approached its end there was more good news for Neil. He was promoted to the rank of acting flight lieutenant and given command of 'B' Flight, his promotion coinciding with the news that Butch Barton was now officially to command the squadron following the departure of John Grandy who was off to a staff tour on promotion.

The weather throughout the rest of the month was miserable with low cloud, fog and drizzle. There was yet another squadron rotation as 46 moved north to make way for 56 Squadron, which returned to its home station after its short time away with No. 10 Group. Otherwise, 249 Squadron flew whenever it could, but there was little for Neil to write home about.

He had, however, been introduced to the Officers' Sunday Club in London, effectively a superior tea party held each week at the Grosvenor House Hotel in Park Lane. It was somewhere he could spend the afternoon and evening enjoying the riches of life with company that he could only ever have imagined before the war. These were moments away from the heat of battle that he would never forget. The question 'What war?' springs to mind.

With the decisive year of 1940 all but over, Neil could sense the country's mood was changing. After months of long and hard fighting over southern England, it was now time for Fighter Command to go on the offensive. Neil was amongst the first to hear the news, announced during a gathering of commanders at Hornchurch on Christmas Day.

Everyone important from No. 11 Group seemed to be there, from the new AOC, Leigh-Mallory, to his squadrons' flight commanders, now including Neil. The assembled audience was told that the RAF had clobbered the Luftwaffe, the threat of invasion had been averted, and now it was time for the group's squadrons to take the offensive to the enemy. This was to be achieved in several ways, such as flying fighter sweeps across the Channel to draw the enemy fighters into the air, by carrying out fighter-escort missions for the bombers against targets in occupied Europe and carrying out low-level attacks against any and every legitimate target within striking range. This, it was said, would keep the enemy constantly on the alert and would take the initiative away from the Hun. And it was all to start the following day!

Sitting in the car on the way back to North Weald, Neil had mixed feelings about what he had just heard. Everyone else, though, seemed to be totally in favour of the idea and so he went along with it. However, the roles of the RAF and Luftwaffe were about to be reversed. Whether this would be a good thing remained to be seen. Neil initially remained unconvinced, particularly when it came to the idea of flying as escort. He did not like the thought of being tied to the bombers, in the same way that the idea had not worked for the Luftwaffe. After all, flying as escorts had not exactly turned out well for the 109s, and so Neil was concerned that No. 11 Group might be about to make the same mistake. There was also the fact that the air battles would now be fought over an extremely hostile occupied Europe instead of above the friendly green countryside of southern England. And there were several miles of freezing cold water in between. These were not overly pleasant thoughts and time would tell.

As he gave it all more thought, he started to warm to the idea. At least with the enemy fighters having to climb up from below, he would find himself more often in a position of advantage. But, for now, such thoughts were put to one side. It was Christmas Day and once back at North Weald there was good food to eat and fine wine to be drunk.

Fortunately for those with sore heads, including Neil, the weather was awful the following day and what should have been the squadron's first offensive mission was cancelled. Two days later Neil went home on leave. New Year's Eve was a special night, spent in style with plenty of champagne in the company of a beautiful dark-haired companion. It had been a difficult year, but the worst was over and there was much optimism for the future. Or, at least, that is what he told her.

And so 1941 began with 249 going on its first escort mission, codenamed Circus One. It was a bitterly cold 10 January, and around midday when the large force of more than a hundred fighters, protecting just six Blenheim light bombers, set off for northern France, the target being an ammunition dump in the Forêt de Guînes, just a few miles inland from Cap Gris Nez in the Pas de Calais.

Flying ahead and slightly below the Blenheims, 249 was led by Victor Beamish with Neil leading the rear section of four. As they crossed the enemy coast at just 5,000 feet, Neil was fully expecting the worst, but nothing happened. He looked down at the snow-covered landscape below. Everything was quite still. There was no one around, although someone claimed to spot a small formation of 109s in the distance. Whether they had or not was not clear. In any event, no engagement took place.

With all the Blenheims safely overhead their target, 249 turned for home. The only excitement occurred on the way back. While crossing the coast at low level near Calais they came under fire from enemy patrol boats. Neil remembers the sight of the flak:

> It started coming in the shape of white streaks and red balls, the latter rising obliquely in clutches of five or six, curving quickly towards me then whipping past. On my right mostly, where there were other Hurricanes in an untidy gaggle. In a moment of naked fear, I pulled back and climbed steeply.

Suddenly, the Hurricane in front was hit and fell away. Neil finally levelled out and soon after was relieved to find himself back over the snow-covered Kent countryside.

Back at North Weald it turned out that two Hurricanes had been hit by the flak encountered over the enemy coast, but both had managed to return home. Neil even discovered that his own aircraft had been hit, the only obvious damage being a minor hole through the elevator. But a couple of Hurricanes were missing.

It later emerged that one of the Hurricanes had been bounced by a 109 mid-way across the Channel and had crashed into the cliffs near

Dover, although Pilot Officer Mac McConnell baled out into the sea and was later picked up by a rescue launch. The other Hurricane had put down at Hornchurch. While it was a new start and still very early days, there was clearly much to learn. Neil was critical of the whole affair and felt it had all been a pointless exercise. He would later write: 'Six bombers, 108 fighters, one squadron aircraft lost and the pilot in hospital, all for what? A few twigs off some trees in the Forêt de Guînes and very little else. And I had not even seen a Hun!'

Another type of offensive mission was given the codename Mosquito. This involved a pair of fighters crossing the Channel to hit whatever targets could be found, such as small boats, trains, or enemy vehicles. The senior commanders hoped these missions would provide pilots with the opportunity to prove themselves over hostile territory, and so they were left to volunteers. The reality was, however, somewhat different and they generally proved unpopular for obvious reasons. There was a high risk of being shot down and little could realistically be achieved by a fighter armed with just eight machine guns.

With 150 or so operational sorties already under his belt and with two DFCs, Neil felt he had nothing to prove but he chose to fly the squadron's first offensive patrol over northern France on the morning of the 12th. He went off with 'Appy 'Arry Davidson, but they arrived over the enemy coast to find hardly a cloud in the sky. Deciding it would be madness to continue without any cloud protection whatsoever, the two Hurricanes turned for home. Neither pilot wished to become a dead hero.

Neil would become increasingly critical of some of the tactics used during these early offensive missions over northern France where the RAF's fighters were vulnerable to ground fire:

> Not one little bit did I like being shot at sneakily and anonymously from the ground. Too many of my friends and colleagues had been lost that way, doing damn silly ground attacks against targets that were either dangerous and shot back or did not warrant being attacked anyway.

Neil with John Beard (*seated*) in the dispersal hut.

It was also during January 1941 that Neil and the other recognised pilots of 249 – Barton, Lofts, and the newly commissioned Beard – went to Duxford to receive their decorations from HM King George VI at a ceremony held in one of the hangars. Beamish was there too, to receive a DFC to add to his Distinguished Service Order awarded for his leadership at North Weald and the AFC that he had been awarded before the war. He had flown with the squadron whenever possible and had now been credited with shooting down at least five enemy aircraft.

As would be expected for such an occasion, it was stiffly formal at first, but things then lightened up when the King and Queen were invited to play shove-ha'penny. Neil remembers their majesties as: 'Relaxed, charming, and utterly normal, personifying for me in a quite remarkable and emotional way, the spirit and steadfastness of the nation.'

As a twice-decorated fighter ace, Neil was now well and truly in the public eye. He would be for the rest of his life. Tall, young, brave, good-looking, and impeccably smart in his uniform with wings and decorations, and with his flawless English accent, he was everything the British public would imagine a fighter pilot and hero of the Battle of Britain to be.

To the nation, Neil was a hero. And understandably so. He had already sat for two prestigious war artists, Cuthbert Orde and Eric Kennington, and had been captured on film by numerous photographers. The nation needed to see its heroes and so Neil was now sent north as part of a Cotton Industry War Exhibition in Lancashire. He was a local boy and he had done exceptionally well. It was time for the public to hear his stories and to meet him in person. He would be required to give talks and speeches to various official bodies while touring the cotton mills in the area. Which he did. He ended up addressing all sorts of dignitaries – members of parliament, mayors and mill managers – and broadened his education no end along the way.

After his tour, Neil returned to North Weald. Little had happened during the couple of weeks he had been away. The weather had been truly dreadful, very cold with lots of snow and fog. There were still defensive patrols being flown, such as for the protection of convoys in the Thames Estuary and along the east coast, as well as the interception of lone intruders by day and by night.

The combination of the winter weather and the switch to flying more offensive missions provided some much-needed time to evaluate tactics and operating procedures. There had been several new additions to the squadron since it had re-formed, but the frenzied activity of the past six months meant there had been little or no time for consolidation, until now.

There was also the fact that 249 Squadron was still equipped with Mark I Hurricanes whereas other squadrons were being re-equipped with the better-performing and better-armed Mark II, while some of the Spitfire squadrons were even looking forward to receiving the new Mark V. It was the subject of many a conversation and things came to a head following Circus Four on 10 February, again involving six Blenheims, this time to bomb the docks at Dunkirk.

249 was one of the escorting squadrons with Neil leading the rearmost section of Ossie Crossey, Gerald Lewis, and the newly commissioned Bill Davis. As the Blenheims carried out their attack, 249's Hurricanes were suddenly bounced by 109s. However, the whole event had gone unnoticed by Neil. The Hurricanes had become scattered over the target area, although there was nothing unusual in that, but it was only when he got back to North Weald that Neil first noticed Lewis's Hurricane had been severely damaged 'as if a mad axe-man had been to work', and then realised that Davis was missing.

It would later emerge that Bill Davis had been shot down, although he had managed to bale out, despite wounds, to become a prisoner of war. But Neil had had enough. Full of what he later described as 'suppressed annoyance', more from his own lack of involvement than anything else, he headed straight for Beamish's office to vent his frustration at being expected to keep taking on the 109s, which were improving all the time, in an old Mark I Hurricane. It could not catch anything, nor could it run from anything. Neil even stated that he would rather be anywhere else – even in the Western Desert; at least the weather would be decent there.

Beamish listened sympathetically, more than Neil had expected. The next week was spent back up north again as part of his tour of the cotton mills, not as a punishment but it was all just part of the plan. While he was away, the first Mark II Hurricanes arrived at North Weald.

Chapter Eight

Malta

Eighteen Mark II Hurricanes were delivered to 249 Squadron and so the old Mark Is were gradually phased out. However, the fact that the squadron now had a better-performing aircraft, particularly when operating above 20,000 feet, would, in the short term, make little or no difference. The squadron's overall activities remained the same, although patrols were now more often being flown at 30,000 feet rather than at 20,000 feet as had been the case before.

There were still occasional excursions across the Channel but mostly it was endless patrols, including some at night, with many hours spent protecting convoys. These patrols typically lasted an hour and a half, but for most, including Neil, it was one and a half hours of boredom. It was all necessary stuff, of course, but his memories of March 1941 are more about the changing faces of the squadron, and the wind and rain. There were certainly no engagements to write home about.

Life had become something of a routine at North Weald, although the sad loss of the smiling, level-headed and experienced Dicky Wynn provided a stark reminder that complacency was a dangerous thing. The squadron was returning from a convoy patrol early in the evening and was not far from North Weald when, for no apparent reason, Wynn's aircraft was seen to plunge straight into the ground. It was a sad and sudden end to such a splendid young man's life.

Then, in mid-April, came news that everything was about to change. 249 Squadron was told to prepare for a move to the Middle East.

As part of the preparation, the squadron's foreign pilots – the Poles, the Czechs, and the French – were quickly moved to other units. The reason for this, as explained in Brian Cull's *249 at War*, the authorised history of the squadron, was because 249 would most likely be in action against the Italians and their countries were not officially at war with Italy. Also, in line with Air Ministry policy at the time, married officers, whenever possible, were to remain at home and so they were posted from 249 as well.

All this, of course, meant several comings and goings in a short period of time. As for those who were preparing for service overseas, including Neil, they had absolutely no idea where they were going. All they knew was that they were to revert to the old Mark I Hurricane once more, albeit modified to the tropical standard, and that their aircraft were to be fitted with long-range external fuel tanks because they would be required to fly off a carrier. And there was further bad news when they found out that the tropicalised Mark I was even slower and less capable than the Mark I flown during the summer of 1940. There was no point moaning. The decision had been made and that was that.

So that the pilots could become familiar with flying the modified Mark I, two Hurricanes, each with two forty-four-gallon underwing drop tanks and a bulky air filter disfiguring the nose, were delivered to North Weald. In this configuration, the pilots were told, the Hurricane could fly over a thousand miles or stay in the air for more than six hours.

Apart from agreeing that such endurance seemed hardly possible, their 'new' aircraft, it was decided, looked ugly. Malta was not even mentioned at this stage, but everyone knew they were off to the Mediterranean or North Africa. Outside north-west Europe, that was the only other theatre where the war was being fought.

Groans and moans apart, the new 249 Squadron was soon beginning to take shape. Besides, many old faces of the original squadron remained – Barton, Neil, Beazley, Wells, and Crossey – while others, such as 'Cass' Cassidy, Tommy Thompson, and the newly-commissioned Jack Mills and 'Tich' Palliser, had all been with the squadron since the autumn. There were twenty-one pilots overall.

During the days that followed there were the inevitable inoculations and kitting out to do, and the packing of bags, although their luggage was to go separately by other means, whatever that meant. Once they were ready, a week of embarkation leave was granted, with everyone told to report to London's Euston railway station on 8 May, from where they would travel to Liverpool by train and then board the old carrier HMS *Furious* for their onward journey. Their ground personnel, however, were not going with them. They were to travel separately, which was not good news as no one liked the thought of the squadron being split up.

It was a damp foggy afternoon when they arrived in Liverpool. The journey from Euston had gone as planned and had been full of the kind of stories that might be expected from a group of young men after a week apart. For most, it was their first time in Liverpool. Even for Neil, the city had a very different feel to it since his childhood years before.

They had arrived during a period of intense bombing, with the peak of enemy activity having occurred only the week before. More than 2,000 high explosive bombs had fallen on the city plus hundreds of incendiaries, putting around half of Liverpool's 150 cargo berths out of action and causing nearly 3,000 civilian casualties. And it was not just the docks that had suffered. More than 6,000 homes had been destroyed, leaving thousands homeless. Bootle, where Neil had been born and raised, was just one area to suffer heavy damage and loss of life. Only three days before Neil and his colleagues arrived in the city, the Luftwaffe had carried out a major raid involving hundreds of bombers, the Germans later admitting it to have been one of the largest air raids ever carried out against a target in England.

Neil could see many of the buildings and warehouses where he had once so happily played now left in ruin. He later described the 'columns of smoke spreading like a dark stain'. Everywhere seemed deserted, apart from all the emergency services, and the stench of war was abominable. He was stunned into silence. Even the flat-topped

With George Barclay (*right*) at North Weald shortly before Neil left for Malta.

HMS *Furious* proved to be a disappointment, smaller than expected and, in Neil's words, 'Her spectral outline suggested a breaker's yard rather than a major ship of war.'

Their arrival was greeted with total indifference. Laden with luggage, they stumbled up the gangway and then pushed and shoved their way through the crowded corridors to their quarters. Being a flight commander, Neil had a cabin to himself; all of six feet square. But he was lucky. The ship was crammed full, with three squadrons on board; the others being 213 and 229. There was so much going on. The Hurricanes were lashed down in the carrier's hangar, and the maintenance personnel were busy fitting the long-range tanks and testing equipment in preparation for war.

A carrier stationary in dock was always vulnerable and so, within the hour, they set sail. Being on board a ship was a new experience and so, for Neil, memories of the first night at sea are those of noise and a total lack of sleep. The following morning was greeted with an unexpected silence. Neil went up on deck and could then see why. They were anchored off Greenock in Scotland and were now surrounded by dozens of ships. It was a convoy forming up. There was even time to go ashore briefly for one last moment on British soil before the long journey south.

It was then that Neil became fully aware of the extent of the Luftwaffe's bombing raids that were happening all over Britain. The bombing of London was understandable, and Liverpool, but the sight of a long funeral procession in Greenock, with twenty or more hearses, left an everlasting impression on Neil. He had not expected to see that.

By the following day, the convoy was well out into the Atlantic. In the days that followed the weather deteriorated to the point that it was awful, which was probably a good thing as it would make it difficult for any prowling U-boat crew looking for a big target and, therefore, increase the convoy's chance of safely reaching its destination.

The ship was vastly over-crowded and so conditions down below were terrible, the only escape for the officers being the wardroom. The pilots were now briefed on the plan. In short, they were to switch ships at Gibraltar with 249 Squadron being transferred to HMS *Ark Royal*. They would then sail into the Mediterranean under the cover of a large convoy, with the squadron's Hurricanes remaining on the flight deck ready to be scrambled should an enemy attack occur. Then, once within 450 miles of Malta, the Hurricanes were to fly off the carrier and after a refuelling stop on the island they were to fly on another 850 miles to Mersa Matruh in Egypt. That was all there was to it. At least that was how the briefing officer saw it.

But Malta was an island under siege. Its position – 50 miles to the south of Sicily, 200 miles north of Libya, and 175 miles east of Tunisia – had made it of great strategic importance as a naval base for a succession of powers. Britain's Prime Minister, Winston Churchill, certainly could not give up on the island. Lying at the crossroads of the Mediterranean where the supply route between Italy and the Axis armies in Libya crossed the Allied sea route between Gibraltar and Alexandria, almost at its mid-point, Malta held the key to the door of the desert war being fought in North Africa.

However, Axis forces in Italy, Sardinia, Sicily and Libya dominated the central Mediterranean and were doing all they could to batter the small island into submission, and so any attempt to resupply Malta was full of obvious risks. It was a difficult period for the Royal Navy, with the loss of many ships, but everything needed to fight a campaign – people, food, fuel, ammunition, medical supplies, aircraft and spares – had to be delivered to the island by sea, in sufficient numbers and on a regular basis. It was a monumental air and maritime effort just to survive, let alone hit back, and to manage both required those in command carefully to balance precious and limited resources.

Much had already been learned about delivering Hurricanes to Malta since the early days. The first Club Run, as they were known, had taken place the previous August when twelve Hurricanes were successfully delivered to the island off HMS *Argus*. The second during November, however, called Operation White, had been a disaster. Eight of the twelve Hurricanes launched off the same carrier failed to reach the island, having ditched in the sea, with the loss of seven pilots.

An official enquiry following Operation White blamed many factors, including the weather, a lack of co-ordination and co-operation between the RAF and the Royal Navy, and the fleet's reluctance to take more risk and get the carrier closer to Malta before flying off the fighters. The harsh lessons learned meant that future ferry flights would never again be planned and conducted in such a manner. But even so, the more Neil thought about the plan the more there was for him to be concerned about. Flying off a carrier was something he had not done before, and he had never flown 1,300 miles over the sea in a single-engine aircraft. The Mediterranean was a hostile place to be, with little chance of being rescued should something go wrong. There was far more to it than the briefing officer had tried to lead them to believe.

It was eight days before the weather started to improve and eventually, after ten days at sea, they arrived at Gibraltar. That night, while the Hurricanes were being transferred across to the *Ark Royal*, the pilots enjoyed the bright lights and warmth of Gibraltar. After twenty months of blackout back home, it was all very different. And the *Ark Royal* was very different, too. It was bigger, cleaner, and far more orderly than *Furious* had been. It was, Neil said, a real warship.

The huge convoy was soon under way for the second leg of 249's journey. Called Operation Splice, the convoy was protected by the Royal Navy's Force H, which included a third carrier HMS *Eagle*. The *Ark* and *Furious* between them had forty-eight Hurricanes on board. Fortunately, their voyage coincided with the Luftwaffe's reduction of forces in Sicily, which, only very recently, had peaked at nearly 250 aircraft. The majority had just left to support Hitler's invasion of the Soviet Union, now only a month away.

By dawn on 21 May the ships were in position and ready to fly off the Hurricanes. First to launch was 213 Squadron from *Furious*, followed by just six aircraft of 229 Squadron; the rest were not able to get off in time before the carrier had to turn back for Gibraltar. All but one reached Malta safely; the other one had gone down in the sea, although the pilot was picked up to become a prisoner of war. After a quick stop-off on the island, the Hurricanes continued their journey on to Egypt.

Meanwhile, on *Ark Royal*, it was 249's turn. The first group was led off by Barton; all the Hurricanes would reach Malta safely. Neil was to lead the second group of eleven aircraft. He fixed his eyes on the flight deck mechanic holding the all-important wand, who would signal when it was his turn to go.

In his book *Onward to Malta*, Neil describes what it was like to take off from a carrier for the first time:

> My mouth dry, I opened up and taxied forward, straightening on the centre-line. The wands gyrating, urging me to rev up. Up! Up! Then suddenly, with a sweep of the arm – Down! I was off! With full throttle but only a modest 6¼ lbs showing on the boost gauge and my tail up almost immediately, I set off down the deck at a smart walking pace, my Hurricane feeling ridiculously light. The island drifted by, faces gawping. At this rate I would be airborne in seconds. This really was a stroll! A moment later I was in the air, despite the extra eighty-eight gallons of fuel, the deck dropping away beneath.

To reduce the risk of being detected, the long transit to Malta was to be made at low level and in radio silence. Their route would take them to the north of Cap Bon on the northern tip of Tunisia, followed by a dog-leg to avoid enemy fighters based on the island of Pantelleria, then avoiding the enemy-held islands of Lampedusa and Linosa before heading straight in towards Malta.

But Neil's formation soon had its problems after losing sight of their escorting Fairey Fulmar when, without warning, it suddenly pulled up and accelerated away. They had already been airborne for nearly an hour and after it became obvious they would not see their guide again, Neil decided to head back towards the ships so that he could either resume contact with the carrier or, if that was not possible, take his formation all the way back to Gibraltar.

Fortunately, the fleet was sighted, and a second guiding aircraft launched. But the Hurricanes were now a hundred miles further from Malta than they should have been and already on the extreme limit of their range. Luckily, the rest of the transit went well and eventually, after more than five hours in the air, Malta appeared with magical suddenness out of the mist.

Desperately short of fuel, Neil took his section towards Luqa while others broke off to land at Ta Kali and Hal Far. As Neil approached the island he noticed he had less than ten gallons of fuel remaining, but that was enough for a straight-in approach. Then, suddenly, there was chaos. Glimpses of brilliant flashes were first seen coming from somewhere on the cliffs. He then noticed flame-centred puff balls exploding on the far side of the airfield, followed by the sight of a large twin-engine aircraft disintegrating in front of him. And then there were bombs going off, right where he was about to land.

The Hurricanes had arrived in the middle of an air raid. Ten gallons of fuel or not, Neil had only one thought on his mind – to get out of there as quickly as possible. He immediately opened the throttle and quickly raised the wheels and flaps in almost frenzied movements, and then fled away southwards at tree-top height back out to sea.

Having made his way safely back to the rendezvous point of Filfla Rock, just off the south-west of the island, he only had seconds to decide what to do next. There was no point going further out to sea because he would never make it back. Besides, if he was to go down anywhere then he would prefer it to be over land.

Approaching Luqa for the second time, he was relieved to see the raid was over, but its results were still there for all to see. The twin-engine bomber was producing a pillar of smoke, there were fires burning elsewhere and a cloud of dust was still loitering above the airfield.

Once safely on the ground there was then the small matter of where to park. He taxied towards some buildings in the hope of seeing someone. Eventually a khaki-clad figure emerged. Neil finally shut down having been airborne for five hours and twenty-five minutes. It might well have been the longest operational flight made by a Hurricane at that time.

Those who had landed at Luqa were transferred to Ta Kali by bus. Ta Kali was the furthest north of Malta's airfields and, therefore, the closest to Sicily. It had been constructed just before the war but had no facilities of note. Its grassy facilities, like Hal Far, deteriorated quickly in bad weather, to the point that it was sometimes unusable.

It was while they were all gathered at Ta Kali that the bombshell was delivered. 249 Squadron was to stay on the island. Malta's resident fighter unit, 261 Squadron, had been on the island since the previous August and had suffered a terrible beating at the hands of Bf 109s operating from Sicily. Despite 261's gallant efforts, including having claimed more than a hundred victories during its time on the island, it had been a costly campaign. Twenty-one of the squadron's pilots had been killed. As of now, 261 Squadron was effectively disbanded, its survivors were leaving for the Middle East for a well-earned rest, and 249 Squadron was to provide Malta's air defence.

The news came as a shock. 249's pilots had nothing with them. Everything was on board a ship with their ground crew bound for Egypt; neither kit nor ground crew would be seen again. Worse than that was the news that they were to fly the well-worn Hurricanes of

261 Squadron. The Hurricanes brought in by 249 were to be flown out by the departing pilots of 261.

In search of some good news, they did find out that just three weeks before, twenty-four Hurricanes had arrived as part of the island's much-needed reinforcements and so 185 Squadron had been re-formed. And so, with the arrival of 249, there would now be two Hurricane squadrons responsible for Malta's air defence. Furthermore, there was a radar site situated high on the cliffs at Dingli on the west coast, about 830 feet above sea level, to provide early warning of any attack.

The early warning system put in place on the island of Malta was based on the RAF's success during the Battle of Britain. Details of suspect plots detected from high up on Dingli Cliffs were passed to Malta's war headquarters at Lascaris, beneath the Upper Barrakka Gardens in Valletta. From this underground complex of tunnels and chambers, built into the bastions overlooking Grand Harbour, the defence of Malta was being co-ordinated and conducted. Down among the passageways and tunnels there were rooms for each of the fighting services, and from the RAF operations room a fighter controller would ring the airfields and scramble the fighters. It was primitive compared to Fighter Command's set-up back home, but it worked.

The next few days were spent settling in and finding their way about. Malta is not a big island. Measuring just 11 miles by 9 miles, it is a bit smaller than the Isle of Wight and, with most of its population (around 250,000 at the time) living in and around its capital Valletta, Grand Harbour, and the so-called Three Cities, it is one of the most densely populated areas in the world. On his second full day in Malta, Neil went into Valletta with others. They toured the narrow streets and looked out over the harbours and inlets crammed full of naval warships and other craft, before introducing themselves to the Union Club to enjoy afternoon tea.

Malta gradually began to take on a more favourable aspect despite the oppressive heat and lack of facilities in the mess, which was situated less than a mile from the airfield in a rather sombre-looking stone building known as Torre Cumbo. But if Neil had been

249 Squadron's first period of operational readiness in Malta nearly ended in disaster, 25 May 1941.

quietly impressed by what he had seen of Valletta, his enthusiasm was completely dashed when he and Barton toured the airfield at Ta Kali.

When it came to any facilities of note, there were next to none; just a single tent for operations and a second tent for the ground crew. The squadron's inherited Hurricanes, of which there were only nine, were in poor shape. They carried no squadron markings, were in various states of modification and in a poor state of repair, having seemingly been patched up by any means.

These were not criticisms but observations, such was the desperate situation that Malta was in. Neil often thought back to what his father had once told him: 'When you are in the services, the further away from London you are, the worse off you are likely to be.' He was right. And if all this was not bad enough, then there was a particularly nasty form of dysentery kicking around, known as 'Malta dog'.

The squadron would eventually muster ten aircraft at any one time, including a couple of Mark IIs, but with there being so few aircraft available on the island and a full complement of twenty-six pilots on the squadron, Barton and Neil decided to operate in two flights.

Neil would lead 'A' Flight while Barton would command 'B'. The task was going to mean cover around the clock, which meant maintaining readiness at night as well, and so they decided to split the day into two, with each flight covering half of the period.

249's introduction to enemy action came as soon as 25 May, during the squadron's first period of operational readiness. It was all very sudden. Barton's flight had held the morning slot since dawn and it was now the turn of Neil's flight to hold readiness. It was a blistering hot day and just before 2 p.m. the air-raid sirens wailed.

Neil ordered his flight to cockpit readiness. But there was no order to scramble. Minutes passed. Nothing. Neil then jumped out of his cockpit and hurried to the tent to find out what was going on. Then, suddenly, a group of 109s screamed low overhead, shooting up the airfield, one seemingly pointing straight at the ops tent. Neil recalls: 'Shocked absolutely into a numbed paralysis, I closed my eyes and cringed, waiting for the impact of bullets and shells, wondering quite stupidly meanwhile whether they were likely to go right through my body or only partly so.'

Then, the 109s had gone, as quickly as they had arrived. Scrambling to his feet, Neil rushed outside the tent. He could see at least three Hurricanes getting airborne in the distance, while one aircraft was on fire and another was shedding smoke. There was nothing to put out the fires. All they could do was watch the flames spread.

Two Hurricanes were destroyed in the raid. The unlucky Pat Wells had been in the cockpit of one when the 109s attacked. He was wounded in the foot. It was only when he leapt out of his burning aircraft that he realised he had been hit. Two other Hurricanes had also been hit during the raid and it looked like they were unrepairable.

It was a bad start to 249's war in Malta but, fortunately, it would be the Luftwaffe's last appearance over Malta for a while. The attack on Ta Kali that afternoon had been carried out by the last fighter unit to leave Sicily and by the end of May most German units had left the region, leaving the Italians to continue the campaign.

However, little was seen of the Italians during the following days. It was a most welcome respite for Malta's defenders. A day-on, day-off arrangement was agreed with 185 Squadron and for a while the biggest risk of being hurt was by sunburn, and the only enemies of note were plagues of mosquitoes and fleas. Malta was enjoying a period of relative calm. There was time to go swimming in the sea and even the locals were getting out.

Being the new boys in town was all very exciting. There were plenty of invites to parties and functions in Valletta and Sliema, as well as swimming parties at the Dragonara Palace in St Julian's, noted for its magnificent scenic position and private swimming pool. And the evenings were blissfully pleasant. Even in war there were moments of utter peace and deep, sensual tranquillity. Furthermore, more Hurricanes were on their way to the island as part of the planned Club Runs and even though most would fly on to Egypt, those that stayed would soon mean the addition of a third fighter squadron, 46 Squadron, to Malta's order of battle.

It was not as if the war had suddenly gone away. There were still the frantic scrambles, but by the time the Hurricanes got anywhere near the Italians they had usually turned away. However, on 3 June, a three-engine Savoia-Marchetti SM.79 bomber paid the price for flying too close to the island while transiting from Sicily to Libya. Butch Barton shot it down to claim 249 Squadron's first success in Malta. Barton was again successful during the early hours of 8 June when he shot down an Italian twin-engine medium bomber, the squadron's first success at night.

When operating at night, the general tactic adopted was to use two Hurricanes backed up by the searchlight batteries to illuminate their target. Because the Italian bombers approached Grand Harbour or one of the airfields alone and chose to spend as little time over the island as possible, pairs of searchlights were set up at both ends of Malta. The Hurricanes would then circle these in the hope that an enemy bomber would be 'coned' by the lights. Using the combination of the radar controller's information and the searchlights, and simply looking out, the night fighters would position themselves above where the intruder was believed to be. Then, once he was spotted, the Hurricanes would attack.

Four days later, eighteen Hurricanes, nine each from 249 and 46 Squadrons, were scrambled to intercept a reconnaissance SM.79 that was being closely escorted by fifteen single-engine Macchi MC.200 fighters, while a further fifteen MC.200s lurked nearby. Leading 249, Neil climbed away to the south to gain as much height as possible before turning back north.

From 17,000 feet, he could see bursts of ack-ack above Valletta and then a group of enemy aircraft caught his eye slightly below and heading in the opposite direction. As they passed underneath, he reared up and dropped down on them. He could clearly see the SM.79 surrounded by fighters, which he thought might be Bf 109s. Aircraft soon began to scatter in all directions. Hanging on to one, he saw it suddenly rear up and point its nose straight to the heavens:

> I attempted to follow but was losing ground when, to my surprise, it did not pull away as expected but turned over and in the act of so doing, presented itself as an almost stationary target. I fired. My tracer with its familiar flecks of curving, whipping red, reached out and clutched both fuselage and wings in a brief rippling embrace. After which it was gone. Below my tipping wing. Downwards. Turning. Diving steeply.

Neil followed it down towards the sea, firing again. He could see Filfla below, then a blob coming from the aircraft, followed by a parachute. He pulled away, climbing, breathlessly elated, but vibrantly tense. He soon spotted some more aircraft in the distance, but the enemy had gone.

Back on the ground there was much excitement but differing stories. Neil's success had been witnessed, but worryingly two of the squadron's aircraft were missing. One of the pilots had baled out but the other, Pilot Officer Hamish Munro, was killed; he was 249's first pilot to be killed in Malta.

Although he claimed a Bf 109, Neil had shot down a MC.200, not that he was convinced at the time. Either way, it was another success. He had hoped, though, that the enemy pilot had been picked up. With Malta being such a small island, plenty of aircraft ended up in the sea and being left to drown was one of his own fears. There was also the fact that they had been ordered to shoot down enemy floatplanes sent out from Sicily in search of downed pilots. For a while the thought played on his mind. War was not nice.

More RAF aircraft passed through Malta on their way elsewhere. The Hurricanes were always airborne to escort them in to the island and prevent them from being attacked once they were on the ground. And when two aircraft failed to arrive on 14 June, 249's Hurricanes were sent out to search for the missing pilots. Neil's section found one, some forty miles to the south-east. He later recalled:

> Leaving Crossey to circle the tiny yellow dot in the water, I returned and made contact with the rescue launch, which was crashing and bouncing its way towards us at maximum speed, and after pointing it in the right direction, flew backwards and forwards endlessly, acting as a guide. After hours, it seemed, we watched it successfully make the pick-up, after which we left, full of warm feelings. It was nice to be able to save a life for a change!

Combat sorties from Malta were generally short, sometimes as short as twenty minutes or so, but operating from Ta Kali during the height of summer was not without its problems. 249's dispersal was at the southern end of the airfield and so the Hurricanes usually took off in a northerly direction to avoid wasting time taxiing across the uneven ground and to prevent columns of dust and dirt from entering the engine and cockpit. The problem was, though, the ground was not particularly flat in that part of the island and so the pilots were faced with rising ground at the end of the airfield, plus a mass of ridges and stone walls. Neil recalls: 'Every time my wheels left the ground, I prayed that my engine would keep going and that I would not end up ploughing into the hill or crashing through a score of obstructions.'

During take-off on one scramble he had a lucky escape when it was obvious there was a problem with his engine. No more than a few feet off the ground, he made the bold decision to turn back. For some moments, and with his heart in his mouth, he feared he would not make it. But he did, just. The Hurricane somehow dragged itself around and seconds later he was back on the ground.

While his Hurricane, Z4048, was having its engine problem investigated, Neil swapped with 24-year-old Sergeant Jock Livingston who had been allocated one of the Mark IIs. When the next scramble order came, everyone except Neil got airborne. He had suffered yet another engine problem on take-off, this time the boost capsule was stuck. It happened all the time apparently, or at least that is what his flight sergeant told him. Neil was again left standing around the aircrew tent to wait for his flight to return. This time there was an engagement, he knew that, and so he waited patiently while staring out towards Valletta to get the first glimpse of the returning Hurricanes.

A pair soon appeared in the distance, then another, and finally more. One was on its own, though, and slow. It was less than a thousand feet off the ground and seemingly struggling. As it got closer, Neil could see it was trailing the familiar thin white stream of glycol and as it reached the airfield boundary a black dot appeared from the cockpit, just seconds before the aircraft fell to the ground. There was the small sliver of white as the parachute streamed, but it never fully developed. The black dot got bigger and thumped into the ground, motionless, the parachute gently subsiding alongside.

Neil and others could only stand and watch in silence, helpless and, frankly, feeling sick. It was Livingston. For the rest of his life Neil would wonder whether the aircraft had crashed because of battle damage or if Z4048 had suffered another engine problem. No one ever knew. It was another of those unhappy tales of war.

By the end of June more replacements had arrived. A new airstrip at nearby Safi allowed 249 to disperse its aircraft. Meanwhile, most of 46 Squadron's pilots were transferred to form the nucleus of 126 Squadron, which re-formed at Ta Kali as 46's ground component left for Egypt by sea, while 185 Squadron moved to Hal Far. There had also been a change in command at the top with the arrival of Air Vice-Marshal Hugh Pughe Lloyd as the new Air Officer Commanding Malta.

Known simply as Hugh Pughe, the new AOC soon became a regular visitor to the squadron. The island was now home to several different aircraft types, operating in a variety of roles – Blenheims, Vickers Wellingtons, Bristol Beaufighters and Beauforts, Fairey Swordfish and Albacores, Martin Marylands – all allowing Malta to hit back harder than ever before. 'Carry the fight to the enemy! Strike them everywhere! Bomb them out of their stride, that's the ticket!' Lloyd used to say.

Neil would often listen to the AOC's fierce exhortations in mild wonderment and dismay. There was, he felt, a considerable gap between Lloyd's expectations and 249's capabilities. The squadron was still flying clapped-out old aircraft. And if the Luftwaffe were suddenly to arrive back on the scene, what then? It was all very worrying. Malta at least needed cannon-armed Hurricanes or, better still, Spitfires. And the sooner they arrived the better.

But re-supplying Malta was already a huge drain on resources in the Mediterranean, it always would be. However, every effort to keep the island topped up with what it needed was made. Hardly a ship or submarine sent through the Mediterranean failed to stop off in Grand Harbour to unload supplies, no matter how small or seemingly insignificant they appeared to be.

The Italians were now mostly operating over Malta during the late evenings and early hours, and so for 249 much of July was spent on duty at night. It was a joy to fly over the island on a moonlit night, but as far as shooting down the enemy in the dark was concerned, it was all proving rather frustrating. Apart from the occasional glimpse of an enemy intruder, and then a burst of fire, the squadron recorded just one success at night during the entire month, the successful pilot being Flying Officer Cass Cassidy.

The difficulty of operating at night led to the formation of the specialist Malta Night Fighter Unit at Ta Kali with eight Hurricanes. This was good news for those like Neil who preferred to fly during the day. The not-so-good news, though, was that many of the pilots forming the MNFU were drawn from 249 Squadron, including both flight commanders, Cass Cassidy, and Donald Stones, as well as Tommy Thompson and Jack Mills. All were very experienced pilots and their departure was a significant loss to 249 at that time.

The summer of 1941 was desperately hot and humid. Many hours were spent sitting in the shade of the dispersal tent, gasping for water in the dusty conditions, and trying to keep cool, while quietly praying for rain. It was hard work for everyone, including the ground crew who worked tirelessly to keep the Hurricanes serviceable. Although there had been several re-supplies of aircraft during the past few weeks, spares were always a problem, which often meant cannibalising one aircraft to keep others in the air. While some aircraft might well have been facing the scrapheap if they had been back in Britain, Malta's fighters were far too precious for that.

When not on duty, Neil and others would walk the dusty road to an estaminet in Rabat, called the Point de Vue, for regular gatherings with a bevy of local daughters. Neil would later pay compliment to the ladies of Malta who, in his words, 'played their part in the defence of the island to a greater extent than they ever realised'. There was also the Union Club and the RAF rest camp at St Paul's Bay where the officers could go for a few days of leave. But because the rest camp was all about swimming and sunbathing, Neil would only ever stay a day or so. Being so fair-skinned, he burned badly in the sun and wearing a parachute harness and strapping into a fighter with sunburn would have been pure hell.

Neil celebrated his twenty-first birthday on the island. He was determined that his parents would not have to remember his birthday as being the day he was killed and so he chose not to fly that day. As the day was to turn out, though, he need not have worried. Nothing happened.

In truth, it was the quietest period of the air war over Malta since the outbreak of hostilities. Little would be seen of the Italians over the island until late August. It was almost as if they had gone on holiday. And good luck to them! Unlike the Germans, Neil said, the Italians were a most civilised enemy.

Neil had flown forty-four operational sorties since arriving in Malta, which had, in the main, resulted in masses of adrenalin expended for remarkably few results. He had also suffered five engine failures during those eight weeks. And he was not the only one to suffer the dreaded engine failure on take-off. Butch Barton, for example, had a lucky escape when he crash-landed from 300 feet after his engine had failed on take-off.

There were few places in Malta to force-land. The island's small fields are criss-crossed with low stone walls and the uncultivated land tends to be rocky and uneven, and so to bale out was the only sensible course of action. But to attempt to jump out below a thousand feet was extremely risky. And at just 300 feet, Barton had no choice. He did not have the height or power to try and turn back. He simply had to stay with his aircraft and hope for the best.

Barton's Hurricane ploughed through several stone walls, and for a while he was trapped in the cockpit. But, fortunately, he got away with his life. Few people have survived such an experience. Even so, Barton ended up in Mtarfa Hospital having suffered second-degree burns from acid, glycol and petrol. Neil went to visit him the following day and later wrote:

> Looking tiny and waif-like in his hospital bed, he was childishly relieved at his deliverance. I was all too conscious of the squadron's debt to the little man. Small and slight in stature, in no way a heroic figure and unassuming to a fault, he was one of the best leaders and fighter pilots it would be my good fortune to meet. Having flown together for more than a year, including the whole of the Battle of Britain, my admiration for his ability and devotion to duty was unbounded.

Barton would be out of action for several weeks and so Neil suddenly found himself commanding the squadron, albeit on a temporary basis as far as the official record is concerned. While he was in temporary command of the squadron Neil received a telephone call one morning in mid-August. It was the duty controller. An aircraft carrying a so-called 'special passenger' was due from the direction of Greece and so 249 was required to provide a section to escort it to Malta.

Neil led three others to a designated holding point to the north-east of the island to wait for the aircraft, even though another engine problem, this time an oil leak, had threatened to cut his sortie short. He could barely see forward because of the oil stain, but the other members of his section were relatively new and inexperienced, and so he decided to stay. Besides, he did not want to miss this rather special, and somewhat different, show.

They had not been waiting long before the dark shape of a twin-engine aircraft of one sort or another was spotted in the distance, flying in the opposite direction at low level just above the sea. Assuming it to be their guest, Neil turned after it.

Although Neil was barely able to see their guest, they escorted the visiting aircraft towards the island with two Hurricanes stationed either side. But when Malta came into sight, the aircraft did not head towards Luqa where it had been expected to land but instead approached Kalafrana Bay, on the southernmost tip of the island, where a seaplane base was located. Neil later recalled:

> At this point, although I had no grounds for suspicion, the faintest shadow of doubt crossed my mind, causing me to look more closely at the aircraft beneath. I couldn't immediately recognise the type, on the other hand I hadn't needed to, the information we had been given, both on the ground and in the air, being so specific. Then, whilst I was still toying with my doubts, and with the 'visitor' entering the jaws of Kalafrana Bay, something splashed down into the water and the aircraft upended itself in a steep turn to the right so that it passed directly beneath me.

Neil's mouth fell open as he instantly registered what the splash had been. Their 'visitor' had just dropped a torpedo. The aircraft they had been escorting was an Italian torpedo-bomber.

Having reported what he had just seen, Neil was ordered to shoot down the Italian immediately. But it was off in a flash and heading towards Sicily. It took several minutes for the Hurricanes to catch it up. Still with an obstructed view, Neil ordered his section to carry out the attack but although several hits were observed, and smoke was seen trailing from the enemy aircraft, it kept going and was last seen heading home, severely damaged. The circumstances relating to this strange incident were never discussed thereafter. But Neil was left furious.

Neil flew just nine operational sorties during August. It was all quite different to the year before. And it was to be a similar story the following month. Although there were still some daylight combats being fought, Malta's defenders enjoyed plenty of time off. The air war was now being taken forward by the offensive squadrons.

It was also decided that 249 should go on the offensive. The long-range external fuel tanks were re-fitted to the Hurricanes, which would enable them to fly extended patrols of up to three hours in search of enemy aircraft transiting to North Africa, while temporary racks were fitted beneath each wing for the carriage of four small 40-lb bombs so that offensive sweeps could be flown over southern Sicily. These latest adaptations did not please everyone, including Neil: 'Bombs! Long-range tanks! What next, mines and torpedoes? What were we, fighter aircraft, or a one-engine Blenheim?'

His frustrations were not helped by the dismal weather that marked the beginning of a new month. Then, on the night of 6/7 October, 249's Hurricanes were sent off to bomb targets in Sicily. The last time Neil had dropped any form of bomb was during his training at Montrose and, even then, it had only been an 8-lb smoke bomb dropped from an Audax by day. Now he was expected to bomb the railway station at Gela at night.

Neil took off just before midnight and flew northwards, fully expecting to find his target with little trouble. Hoping that the Italians would reveal their known defensive positions by shooting at him, he was disappointed that they did nothing of the sort. And so he was left to wander about endlessly over Sicily, not just looking for his target but trying to work out exactly where he was. He recalls:

I never did find the railway station but, by sheer good fortune, came across the railway line that presumably led to it, which I saw dimly beneath me from a height of 1,500 feet. By this time, remembering the thousands of tons of bombs that had been dropped on London to such little effect and deciding that dropping my eight insignificant bangers was a howling waste of time, I did a gentle dive in that direction and disposed of my load.

The rest of October was spent flying lengthy patrols in search of enemy transport aircraft carrying out re-supply runs between Sicily and North Africa. These aircraft tended to transit well clear of Malta and so there was little in the way of control. It was more a case of get airborne, go, and then look. And, of course, hope.

Neil and Crossey flew the first of these patrols and landed after nearly three hours of stooging around without seeing a thing. However, three days later, and in the same area, the squadron did shoot down an enemy transport aircraft. But in the absence of any real reward for the effort they took, these patrols soon petered out and 249 was back to roaming over Sicily looking for something to attack.

The weather had changed too. It was now much cooler, and there was plenty of cloud and rain to hamper operations. Ta Kali even flooded for a couple of days, meaning that 249 operated from Luqa, which all seemed rather odd in such a climate. But the lack of any drainage had caused the airfield to revert temporarily to its one-time existence as a lake. Life was seldom dull, though. Scarcely a day passed without the air-raid sirens heralding the inevitable sound of guns blasting into the sky.

Neil had thoroughly enjoyed his time in Malta, but the truth was he had now become bored. He was getting more frustrated by the day at not having a decent aircraft to fly. And his spirits were further dampened when he was asked to test the performance of his Hurricane against a newly arrived photo-reconnaissance de Havilland Mosquito. He should have known better!

Also, he was one of just a handful of 249's old brigade left. Most of his good friends – those who had not been killed or wounded – had been rested from ops long ago, but he was still soldiering on. After more than eighteen months of continuous operational flying, Neil had more than done his bit. He later wrote:

> Willing to admit to staleness, I did not feel spent exactly nor in any way unhappy about fighting; never having been mauled by enemy aircraft, I could honestly say they had never held any terrors for me; flak yes, but never aircraft. I was just less enthusiastic, without that extra edge that made the difference between success and failure, between surviving and being killed. But more than that, I was fed up with engine failures, fed up with flying over endless miles of sea in lame-duck aircraft that sank like a stone as soon as they were forced to ditch, weary of the terrible sameness of scramble, climb, and the pursuit of an enemy who seemed always to be out of reach.

He was fed up, too, with sitting about at dispersal for endless hours in the heat and dust, eating indifferent food, and with the mosquitoes and man-eating fleas. He knew there were worse places to be, but he also knew that he was probably due for a change. And he was certainly ready for a change of aircraft type.

249 Squadron had definitely played its part in the defence of Malta. In a matter of just a few months, the island had gone from being on the ropes and about to be battered into submission to be an island from where successful offensive operations were being carried out on a regular basis. Every day, small formations of aircraft, ships or submarines were seeking ways of harassing the Axis supply lines. Between them all – the Royal Navy, the Fleet Air Arm and the RAF – Malta's forces were crippling the Axis supply chain between Italy and North Africa as they had never done before.

The fortunes of the land war in the desert and the battles being fought above and around Malta were irrevocably intertwined. Never again would Malta's forces achieve so much success, although there were still devastating losses being suffered in the air and at sea; one of the biggest was *Ark Royal*, from which Neil had flown off just a matter of months before, while returning to Gibraltar after yet another Club Run. Furthermore, Malta's darkest days were far from over. The Germans would soon return and so the next year would be a defining one. Nonetheless, for now at least, the pendulum in the desert war had swung in favour of the Allies.

It was time for Neil to leave Malta. And Butch Barton, too. Pat Wells had already left, although Tich Palliser, John Beazley and Ossie Crossey would all have to wait another month or two on the island. Barton, in fact, now with a Bar to his DFC, left before Neil. He returned to England in early December for a well-earned rest having handed over 249 to Squadron Leader Edward Mortimer-Rose.

Neil was also to return to England. He had been concerned that he might be posted to the desert or even further east, but he was relieved to find out that was not going to be the case. He would, however, need to wait a few more days until his replacement, Sidney Brandt, arrived on the island before he could leave.

The recent poor weather meant the Italians had continued to stay away from Malta, and so Neil's last few operational flights with 249 were mostly flown over Sicily. On 7 December, the day the United States was brought into the war by the Japanese attack on Pearl Harbor, Neil bombed Ragusa railway station: 'As my target was within spitting distance of the fighter base at Comiso, I half expected to run into a clutch of hostile Macchis, or 109s even, but in the event I saw nothing, not even a burst of flak.'

It was to be his penultimate flight with 249 Squadron, his last being four days later, another uneventful patrol to the west of Malta. When Neil brought his flying log book up to date, he noticed that he had flown eighty-nine operational sorties during his time in Malta, to add to all those he had flown with the squadron since the start of the Battle of Britain. He had more than done his bit. It was time for a well-earned rest before his luck ran out. Under his final entry in his log book for Malta, Neil wrote: 'Good Bye Malta & the most enjoyable 7 months I have ever spent.'

With Brandt having arrived on the island, Neil spent his final few days in Malta watching 249 prepare for the onslaught that was surely to come with the expected return of Luftwaffe forces from Russia. He had mixed feelings. He had sympathy for his successor because he was about to find out what it was like fighting in an aircraft vastly inferior in performance to that of the enemy, and a feeling of regret, regret that for the first time in eighteen months he would not be taking part.

Chapter Nine

A Rest from Ops

The start of a new year would bring a much-needed change of scene. However, unlike senior officers who seemed to manage to escape Malta the quick way, by jumping on a flying boat heading straight back to Gibraltar from where they could make their onward passage to Britain, Neil was to make the journey home the much longer way, by sea via Egypt.

There seemed to be little to celebrate at Christmas. The Luftwaffe had re-appeared over Malta just as Neil was preparing to leave, signalling the start of another difficult period for the island. Nonetheless, he had woken on Boxing Day with a sore head. But any thoughts of spending the day recovering in his bed were quickly put to one side when he was told that he was finally off home.

It was late in the afternoon by the time he and three other pilots, including Cass Cassidy, arrived at Grand Harbour carrying whatever luggage they had managed to gather together. The harbour was a hive of activity and crowded with warships – cruisers, destroyers and submarines – in addition to the merchant vessels of a convoy that had arrived on Christmas Eve with much-needed supplies. With air raids always likely, there was little time to turn the merchantmen around ready for the dash back through the eastern Med to Egypt.

It was all very new to Neil. He had been to Valletta many times, but never to the heart of the dockyard. One of the merchantmen, he was told, a 13,000-ton refrigerated cargo liner belonging to the Blue Star Line called the SS *Sydney Star*, was to be his home for the next few days.

The patched-up *Sydney Star* had originally sailed from its home port of Liverpool in July but had been severely damaged by Italian torpedo boats during the first of the convoys from Gibraltar to Malta. Somehow its crew had managed to get the crippled liner to Malta, where it was then dry-docked to undergo repairs. But it had been languishing in Grand Harbour far too long, constantly shifting its moorings to fool Italian reconnaissance aircraft and to frustrate any attempt to bomb it. Now the *Sydney Star* was ready to sail to Egypt with three other merchantmen under the convoy designated ME8 (standing for Malta East, Number 8).

The news that he was to travel to Egypt on a merchantman had come as something of a shock to Neil. Many merchant vessels were already at the bottom of the Mediterranean and his spirits were hardly raised when someone tried to offer some comforting words with 'Hopefully this one will get through'. The reality of the perilous Malta convoys suddenly hit home!

Having made his way down below, Neil was shown to his cabin, best described as tiny and furnished in mahogany. Being in the central part of the ship it was very noisy and there was a distinct lack of fresh air, but at least he had the space to himself. He then went back up on deck to take in the scene for one last time, and moments later they were under way.

They had hardly moved when, suddenly, guns from the escorting ships opened fire. A Ju 88 swooped low overhead. News that another convoy was leaving Grand Harbour would have been transmitted in seconds. There was nothing Neil, or anyone else for that matter, could now do but hope. At least, though, he was finally on his way home.

Fortunately for those sailing with convoy ME8, the weather was overcast and for the first couple of days nothing of note happened. But then, when they were passing through the dangerous waters to the south of enemy-occupied Crete, the air-raid alarm sounded. Up on deck, Neil could see the puffs of ack-ack following a Ju 88. Within minutes the 88 vanished but the significance of its appearance was all too obvious. The convoy was being tracked.

Sure enough, within the hour, the attack started. Neil watched a Ju 88 begin its shallow dive towards him, amongst a flurry of ack-ack bursts, before it released its stick of bombs. He then remembers seeing the columns of white spray rising magnificently into the air less than a hundred yards away:

> This was exciting stuff; and how lovely to see someone else being shot at for a change! It had not occurred to me for a moment that my life might be in jeopardy, the bombs had looked so innocuous, the incident simply adding spice to what had thus far been a fairly hum-drum voyage.

With the attack over, talk was about nothing else for the rest of the day. Neil's small group of fighter pilots were not only critical of the standard of bombing, but they also offered their uninformed opinions when discussing the accuracy of the anti-aircraft fire put up by the merchantman's machine gunners in return. The banter went on until the challenge was laid down. If the pilots thought they could do better, then they should be given the chance to show it.

And so, the following day, Neil found himself being trained on how to work one of the ship's single machine guns, an American-built Marlin. It was then just a matter of waiting for the next attack to begin.

The first indication that something was about to happen was the sound of the escort's guns. Looking northwards Neil could see the specks of incoming aircraft, low down and just above the horizon. But they were crossing left to right and so were not coming their way. So far so good.

The specks were then seen to head west and then make a wide circle to the south. That was not good news. As they got bigger they were identified as Italian Savoia-Marchetti SM.79s, half a dozen of them and just fifty feet above the waves. And now they were coming their way. Neil recalls:

> For the first time I felt a chilling spasm of naked fear. It looked as though we were going to be torpedoed and there

149

was nothing whatever we could do about it. Then it started, three of the noisiest and most hair-raising minutes of my life.

The ship opened-up with everything it had as the shriek of shells ripped through the rigging above Neil's head. But through it all, seemingly unscathed and with magnificent, even foolhardy bravery, came the Savoias. Line abreast, their range closed on the merchantman.

Remembering what he had been told and to wait until he could see the 'whites of their eyes', Neil waited patiently but nervously until the attackers were within range. Then he began to fire, the Marlin shuddering and rattling in his hands:

> One Savoia directly in front of me now, two hundred yards distant and coming my way. I could see the three engines and cockpit quite clearly, the pilot almost. Still everyone firing like madmen. Deafeningly. The sharp stink of cordite everywhere. The Savoia almost in touching distance. And something falling, rearing up in slow motion, before splashing into the water. A torpedo! Aimed straight between my legs. It couldn't miss. I was going to die. Die! In five seconds, I was going to die!

There have been very few occasions in Neil's life, even in wartime, when death seemed inevitable, with nothing that could be done to halt the process. But this was one of those moments. The torpedo had been dropped, Neil thought, less than a hundred yards away and, realising there were probably only around five seconds to impact, he started to count. He passed five, then six, seven, and eight, still nothing as the Savoia flashed across the stern of the ship. The torpedo must have passed harmlessly underneath. It was a huge relief!

The next thing he saw was a naval Wildcat, one of several that had suddenly appeared, probably from a base somewhere in North Africa, fly through all the anti-aircraft fire, and pass low overhead. He then watched the Savoia stagger like a wounded animal before it cartwheeled into the sea about half a mile away. His attention was then drawn elsewhere. The attack was still going on. It seemed like it would never end.

Finally, the attack was over. Limp with emotion, Neil was left to survey the scene. The sky was clear, and the ships were moving as quickly as they could back into position. That evening he reflected on what he had witnessed during the day. The noise, and the guns. Once they had started it had been impossible to stop them. He was left feeling very unhappy about the whole affair.

The following day was bright and clear. Despite all that had happened the day before, the hard-pressed convoy had successfully got through unscathed. While the escorts went into Alexandria, the merchantmen sailed on, reaching Port Said at dawn on 30 December. Although Neil did not know it at the time, his successor in Malta, Sidney Brandt, was already dead. He had been killed the day before in what proved to be the fiercest day of action since the Luftwaffe returned.

After being deposited on the quayside with what few belongings they had, Neil and the others were told they were next off to Cairo, by road, a journey of some 200 miles. This would mean five or six hours in the back of an open-top lorry sitting on their luggage. After that, only time would tell, but they could expect to be in Cairo for anything up to six weeks before continuing their journey home. It might even be longer, no one really knew. And, of course, it was always conceivable their postings might be changed. Things were not going well in the Far East, and so anything was possible. Neil shook his head in despair. Thoughts of returning home, and the prospect of flying again, were fast disappearing over the horizon.

The road south to Cairo followed the Suez Canal and for a while the journey seemed rather pleasant. They passed through Port Said, giving Neil a chance to observe the people and their way of life. But as the journey went on, he looked more inland. Beyond the thin strip of pleasant and fertile green, lined with palm trees, that ran alongside the canal, he could see nothing except an endless expanse of desert.

It stayed like that for several hours until they reached the built-up area of Ismailia, and after a brief stop they left the canal behind and turned inland towards Cairo. There was then a short stop at the RAF airfield of Abu Sueir where, ironically, 249's baggage from North Weald was being held. They were even given some time to look for any of their personal possessions that never made it to Malta. The irony was that, having found his suitcase, Neil discovered that most of his belongings had been stolen.

Cairo was eventually reached. Neil was then taken to his accommodation at the very grand Metropolitan Hotel, where he finally collapsed exhausted onto his very plush bed.

Life in Cairo was very different to what Neil had left behind in Malta. Apart from enjoying the obvious luxuries of the hotel, there were all the usual sight-seeing things to do, the pyramids and the Sphynx being amongst the most popular attractions. The history of the place fascinated him. It was also in Cairo that Neil saw the enemy at close hand when he got his first glimpse of German prisoners of war, but his memories of his time in Cairo are tarnished by the sight of drunken Allied troops. It was not something that he had particularly expected to see.

It was only a short stop-over in Cairo. Five days later they were moved to the RAF airfield at Helwan, just to the south of the city alongside the Nile. It was a relaxing week there, giving Neil the time to catch up on writing letters and to do some drawing. It was far more pleasant than the noise and bustle of Cairo, and there was plenty of time to reflect on all that had happened during his time with 249. All those friends.

It was then time to continue his journey home, first by train to Port Tewfik on the Red Sea coast and then by sea to South Africa on board the beautiful and quite luxurious Dutch liner SS *Nieuw Amsterdam*. However, the first two days of bliss were followed by days of vomiting courtesy of a serious bout of food poisoning. Neil recalls:

> At this point in the voyage, I was past caring and just
> wanted to die, thinking at the time how unfortunate

I was that, after two years of hard fighting in lame-duck Hurricanes, I might die painfully as the result of eating some wretched piece of salad or chicken.

Confined to his cabin, Neil missed the run ashore in East Africa and it took him until the day before they arrived in Durban to recover.

They were now due to change ships, but the next part of the journey home would have to wait because the next ship had yet to arrive. And so Neil could enjoy a few wonderful days in Durban, a place seemingly untouched by war. Unfortunately his short stay in paradise had to end. Still in their small group of four fighter pilots that had sailed together from Grand Harbour, they boarded the next ship, a camouflaged and rusty ocean liner, the SS *Oronsay*.

At 20,000 tons, the *Oronsay* was smaller than the *Nieuw Amsterdam* and with 2,000 people on board was far more crowded. Because it was capable of 18 knots, the *Oronsay* was fast enough to qualify for independent sailing rather than having to be part of a convoy. But the risk of being sunk was greater as losses amongst ships sailing independently were three times higher than those sailing in a convoy. It was a statistic that Neil would have been glad not to have known.

Their first destination was Cape Town and, after a brief stop-over of just a day or two, it was then out into the Atlantic for the long final leg back to England. But they had only got a short way out when the ship developed a problem, and so they returned to Cape Town for a further three days of fun and sight-seeing while repairs were carried out.

They then set off for a second time. After a quick replenishment stop at Freetown in Sierra Leone, the *Oronsay* set sail for the mid-Atlantic for what would be the most dangerous part of their voyage home. German U-boats were always prowling the Atlantic, and recent shipping losses had been excessively high. The Battle of the Atlantic was a hard-fought and costly campaign.

Keeping well clear of the known convoy routes in the hope of avoiding the U-boats, the *Oronsay* zig-zagged its way towards home. There followed a couple of awful days because of high winds and a rough sea. The ship had to reduce speed to a minimum, making it pitch and roll even more, dangerously so at times, to ride out the storm. Understandably, everyone on board was extremely frightened. It was two days of terror before everything began to calm down.

The *Oronsay* ploughed steadily on northwards, almost as far as Greenland, before turning east towards Iceland, it seemed to Neil. The weather remained thoroughly miserable overall, but it was a small price to pay to get home safely. And then, finally, they turned south towards home and eventually made their way through the Irish Sea to dock in Liverpool.

Not only was Neil safely back in England, he was back in Liverpool once more. But, instead of being the joyous and memorable occasion that he had so much looked forward to since leaving Malta, it turned out to be a return that he would not forget for the wrong reason. He had, once again, gone down ill. It would be a further three days before he was well enough to leave the ship.

Eventually, Neil arrived home during the early hours. His parents had been in bed. Understandably, there were tears of joy. Their only son, still only twenty-one years old, was back home again safe and well, for the time being at least. It was early March 1942. His journey home had taken more than two months.

Neil was now given a well-earned rest from operational flying. How long for would remain to be seen, but he was next off to Gloucestershire to take up an appointment as the tactics officer at Headquarters No. 81 (Training) Group, located at the magnificent Avening Court, near Stroud.

Part of Fighter Command, No. 81 (Training) Group had been formed at RAF Sealand during the final days of 1940 under the command of Air Commodore Francis Vincent to control the fighter operational training units. The introduction of OTUs earlier that year had eased the load on the hard-pressed front-line squadrons, meaning that a pilot's specialised training prior to joining his operational squadron was now completed at an advanced training unit. Previously, as had happened to Neil, a pilot was thrust straight into an operational squadron without even having flown a low-wing monoplane. He then had to learn how to fly a fighter and was taught tactics and procedures as he went along, relying on others more experienced to provide the instruction.

Nothing had been in place during the early months of the war to prepare a new pilot for his operational role and so many young lives were lost. One of the key lessons identified during the summer of 1940 had been that new pilots needed to be better trained on their operational type prior to joining a squadron. The OTUs worked well, and by the time Neil arrived at Avening Court the group had eleven OTUs at eleven airfields spread across the country, equipped with a variety of fighter types – Spitfires, Hurricanes, Blenheims, Beaufighters and Defiants – as well as other advanced training aircraft.

While languishing as a so-called staff officer at Avening Court Neil wrote to Victor Beamish, his former station commander at North Weald. Neil felt that he had now had a long enough break and was keen to return to operational flying as soon as possible, and with Beamish now a group captain and leading the Kenley Wing, Neil asked if he might join one of his squadrons.

Beamish wrote a very pleasant reply inviting Neil to Kenley, but sadly their meeting never took place. Just days later, while leading his Spitfire wing over France, Beamish was jumped by a 109. The gallant and highly decorated Irishman, with two DSOs, a DFC and an AFC, disappeared into cloud and was never seen again. So, ended the life of one of the bravest men that Neil ever knew, and Beamish's last letter to him has remained a treasured possession ever since.

It was also during the spring of 1942 that Neil was invited back to his former school at Eccles to give a talk about his experiences during the Battle of Britain. It had been almost four years since he had last set foot in the place and returning to his old school was a strange feeling. Despite two and a half years of war, little had changed at the school, but so much had since happened to him. As for the visit, it resulted in him striking up an unlikely friendship with one of his former teachers. She was considerably older than him and their wartime experience would form the basis of a book Neil would write later in his life under the title *Portrait of an Airman*.

Still keen to return to flying as soon as possible, Neil was well placed at Avening Court to hear about any opportunities that might become available and, in June, he became the chief flying instructor at No. 56 OTU.

The OTU was then equipped with some rather well-worn Hurricanes, a handful of Miles Master advanced trainers and a few Westland Lysanders used for target-towing. The unit had recently left its previous home in Lincolnshire and had now moved north to Scotland to a new airfield at RAF Tealing near Dundee.

However, Tealing had not been constructed in a good location. It lay in a hollow, making it prone to fog as well as flooding during periods of bad weather. There was also the fact that the airfield was in low-lying land at the foot of a range of hills, which meant that night flying was considered very dangerous. Furthermore, the OTU's aircraft, particularly the Hurricanes, were getting old, and so technical problems were all too frequent. It was a busy time, too, with anything up to forty pilots on every course.

As the CFI, Neil was also in command of Tealing's satellite airfield of Kinnell to the north of Arbroath. Apart from being useful as an additional landing ground, Kinnell was used extensively during the final weeks of the course when the students flew from there during simulated interceptions and dummy offensive missions to prepare them for their operational tour.

Six months had now passed since Neil's return from Malta, and he was ready for operational flying once again. Then, in late August, came the exciting news that he was to be given command of 41 Squadron, a Spitfire unit. Neil later wrote: 'Needless to say I was delighted. My new command was one of the oldest and most famous squadrons in the RAF.'

Neil had first seen a Spitfire at the age of fifteen when he watched one close-up while sitting on the grass at the Hendon Air Display. It had produced an everlasting moment of breathless excitement. Now, just over six years later, he was to command a Spitfire squadron.

He had only just celebrated his twenty-second birthday and he was already a squadron leader. It was all such excellent news.

However, Neil had not been near a Spitfire for two years and now he was expected to lead his squadron against the enemy.

Chapter Ten

41 Squadron

From its early days patrolling above the Western Front during the First World War, through the Spitfire and the Battle of Britain, to the high-performance combat jets of the modern era, 41 Squadron has a marvellous history. When Neil took command of the squadron on 3 September 1942 it was equipped with the Spitfire VB and based at Llanbedr on the west coast of Wales, from where 41 flew patrols over the Irish Sea.

Situated on a narrow coastal strip, with the mountainous region of Snowdonia immediately to its east, Llanbedr was then a forward operating airfield for the sector station of RAF Valley, part of No. 9 Group with responsibility for the protection of the industrial north-west and shipping in the Irish Sea. Neil was given command of 41 following the death of its previous commanding officer, Geoffrey Hyde, killed two weeks earlier, not over the Irish Sea but above Dieppe while flying in support of the British Commandos and Canadian troops attacking the French harbour town. Hyde had been in command for just three weeks.

41 Squadron had moved south for the Dieppe raid to operate with the Tangmere Wing but had since returned to Llanbedr under the temporary charge of one of the flight commanders, Flight Lieutenant Douglas Hone. A somewhat quiet man, the experienced and highly capable Hone would remain in command of 'B' Flight for the next year. There would be far less continuity when it came to 'A' Flight, however. Malta Stepp Jr, a 22-year-old American who had been with the squadron for four months, was in post when Neil arrived, but he

was about to be transferred to the United States Army Air Force to be replaced by Charles Chappell. It was the first of several changes of 'A' Flight commanders.

Continuity, in fact, would always be a problem. Neil would be constantly fending off personnel staff looking to transfer his pilots elsewhere. It was as if 41 Squadron was not considered to be on the front line and was seen to be a breeding ground for training young pilots before they went off to other squadrons more in need.

But leaving personnel issues to one side, Neil was delighted to fly the Spitfire once more. Powered by the Merlin 45 engine, the Spitfire V had become the RAF's principal fighter and had been developed to rival the Messerschmitt Bf 109F, probably the best variant of the 109 to have been built. With a top speed of 370 mph at 20,000 feet and an operational ceiling of 36,500 feet, the Spitfire VB sub-variant with which the squadron was equipped was armed with two 20-mm Hispano cannon and four 0.303-inch Browning machine guns.

The Spitfire had not been designed with cannons in mind, but as the war progressed it had become increasingly clear that a much heavier calibre weapon than the aircraft's original 0.303-inch Browning machine guns was required. The only 20-mm cannon around at the time was the drum-fed Hispano, which was neither reliable nor available in the numbers required. It also meant that much thought had to go into the housing of the cannon. There were inevitably problems but by the time Neil joined 41 Squadron, cannon trouble had largely been resolved, although stoppages were still quite frequent. Neil would later write:

> I was never really comfortable using the cannons in a Spitfire, as they thumped quite violently when fired, the aircraft slewing sideways when, for whatever reason, one of them stopped. I am bound to add, however, that when a target was hit with 20 mm shells, the effect was almost frightening.

Such was the rapid development in aircraft performance and armament at the time that the more powerful Spitfire IX was already being introduced into service to replace the Mark V. This improved variant had been designed to counter the Luftwaffe's Focke-Wulf Fw 190, which was outclassing the earlier Spitfires and was now appearing over north-west Europe in increasing numbers. While squadrons in the south of England were already being re-equipped with the Spitfire IX, being in west Wales meant that 41 would have to wait for new aircraft, although the Spitfire VB was perfectly adequate for the squadron's task.

Other than being keen to emphasise the importance of discipline to his squadron, Neil went into his tour in command with no perceived plan. As far as how the squadron operated was concerned, he was happy to go along with the norm. This meant having one flight on operational readiness at dawn, around 5.30 a.m. at that time of year, and the other flight at thirty minutes' readiness.

The squadron's main operational tasks were flying patrols, mostly to cover the many convoys transiting in and out of Liverpool, carrying out local reconnaissance sorties and supporting any air–sea rescue operations in the area. When not conducting an operational task, aircraft still had to be maintained on readiness but otherwise there was plenty of time for training flying, something that Neil had not done on an operational squadron since before the summer of 1940.

Neil believed training flying to be important as it would keep his pilots sharp and provide the opportunity to develop tactics. Even his newest pilots had around 300 hours of flying time, and all had been through an operational training unit and so they were far better prepared than their predecessors. He led the squadron for the first time during the afternoon of 10 September for an hour of formation flying. It was the first time the whole squadron had been airborne together under his leadership. And then the following week he led six aircraft to Valley for a night-flying exercise before returning to Llanbedr the following morning.

With the weather deteriorating rapidly towards the end of September, mainly mist and low cloud, there was little or no flying to be had from Llanbedr and so Neil took 41 off to Eglinton, on the southern edge of Lough Foyle in County Londonderry, for Exercise

Punch. Not only would the detachment provide some better weather for flying, he hoped, but it would also give him an early opportunity to see how rapidly the squadron could be deployed.

Like all fighter squadrons at that time, 41 was a completely self-contained unit. It could quickly move anywhere and then operate independently from wherever it was based. Some of the pilots would take the Spitfires, while the advanced party of ground personnel would travel in one of the RAF's lumbering transport aircraft, such as the twin-engine Handley Page Harrow, a high-wing monoplane heavy bomber of the 1930s now being used in support roles. The rest of the ground and support personnel, and those pilots who were unlucky not to fly the aircraft, would move by rail or road in one of the squadron's many vehicles of varying sizes. All in, the squadron had around 200 personnel.

Exercise Punch was to be a week-long army, transport, and shipping co-ordination exercise. After first stopping off at Ballyhalbert in County Down to refuel, twelve Spitfires arrived at Eglinton during the early evening of the 22nd, with the ground personnel following behind in a pair of Harrows. For them, it was an all too familiar occurrence. This was already the squadron's ninth move that year.

The exercise began the following day, but the continuous rain and low cloud in Northern Ireland meant the weather turned out to be no better than what they had left behind on the west coast of Wales. It did, however, pick up to the point where some good training could take place, but mostly the flying was hampered. Worse still, by the end of the week one of 41's young pilots had been killed. On the second day of the exercise, twenty-year-old Sergeant Russel Oxenham was carrying out a simulated attack against shipping in Dundrum Bay when his wing-tip clipped a wave and the Spitfire plunged straight into the sea just a mile off the beach.

This tragic accident marred the exercise and more dreadful weather then postponed 41's return to Llanbedr, although the resulting diversion to Andreas on the Isle of Man led to a wonderful and unforgettable night, the station's personnel looked after the squadron so well. A dance was soon arranged, some very nice members of the

Women's Auxiliary Air Force appeared, and beer was available at eight (old) pence a pint.

October was to be no better and is best summarised as another bad month, plagued by more poor weather and tragically remembered for the loss of three more pilots. Firstly, though, there was another exercise, Exercise Aflame, just a week after the end of Punch and this time at Tangmere. But it proved to be a difficult week. For a start it took five days for 41 to move south. The bad weather resulted in the Spitfires diverting to Honiley in the Midlands, where they ended up being grounded for four days because of fog. Having finally arrived at Tangmere, they spent the next day preparing the aircraft only for Neil to be told that 41 could not take part because of their late arrival!

The squadron did manage some flying from Tangmere, though, acting as spotters and flying defensive patrols for those forces taking part in the exercise. Neil led the first of nine patrols that day, his sortie over St Catherine's Point at 3,000–4,000 feet lasting nearly an hour, which constituted the squadron's best day of flying for the entire month. It then took 41 another two days to get back to Llanbedr, again because of poor weather.

Back in Wales, the operational patrols continued with only the occasional glimpse of an enemy aircraft and no engagements. One of the squadron's regular areas to patrol was off Carnsore Point, the south-eastern most tip of Ireland, about a hundred miles to the south-west of Llanbedr. The round-trip, including time on task, was typically around an hour and a half.

Operational flying was achieved on just nine days that month, the squadron's total effort amounting to fifty-five operational sorties. But October would be remembered for the wrong reason when around midday on the 22nd, tragedy struck the squadron for the second time during Neil's short spell in command. This time, three pilots were killed: 23-year-old Flight Lieutenant Gilly Gillitt; 22-year-old Flying Officer Ronald Harrison; and 20-year-old Flying Officer Thomas Scott. All three had taken off that morning to practice cloud flying. There was plenty of cloud about, in layers from the ground up to 18,000 feet, and so the three Spitfires first flew out over Cardigan

Bay and then along the Welsh coast. They were last seen in formation to the south of Llanbedr, but then radio contact was lost and soon after they were reported overdue.

A thorough search of the area found nothing. Bad weather the following day prevented the search continuing, but finally, two days after they had gone missing, aircraft wreckage was found on the side of the 2,000-foot Tarrenhendre. It seems the pilots had flown straight into the side of the mountain. Two days later Neil led the funeral party of Thomas Scott at Portmadoc Cemetery with the chaplain, Squadron Leader Reginald Parkes, leading the ceremony. Attending the funeral were Scott's parents and sister. Gillitt and Harrison both had private ceremonies, with the squadron sending a representative to each.

It was a bad end to the month, but there was still another potentially difficult incident to deal with when 23-year-old Sergeant Jan Zimek, who had joined the squadron just five days before, force-landed in neutral Ireland. He had apparently become separated from his leader after suffering a radio failure and then ran low on fuel. His injuries meant he was hospitalised for several weeks, but instead of being handed back across the border to Northern Ireland, as would normally be the case, the young Pole was interned in a military camp. In what appears to be a separate story of mystery and intrigue and political squabble between London and Dublin, it would be nine months before Zimek was released, by which time Neil had left the squadron. Fortunately, he did not have to become involved.

November was another quiet month as far as the number of operational sorties was concerned, but whenever the weather was good enough there was plenty of flying to be had. It was a record month for night-flying hours and daytime training included practice air-to-air gunnery, fighter–bomber affiliation exercises and flying in large formations. Time was also spent in the Link trainer as well as brushing up on aircraft recognition skills. There was even an All-Star Variety Concert at Valley, hosted by BBC artists. Life was very civilised indeed.

As the month drew towards a close, Neil took seven aircraft to RAF Woodvale, near Southport, to take part in an operation called

Fighter Night. Another night attack was expected on Liverpool and so more fighters were brought in to protect the city and its docklands. Throughout the night, fighters were constantly airborne with patrols layered every 1,000 feet at the heights at which the bombers were expected to carry out their attacks. As things were to turn out, though, only two unidentified aircraft were spotted over the area that night. One was almost intercepted by Neil, but by the time he had dived down from his patrol height at 24,000 feet to the intruder's reported height of 15,000 feet, it had disappeared.

Frustrated, Neil returned to Woodvale. It was another example of a day fighter's limitations when trying to operate at night. There were specialist night-fighter units equipped with Beaufighters and Mosquitos already in service, but single-engine fighter squadrons, such as 41, were still being regarded as day and night interceptors. In his book *From the Cockpit: Spitfire* Neil records his frustrations:

> The prospects of intercepting anything, though, were remote. Without airborne radar, the Spit was almost useless in the dark; even in the most favourable conditions of moonlight and weather, the pilot could see next to nothing in the air. Even so, the citizens of Britain, who were constantly having bombs dropped on their heads, liked to hear the sound of their own aircraft and in this respect our involvement was justified.

It was to be Neil's last night operational sortie in a Spitfire. The rest of 1942 drifted to an end with no reported enemy activity in the Valley sector at all. The weather was so bad that on nine days, nearly one-third of December, not one aircraft flew from Llanbedr, and on a further seven days flying was severely restricted. Several pilots went south to Westhampnett in West Sussex as part of an operational training programme, which generally consisted of flying defensive patrols along the south coast, while four pilots also took part in an offensive mission across the Channel to northern France, called a Rhubarb, to look for targets of opportunity.

Less than 15 per cent of the squadron's flying hours recorded that month were spent on operational tasks. There had also been another change in one of Neil's flight commanders with Charles Chappell posted to Malta to be replaced as OC 'A' Flight by 22-year-old Rex Poynton, a South African who had been with the squadron since April.

While things might have been quiet on the operational front, Christmas Day was anything but and a great day of celebration was enjoyed by all. The dining hall was decorated, an excellent dinner served and, of course, there was plenty of beer and amusement. There was no flying, although one section was kept at readiness. In the evening there was a station concert party and variety show for everyone to attend. And then on Boxing Day there was a rugby match followed by a concert, cabaret and a dance in the evening.

It had now been exactly a year since Neil left Malta. He was enjoying being in command and all that went with it. Morale on his squadron was certainly very good, but as far as the war was concerned it was not very exciting. Furthermore, it had already been more than four months since the squadron last fought any action. Nonetheless, 41's diarist in the squadron's official operations record book maintained a positive outlook when summing up the past few months:

> Above all, there is a harbinger of a SPIRIT, that something which makes all good squadrons what they are. It is not indefinable. It is keenness, together with team work. The squadron plays well – it is a good sign. Given a month, 41 will do more than well. Everything is here, the guts, the energy and the will. It only remains for us to try just a fraction more, and we shall be at the only worthwhile position – The Top.

The new year started in the same way the previous one had ended – poor weather and restricted flying – with a little over 10 per cent of the squadron's flying during the first month of the year spent on operational tasks; and those hours were flown by the lucky handful whom Neil had sent south to Westhampnett. It was the same story across the entire Valley sector, where there had been just nine scrambles during January without an enemy aircraft being spotted. Again, the squadrons had to be content with extensive training programmes.

It was not as if the winter weather prevented flying altogether. Far from it. The squadron flew a fraction under 500 hours during January, but only fifty-six of these hours were operational flying. The situation got worse the following month. Again, there was flying to be had, but there was no sight of the enemy in the region at all. And another pilot of 41 was killed, once more the result of a flying training accident.

With such little operational activity and twenty keen young pilots to look after, it was important for Neil to maintain the sharpness and morale of his squadron. Then, during the afternoon of 19 February, came a change. And it came out of nowhere. Neil immediately called his squadron together to tell them the news. 41 Squadron was leaving Llanbedr for High Ercall, near Shrewsbury in Shropshire, to become the first RAF squadron to be equipped with the latest variant of Spitfire, the Mark XII. This, he said, would soon bring some long-awaited action. As he had expected, the room was abuzz with excitement.

The Mark XII was the first production Spitfire to be powered by the new and more powerful Griffon III engine. Manufactured from a Mark VC airframe (although the later Mark XIIs would be manufactured from Spitfire VIII airframes), it had been strengthened to cope with the additional stresses and was approximately two feet longer than the Mark V, which allowed the engine to be mounted slightly further forward. In terms of performance, the Spitfire XII was much faster at low level than earlier variants and capable of exceeding 370 mph at 5,000 feet. Although it was still armed with two 20-mm Hispano cannons and four Browning machine guns, the Spitfire XII was otherwise a very different aircraft from earlier variants. And with its four-bladed propeller, a larger pointed-tip rudder, and clipped wings, it even looked different.

Such was the rapid development of fighters at that time that the Spitfire XII was only ever intended to be an interim variant and so only a hundred were to be completed, the plan being to equip just two RAF squadrons.

During the next few days 41 Squadron was busy preparing for the move. Neil, meanwhile, went off to the Air Fighting Development Unit at Duxford, then under the command of the celebrated Olympian Don Finlay, who had led 41 Squadron during the Battle of Britain, to get his hands on the new Spitfire XII for the first time. He later recalled:

> My introduction to the XII was not without incident. First, I had trouble starting the engine; the Mark XII had a cartridge starter to get the big Griffon to work, unlike most other marks which used a 12V external battery. The trick was to prime the engine correctly before firing the gun as it was not possible to squirt fuel into the cylinders whilst it was turning over. Get it wrong and it wouldn't go. My second mistake was to take off on the shortest possible runway towards the hangars. Even now, I can bring on a rash when I recall the sight of the tiles on that curving hangar roof.

Otherwise, Neil found the Mark XII extremely pleasant to fly, finding that it achieved its best performance at around 18,000 feet where the second stage of the Griffon's supercharger was engaged manually, although at low level it seemed remarkably nippy and manoeuvrable. On the other hand, he found it noticeably heavier than the Mark V, with a higher stalling speed and a higher landing speed, and he was always conscious of the whopping great propeller, the tips of which seemed all too close to the ground.

Situated some five miles to the north-east of Shrewsbury, the airfield of High Ercall was another of the RAF's expansion projects of the Second World War. One of its main advantages was that it had been constructed with three hardened runways and so the airfield escaped the effects of rain and mud. Apart from being a night-fighter airfield in the Tern Hill sector, High Ercall was also used as a rear airfield for fighter squadrons, either resting from operations in the

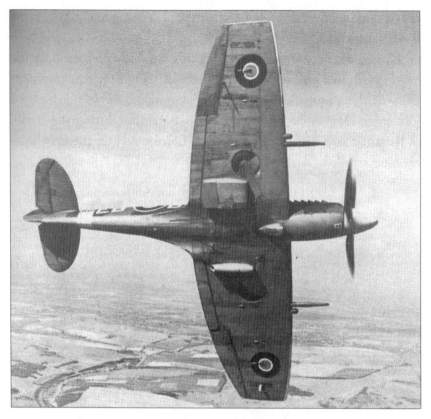

Spitfire XII of 41 Squadron.

south of England or, in this case, for use by squadrons working up with a new type.

41 Squadron arrived at High Ercall during the early afternoon of 25 February 1943 and the first Mark XII was delivered that same day. Neil remembers the occasion well:

> Our collective ego was knocked sideways when our first aircraft was delivered by a pretty, pink-cheeked young female in ATA [Air Transport Auxiliary] uniform, who taxied in with a flourish and stepped out as though she had been flying nothing more exciting than a Tiger Moth.

The squadron was officially declared non-operational whilst converting to the Spitfire XII with Neil given just six weeks to get 41 up to operational status. But the transition was slow. There were no Pilot's Notes for the Mark XII and so instruction consisted of a half-hour presentation by a junior engineering officer. And by the time they were approaching the half way point of the allotted time, just five new airframes had been delivered to the squadron.

Fortunately, the squadron had retained a couple of Mark Vs to help maintain flying continuity and despite it being a slow start, the pilots were full of enthusiasm for the Mark XII and reportedly took an immediate liking to their new aircraft. The Griffon engine was assessed to function perfectly at normal and combat settings, the only adverse comment being it 'cutting' under conditions of positive and negative 'g' at low power.

While this issue was played down in official reports, Neil always considered the problem of the engine cutting in certain conditions to be a major concern. Like the Merlin engine used in the earlier variants of Spitfire, the Griffon III used an SU-manufactured carburettor in which the fuel flow was metered through a float. In most circumstances this proved sufficient, but it was found under certain conditions, for example under negative 'g' during a bunt into a dive, the engine would briefly lose power, or even cut out altogether, through the starvation of fuel.

Neil remembers all too well the famed aeronautical engineer Beatrice 'Tilly' Shilling, a tiny, Bohemian-looking lady, arriving at High Ercall on her ancient and raucous motorbike, and then wandering up and down the flight line to resolve the problem as best she could. Her remedy was to fit a metal diaphragm with a hole in it, like a metal washer, across the float chamber, which restricted fuel flow to the carburettor and so helped prevent the engine cutting out. The idea partly cured the problem although, in the end, the solution for the next series of Griffon engine was a new pressure carburettor, which allowed more precise metering of the amount of fuel used by the engine and prevented starvation, but the problem would never go away for those flying the Spitfire XII.

Despite a relatively slow start to 41's transition, by the beginning of April the squadron was up to its full establishment of nineteen

Spitfire XIIs, a couple of Mark Vs, and twenty-four pilots. Then, with more training complete, specifically gunnery practice, the squadron was declared operational once more. It was now time for Neil to lead 41 Squadron on to its next home: Hawkinge, near Folkestone in Kent. Neil and his squadron were back with No. 11 Group. It was excellent news.

Fighter Command's nearest airfield to northern France, Hawkinge was only ten minutes' flying time from the Luftwaffe's bases in the Pas de Calais. Its forward location meant that its history went back to the First World War when it was first used by the Royal Flying Corps to re-supply forces in France. More recently, though, Hawkinge had been used by Spitfires carrying out offensive operations across the Channel, with many fighter squadrons coming and going from the airfield.

41 Squadron arrived at Hawkinge on 13 April, swapping places with 91 Squadron, which now moved to the Midlands to begin its conversion to the Spitfire XII. Some of 41's pilots were already familiar with Hawkinge having been detached south to fly alongside 91 Squadron, and so it would not take long for the new arrivals to settle in.

The squadron was mostly tasked with flying reconnaissance patrols from Hawkinge. Known as 'Jim Crows', these were flown across the Channel to reconnoitre the French and Belgian ports, with the pilots reporting on the movements of enemy shipping. These sorties would typically involve a pair of Spitfires taking off at first and last light. Having crossed the Channel together, they would then split, with one aircraft flying from Cap Gris Nez north-eastwards up to Ostend, while the other flew south-west to cover the ports of Dieppe, Boulogne and Le Havre, with all enemy activity being reported to Headquarters Naval Operations at Dover. When not flying 'Jim Crows', 41's Spitfires conducted attacks against any enemy targets of opportunity as well as carrying out rather mundane, but no less important tasks such as helping with air–sea rescues and providing weather reports over the Channel.

It was not long before the squadron scored its first aerial victory from Hawkinge. It happened just four days after 41's arrival, during an early evening reconnaissance near Ostend when a Ju 88 appeared and was promptly shot down. It was the first enemy aircraft destroyed by the squadron for nearly a year, but 41 was soon to find out just how risky these patrols were. Enemy fighters were also patrolling the coastline of northern France to counter the RAF's excursions across the Channel, and just ten days after arriving at Hawkinge, 41 suffered its first loss when Rex Poynton failed to return from a patrol. To lose a flight commander was a devastating blow to the squadron. Although Poynton is recorded as being shot down by a Fw 190 off the Somme estuary to the north of Dieppe, it was later suggested that his loss might well have been due to another aircraft design fault that would only become apparent after his death.

To increase the range and endurance of the Spitfire, an external fuel tank, called a slipper tank, usually of thirty gallons capacity, was hung between the undercarriage legs and held so close to the fuselage that it appeared to be part of the aircraft itself. This additional fuel increased the Spitfire's endurance by up to half an hour and enabled operations deeper into occupied Europe. The slipper tank could be jettisoned at will, but a problem occurred sometimes when switching the fuel supply to the internal tanks prior to jettisoning the slipper tank.

The procedure was for the pilot to select the main tanks 'ON' by bringing up the lever on the Teleflex control in front of his knees, while almost simultaneously reaching down to switch off the fuel from the slipper tank and pull the jettison handle. However, in his book *From the Cockpit: Spitfire*, Neil describes the problem encountered:

> Months later, after several more unaccountable losses, it became known that the Teleflex control to the fuel tank was coming adrift in the pilot's hand when changing over from drop tank to mains. Left with the main tanks full, but unable to use the fuel therein, the only option was either to land in enemy territory or fall into the sea.

Whether this happened to Rex Poynton or whether he was shot down by a Fw 190 as claimed, will never be known. He was operating alone at that point and so it is impossible to know for certain what happened. The same applies to other losses as well, but it is entirely possible that early losses of the Mark XII might well have been attributable to this fault. Either way, Poynton's was the first Spitfire XII to be lost over the Channel: 'It was a sad loss. Rex Poynton was a brilliant leader and most enthusiastic pilot who was respected and liked by all the squadron. Everyone had the most affectionate memories of him, a brave and fearless boy.'

There was another problem, too, with the drop tank as Neil remembers all too well. His personal aircraft during this period was EN237, coded EB-V, which he later described as 'a problem aircraft if ever there was one!' It was one of the earliest Mark XIIs and had already suffered a series of engine troubles, but this aircraft also possessed another gremlin affecting the slipper tank.

The normal operating procedure for 41 Squadron was to discard the slipper tank when crossing the enemy coast, but Neil explains the difficulty he often had with his aircraft:

> On being jettisoned, the tank was supposed to drop down fractionally before moving backwards and impinging on two lugs which served to tip it forward so that it cartwheeled away from the belly of the aircraft. Alas, not on mine! On two out of every three trips, my tank would impale itself on the lugs, either sticking there and greatly reducing my aircraft's performance, or whipping off sometime later, when it would whirl like a boomerang between those unfortunate members of my squadron who happened to be flying behind me.

After the loss of Rex Poynton, Richard Inness, who had just arrived at Hawkinge prior to taking command of his own squadron, briefly took over as flight commander before he in turn moved on to be replaced by Hugh Parry, Neil's fifth OC 'A' Flight in just eight months.

The day after Poynton's death, Sergeant John Thomas was also killed, not because of enemy action but while coming in to land at

Portrait of Pilot Officer Tom Neil by David Pritchard.

Left: This image (which has now been digitally coloured) originated as a press photograph taken on 21 September 1940, which was subsequently used in a 1941 Ministry of Information publication on the Battle of Britain. *Left to right:* Percy Burton, Butch Barton, Gerald Lewis, Ossie Crossey, Tom Neil, John Beazley, John Grandy, George Barclay, Keith Lofts.

Below left: North Weald, September 1990, at a 249 Squadron reunion to mark the fiftieth anniversary of the Battle of Britain. Former members of the squadron line up in front of a Harvard to re-create, as far as possible, the iconic image of September 1940. *Left to right:* John Beard, Cyril Hampshire, Peter Rowell, Tommy Thompson, George Stroud, Tom Neil, John Grandy, Charles Palliser, Jerzy Solak, Wally Evans, Ron Smyth, Bill McConnell.

Below: With his first CO, Sir John Grandy (*right*) who became the RAF's only Chief of the Air Staff to have flown in the Battle of Britain. Tom met up with him many times after the war and would often visit him during the final years of his life. Sir John died in 2004 at the age of ninety.

**Wing Commander Thomas F. Neil
DFC*, AFC, AE.**

Top: Tom's medals and wartime log book. The medals are (*from left*): Distinguished Flying Cross and Second Award Bar, Air Force Cross, 1939–45 Star with Battle of Britain Clasp, Air Crew Europe Star with France and Germany Clasp, Africa Star, Burma Star, Defence Medal, War Medal 1939–45, Air Efficiency Award, US Bronze Star, Malta George Cross Fiftieth Anniversary Commemorative Medal. The French Légion d'Honneur is not shown.

Above: Amongst many personal items that Tom has kept from the Second World War is this piece of art painted by one of his ground personnel during his days commanding 41 Squadron.

The First of Four on the Fifteenth

Above: Over the years, Tom has been the subject of many paintings. The example shown here is by Geoff Nutkins in recognition of Tom's outstanding achievement on 15 September 1940, since remembered as Battle of Britain Day, when he shot down four enemy aircraft.

Left: Official programme cover for 'Royal Air Force Display' held at Farnborough in July 1950 and organised by Tom.

Right: The author first met Tom twenty years ago at Bentley Priory when honoured to be the guest of Pat Wells (*far right*) at the annual dinner of the Battle of Britain Fighter Association. Tommy Thompson (*second from left*) also served with 249 Squadron during the battle and then in Malta.

Right: Tom (*fourth from right*) next to Marshal of the Royal Air Force Sir Michael Beetham, at a dinner held at RAF Coltishall, in 2000 to mark the sixtieth anniversary of the Battle of Britain.

Bottom, far right: Tom (*back row, far right*) with former members of 249 Squadron during a reunion at North Weald in September 1990 to mark the fiftieth anniversary of the Battle of Britain. The squadron's former CO, now Sir John Grandy, is seated second from right.

Below: Summer gathering of the Battle of Britain Fighter Association, 15 June 2007. The guests of honour are HRH the Prince of Wales and HRH the Duchess of Cornwall. Tom is seated second from the left.

Inset, above: With Johnny Johnson, Britain's last surviving Dambuster, at the Godmanchester Bomber Command Veterans Day, 25 June 2016.

Above: In 2017, Hurricane LF363 of the Battle of Britain Memorial Flight carried on its left-hand side Tom's personal markings GN-F worn on two of his Hurricanes while serving with 249 Squadron during the Battle of Britain.

Above: Tom and Eileen at one of many formal occasions to mark the anniversary of the Battle of Britain.

Top right: Enjoying a light-hearted moment with HRH the Prince of Wales during an art exhibition of national heroes.

Right: Talking with HM the Queen at the opening of The Wing, Capel-le-Ferne, March 2015.

Tom and Eileen pictured with their wonderful family at their grandson's wedding, June 2011.

Tom's world all but fell apart in 2014 when his wife, Eileen, died a few days short of her ninety-sixth birthday. Eileen was every bit as charming as he and she was everything to him.

Tom with his three sons – Ian (*far left*), Terence, and Patrick (*far right*) – in 2015 after a service at Westminster Abbey to mark the seventy-fifth anniversary of the Battle of Britain.

Above left: Tom pictured in the rear cockpit of Spitfire SM520 at Goodwood, 15 September 2015, Battle of Britain Day.

Left: Over Beachy Head during Tom's flight in SM520.

Above: Tom doing what Tom is so often asked to do – this time signing a canvas.

Above: Tom pictured following the publication of his book *Acts of Fate*, one of three collections of short stories he has written, all based on his own experiences and people that he served with during the Second World War.

After the award of the Légion d'Honneur, presented to Tom in 2016 at a ceremony at the RAF Club in London, in recognition of his services in helping to secure France's liberation during the Second World War.

Hawkinge; his Spitfire was seen to lose power suddenly and plunge into the ground. The resulting investigation showed that the loss had most probably been caused by another engine problem.

But technical problems or not, for 41 Squadron the war had to go on. Early on 29 April, Neil led four Spitfires on another type of mission, called a Rodeo, a straightforward sweep over the enemy coast and 41 Squadron's first offensive patrol with the Spitfire XII. The Luftwaffe had been encountered a few times recently and so the hope was to try and spot enemy aircraft with a view of shooting some down.

Their route was flown at 8,000 feet, starting at Dungeness, then across the Channel to fly coastwise between Le Touquet and Berck before returning across the Channel. Having completed the triangular route once, the four Spitfires then went around again, but to everyone's disappointment no enemy aircraft were seen. After fifty minutes airborne they all landed back at Hawkinge.

Many hours were spent on sweeps and patrols, and despite their best efforts to entice the enemy into a fight, only rarely was anything seen. Poor weather over the Channel during the first half of May, sometimes for days on end, and the Luftwaffe's reluctance to get into unnecessary air combat were the main reasons why. And so the squadron would have to wait for its next aerial action.

Being the squadron commander meant that Neil could not fly as often as he would have liked because of the other duties he was expected to perform as well. One of these was hosting visitors to the squadron and one of the more memorable visits took place one afternoon in mid-May when Marshal of the Royal Air Force Viscount Trenchard, the so-called founder and father of the RAF, visited Hawkinge.

Neil had met Trenchard a few times before, during his days with 249 Squadron at North Weald, and had always found him a very friendly and personable man. On this latest occasion, Neil and Hawkinge's station commander, Wing Commander Fred Barrett, hosted the visit. It proved to be a very relaxed affair. They all sat outside the dispersal hut, the weather was good and Trenchard was in fine form, chatting openly with the pilots.

With its conversion to the Mark XII complete, 91 Squadron was soon back at Hawkinge, meaning that 41 Squadron was on the move again, just five weeks after arriving in Kent. Those on 41 at the time used to joke about how they had become a Bedouin squadron. Even Neil was given little warning of the move. All he received was a telephone call just twenty-four hours earlier telling him the squadron was again being transferred. During the late afternoon of 21 May, 41 Squadron left Hawkinge for nearby Biggin Hill, the Spitfires being followed by two Harrows with most of the ground personnel on board, while the rest were left to travel either by train or road.

The RAF's historic airfield of Biggin Hill needs little or no introduction. Commanding a wonderful location on top of Kent's North Downs, Biggin was one of Fighter Command's principal pre-war stations and arguably the most famous airfield of the Battle of Britain. When 41 Squadron arrived in May 1943, the station was under the command of the legendary South African Group Captain 'Sailor' Malan, a former merchant navy officer and now a highly decorated fighter ace with two DSOs and two DFCs for his near thirty victories, while the Biggin Hill Wing was led by another notable fighter ace, Wing Commander Al Deere, a New Zealander with two DFCs.

It was a formidable line up, but Neil soon found his superiors, particularly Malan, difficult to get on with. The Mark XIIs of 41 Squadron were never going to integrate with the Mark IXs of the Biggin Wing. The Spitfire XII had been designed with low-level performance in mind, whereas the Mark IX was superior at higher altitudes. The two variants were simply incompatible and would never be able to operate efficiently together. Besides, with two fighter squadrons already in residence, Biggin Hill was effectively full, and so 41's temporary facilities were some way away from those of the main station. Consequently, much time was spent either walking from place to place or on a bicycle.

Whilst the Biggin Hill Wing continued operating over northern France, 41 Squadron often stayed behind. Rumours of another transfer soon started to circulate and then, sure enough, six days after arriving at Biggin, it was confirmed that 41 Squadron was, once again, on the move, this time to Friston in Sussex. The squadron was being sent there to guard the coastal towns against the Luftwaffe's 'tip and run' raiders, Bf 109s and Fw 190s flying as fighter-bombers, now becoming a serious problem. And so, having just unpacked, it was time to pack up again, and by the end of May 41 Squadron was at its third home that month.

Situated up on the South Downs just to the west of Eastbourne, Friston was a small satellite landing ground for Kenley. Neil would later describe Friston as 'a lumpy stretch of cow pasture on the tip of Beachy Head'. As Neil's description suggests, Friston was indeed an all-grass airfield and facilities there were basic to say the least. Because it was only ever intended to be a wartime landing ground, there were no permanent buildings at all and no accommodation was provided for personnel serving there, and so the officers were billeted in the village while tents were pitched for the other ranks. While Friston's proximity to the Channel made it an ideal emergency landing ground for any aircraft in trouble, it was also close enough to France to receive some unwelcome visitors from time to time.

As always, though, Neil's squadron rose to the challenge. Everyone soon settled down and people very quickly decided that Friston was a most delightful spot. The Spitfires were parked close to the dispersal hut on the perimeter of the airfield and within two days of arriving, 41 Squadron was operational.

Because of the lack of warning time of any enemy raiders, being at stand-by meant the pilots were in the cockpit at readiness. They were strapped in, the radio was on, and the engine had been warmed up and primed ready to start as soon as the order to scramble was given. A Spitfire could be airborne from Friston in a matter of seconds. In addition to waiting for any order to scramble, airborne patrols were also mounted off Beachy Head, but it was not until 4 June that 41's first action from its new home took place, and it would turn out to be one of the squadron's busiest days for a long time.

The weather that day was overcast but otherwise fair. Twenty-one patrols, each involving a pair of Spitfires, were flown during the day and it was the day when 41 Squadron encountered the Luftwaffe for the first time in five weeks.

It was around 11.20 a.m. when the airfield alarm sounded. Two Spitfires took off to investigate and the pilots soon reported spotting eighteen Fw 190 fighter-bombers heading towards Eastbourne. Six more Spitfires were scrambled from Friston, but the raiders were already about to strike. Considerable damage was caused to the town, killing six civilians and injuring dozens more. One of the raiders was shot down by the lead pair of Spitfires and another reported as damaged, but the other six Spits had arrived too late. It was all over within twenty minutes.

While Friston might well have been a beautiful spot, the reality was that the temporary grass airfield was soon proving to be a problem for the Spitfire XII. The result was a series of damaged undercarriages and several incidents of propeller damage due to the longer blades clipping the bumpy surface. Besides, news had already filtered through that 41 Squadron was about to be moved yet again. This time the squadron was off to Westhampnett to join up with 91 Squadron to form a Spitfire XII Wing, under the overall command of Wing Commander Rhys Thomas.

Unsurprisingly, there were some grumbles amongst squadron members at the thought of yet another move. Even the diarist writing in the squadron's operations record book quipped, 'We could say with certainty that 41 Squadron are the most moved squadron in the Royal Air Force.'

As packing again got under way, an advanced party left for West-hampnett. Then, on 21 June, the Spitfires left Friston for the short flight to West Sussex. The deployment had been hampered by poor weather throughout the day and so their departure was delayed until the early evening, but by 7.30 p.m. the squadron had finally arrived at its new home.

Built on the Goodwood Estate just a couple of miles to the north-east of Chichester, home to the Duke of Richmond for over 300 years, Westhampnett had initially been developed as an emergency landing ground for Tangmere. Since then, facilities had been upgraded and by the time 41 Squadron arrived the airfield had maintenance hangars and a handful of permanent buildings, although accommodation was provided off-base with the officers billeted at the rather wonderful Georgian manor of Shopwyke Hall, just a couple of miles from the airfield.

Within a few days, 91 Squadron, led by Squadron Leader Ray Harries, another fighter ace with two DFCs, had arrived at West-hampnett and by the end of June the Spitfire XII Wing had been established. The creation of this new wing brought a change in operating procedures. In addition to the normal defensive duties and fighter sweeps over northern France, the wing's role was mostly to fly as fighter escort for RAF and American bombers taking part in short-range daylight bombing raids over occupied Europe. These missions, called Ramrods, would see 41 Squadron operate mostly over Normandy and the Cherbourg peninsula, although some would take them deeper into France.

The types of bombers used on these raids varied enormously from the big four-engine heavy B-17 Flying Fortress to twin-engine medium bombers, such as the B-25 Mitchell and B-26 Marauder, to the lighter twin-engine Douglas Boston III and Mosquito. Their main objective was to bomb enemy airfields, and so push back the Luftwaffe from the coast, but strategic targets also included railway marshalling yards and industrial sites. It was also hoped that enemy fighters would react. Fighter sweeps over the Channel had often been ignored by the Luftwaffe, but now its fighters would be forced into the air, which would give the Allies a better chance of shooting them down. It was all part of the preparation plan for the Allied landings in north-west Europe, now less than a year away.

These Ramrods required a great deal of planning and co-ordination. Operational instructions for the following day would normally arrive around 9 p.m. in the form of a teleprinted message, known as a Form D, which also contained the plans for all the other wings and squadrons so that everyone knew what was going on elsewhere.

Neil would always wait around the ops room for the Form D to come in, although sometimes it did not arrive until nearly midnight.

And then there was a mass of information to wade through. The following morning the wing would gather to decide its plan, after which the selected pilots attended the briefing, usually lasting around half an hour, before watches were set to the second. Neil liked to spend the last minutes before take-off alone, chatting only to his ground crew while thoroughly checking over his aircraft.

A typical early mission for 41 Squadron was Ramrod 124, which took place during the late afternoon of 4 July. The target was the railway marshalling yards at Amiens with the RAF's No. 2 Group providing the bombers, in this case twelve Mitchells. As far as the fighter plan was concerned, two squadrons of Spitfire Vs based at Redhill were to provide the close fighter escort, while three more squadrons of Spitfire Vs, from Kingsnorth, would provide cover for the escort, with two squadrons of Spitfire IXs from Hornchurch providing the high fighter cover. Two more squadrons of Spitfire IXs, based at Northolt, would then cover the bombers off-target. Meanwhile, there were to be three fighter sweeps of the area with Westhampnett's Spitfire XIIs hunting as far as Poix to the north-east of Paris, while two squadrons of Mark IXs from Kenley would fly to Pointe d'Ailly and a further two squadrons of Mark IXs from North Weald would head for Ambleteuse. Ramrod 124 therefore involved fifteen squadrons from Fighter Command based at seven different airfields.

The problems of planning, communication and co-ordination are obvious. Westhampnett was tasked with providing twelve Spitfires for Ramrod 124, with Thomas leading the first section of four, while Neil led the second and Parry the third. Their role as the first fighter sweep was to bounce any enemy fighters before they could get anywhere near the bombers.

Setting off towards Poix, the wing crossed the Channel at 500 feet before climbing to 6,500 feet and jettisoning their drop tanks to cross the enemy coast at Berck-sur-Mer. No enemy flak was encountered and, with great visibility ahead, the Spitfires climbed to 10,000 feet.

As they arrived over Poix, around thirty Fw 190s were spotted ahead and climbing through a similar height. Thomas led the wing to engage but the 190s simply turned away to the south and disappeared at full throttle, climbing as they went. There was nothing the Spitfires could do. After turning north and then orbiting for a while, the wing's job was effectively done. With some fuel to spare they went back to the coast, orbited again to see if there was any sign of enemy activity, but nothing was seen. Now getting short of fuel, they all returned safely to Westhampnett, landing an hour and twenty minutes after getting airborne.

As things were to turn out for Ramrod 124, all the bombers reached the target and bombed successfully. The fighter sweeps proved largely uneventful, although there were engagements involving the high cover and escort cover, resulting in two 190s shot down and three 109s damaged for the loss of four Spitfires.

Some of these Ramrods were very big and even more complicated than Ramrod 124. Ramrod 133, for example, flown on 14 July, involved 267 Flying Fortresses, 202 tasked with bombing two different airfields in northern France, while sixty-five provided a diversionary attack on a third airfield. Twenty-three squadrons from Fighter Command, based at twelve different airfields, provided Spitfires, in addition to American Thunderbolts from three USAAF fighter groups.

For this latest mission, Westhampnett's wing was tasked with providing the rear withdrawal cover for the Flying Fortresses. Neil later described what it was like over enemy territory at 13,000 feet waiting for the American bombers to appear on their way home:

> We search for the Fortresses. Then tension heightens rapidly as someone reports four bandits seven o'clock and above, which, because they are behind me, I do not see immediately. I turn, hard. Then much more flak in the distance and suddenly a thick wedge of slow-moving Fortresses coming in our direction, a little above, several straggling. Sector is warning us again of more bandits in our area, but I do not see them.

Neil's formation had already been airborne for fifty minutes. Furthermore, he was flying his EB-V with its usual problem of jettisoning the slipper tank as well as a mis-firing engine. It was not a great place to be. There was then some more chatter on the radio and a bunch of Fw 190s went past them in a fast-moving line. Neil turned instinctively after them and started to give chase, but the 190s were fast disappearing downwards and away. He then spotted some more, instantly turning towards them, but they were climbing and swept over his head. Neil continues:

> Now there are two more about 800 yards away, slanting towards me and looking very unfriendly. As I watch them almost dispassionately, white rods of tracer reach out in my direction to disappear somewhere astern. I pull around so violently that my Spit shudders in a near stall and almost groans. The two 190s flash underneath, for a moment in plain view and so close that the blunt noses and black crosses of one of them are clearly visible.

Neil followed the 190s, trying to get the rear of the two into his gunsight. But the 190 was going too fast and was now too far away for Neil to get a decent shot. Besides, Neil was still heading south and now feeling very alone. Almost as a gesture, he opened fire, but the 190 was safely away.

Turning northwards, Neil could see the tell-tale signs of flak in the distance and headed off in search of the Flying Fortresses. He eventually spotted them and having chased them down he settled alongside a group of stragglers crossing the coast at less than 5,000 feet. After what seemed like an age the Isle of Wight appeared in the distance and, now desperately short of fuel, Neil set course for home.

While Ramrods might have required much planning and co-ordination, they did work in the sense that the bombers were given the best chance of getting through to their target. But being part of such a large mission meant they could, at times, be rigid and uneventful for many of the fighter pilots. Neil, for one, felt that many of the escort and sweep missions were a waste of time. It all depended on what role the squadron was given and where the action took place. Nonetheless, there was always competition amongst his junior pilots to take part in the big shows. With generally only nine slots up for grabs, pilots would even forgo leave to take part in an op.

Being back on ops had buoyed the pilots and there was a renewed sense of urgency amongst the ground personnel. The wing would typically fly a big mission every couple of days, with 41 and 91 taking it in turns to provide the aircraft and pilots; the wing rarely flew as mixed squadrons. Usually, there would be three sections of four, but on the bigger missions the task could require four sections of four; in which case, Thomas would lead one section, while Neil, Parry and Hone led the other three. And when not part of a big mission, the squadrons would take it in turns to be on standby from dawn while the other squadron maintained thirty minutes' readiness, and then switch readiness states at 1 p.m.

Not all Ramrods went as planned for 41 Squadron. On 18 July, Neil was leading the fighter sweep for Ramrod 148, a relatively small mission involving fifteen RAF Hawker Typhoons tasked with attacking the enemy airfield at Abbeville-Drucat in Picardie. The Typhoons reached their target unscathed, bombed successfully and all returned home. But it was a different story for the fighter sweep.

Having taken off from Westhampnett at 5.45 p.m., the wing crossed the Channel and proceeded inland to Poix where fifteen aircraft were spotted ahead and slightly below. On giving chase, it soon became obvious they were the Typhoons, but they were not where 41 had expected them to be. Neil then took his formation back over Poix, but they were immediately bounced from the south, out of the sun, by at least thirty enemy fighters, a mix of 109s and 190s.

The minutes that followed were chaotic, with several individual combats breaking out, during which two 109s were shot down. Neil was leading Red Section and his number three, Flying Officer Joe Birbeck, hit one of the 109s, as did his number four, Flying Officer Bruce Moffett, but neither pilot could confirm their claim.

It was then all over. The wing regrouped, badly shaken, and headed back across the Channel. However, there had been casualties. Two of 41's long-serving pilots had been shot down during the action. Flying Officer Rycherde Hogarth, a popular 21-year-old South African who had been leading Blue Section, which had been bounced first, was killed, while Flying Officer Thomas Slack, flying as Yellow Two, baled out; he would return to the squadron two months later after evading capture and making the long journey home via Spain and Gibraltar.

Neil's days of leading 41 Squadron were over. His operational tour in command was at an end. On 25 July he handed over the squadron to 23-year-old Squadron Leader Bernard Ingham. The operations record book paid tribute to Neil:

> Squadron Leader T. F. Neil came to us on 3 September 1942 and during the time he has been with us the squadron has kept a fine record of training during our long 'rest' in No. 9 Group. The squadron under his command re-equipped with the latest Spitfire XII and the training on these machines was carried out without an accident – a very successful accomplishment. We all wish him the best of luck in his new post – not exciting work, but a very useful job.

The 'not exciting work' mentioned in the ORB refers to Neil's next posting back in the training world to give him another rest from operational flying. This time he was off to No. 53 OTU at Kirton-in-Lindsey in Lincolnshire as chief flying instructor, with responsibility for training the next batch of young fighter pilots, although he would, at least, still be flying Spitfires. But, although it was now time for Neil to take another break from operations, his war was far from over.

Chapter Eleven

The Americans

Neil's time at Kirton-in-Lindsey was enjoyable and rewarding. Leading formations of Spitfires, albeit old Mark IIs, and teaching keen young students the art of formation flying, aircraft handling and combat procedures certainly had its rewards. Exercises like follow the leader, with plenty of loops and rolls, depending on whatever Neil decided to throw in, were fun. They were simple ways of teaching aircraft handling, and easy for an experienced fighter pilot like him, but less so for the young men following behind.

Watching the students leave at the end of the demanding fourteen-week course gave Neil a lot of pride, but he could not help but wonder what might be in store for them. The past four months had gone quickly since leaving 41 Squadron and he was now ready for the next challenge.

The first he knew that a change was in store was late one afternoon in November, having just landed off another training sortie, when the adjutant informed Neil that the station commander wanted to see him. Group Captain John Hawtrey, an old Etonian and something of a thespian, and nearly twice the age of Neil, had not been in post long and so Neil was still a little unsure of him. Having cleaned himself up and put on his forage cap he made the long walk to the station commander's office. He later recalled: 'Little did I know that I was within fifteen minutes of being given instructions that would affect my service career for the following twelve months and, indirectly, my life for many years to come.'

After the normal pleasantries, Hawtrey read out a signal he had received. Neil was to go to the Air Ministry in London for an interview, with a view of him joining the American Ninth Air Force with effect from January 1944. There followed a brief silence, after which Neil admitted to knowing nothing about Americans. It was all a bit of a shock, but within a couple of weeks, he was on a train heading for London.

The interviewing officer, an older wing commander, explained to Neil that the Ninth Air Force was still in the process of establishing itself in Britain. Being new, its pilots were raw in terms of combat experience and so the Americans had asked for experienced RAF fighter pilots to be posted to them as liaison officers for an indefinite period.

The wing commander also went on to explain that, unlike the American Eighth Air Force, which had long been established at bases in and around East Anglia, the Ninth was to be a tactical air force rather than a strategic one. The plan was that once the Allies had landed in Europe, the Ninth would then provide tactical support for advancing troops by destroying the Luftwaffe on the ground as well as in the air. The Ninth would also disrupt the enemy's lines of communication and, in general, cause as much mayhem as possible – all this with a large force of fighters and short-range medium bombers.

In response to the American request, the wing commander explained, the Air Ministry had decided to establish several teams of three RAF officers to be attached to the Americans and that Neil had been selected to be the flying operations member of the first team. But as there was no blueprint for such a role, Neil would have to make it up as he went along. It was as simple as that.

It had hardly been an interview. It was more a case of being told what was happening. Neil was then instructed to make his way to an airfield near a village called Boxted in Essex, which the Americans were in the process of taking over, and then report back to the Air Ministry with what he had observed. At first, Neil did not know what to make of it all. Initially, he admits, the idea of his next posting had not particularly thrilled him, but by the time he left London the following morning his spirits had picked up. However, after eventually arriving at Boxted, an airfield he later described as a 'sea of mud', he found out the Americans were expecting someone to run their operations room.

It turned out to be a simple case of differing terminology between the two air forces. The Americans had misunderstood the RAF's definition of an operational pilot and running an operations room was not at all how the job had been explained to Neil. And so, with his brief introduction to the Americans over, he returned to London to inform the wing commander of his rather disappointing visit to Boxted.

While others more senior than him decided on what should happen next, Neil went back to Kirton-in-Lindsey for Christmas. It took until the new year for the situation to be resolved, but, after a few weeks of uncertainty, Neil was officially posted to the 100th Fighter Wing, XIX Tactical Air Command, Ninth USAAF, with effect from 10 February 1944.

Headquarters 100th Fighter Wing had been established at Ibsley, near Ringwood in Hampshire. The airfield had been constructed on low ground at the western edge of the New Forest as a satellite airfield of Middle Wallop, and by the time Neil arrived it had all but been vacated by the RAF to make way for the Americans. He arrived to find elements of the headquarters already in place, but more people and equipment had yet to arrive. As a satellite airfield there were few permanent buildings and so the wing's headquarters had been set up in a group of Nissen huts on the edge of the airfield.

An American fighter wing during the Second World War was broadly equivalent to an RAF tactical group, with each American wing having four or five fighter groups, and with each group consisting of three squadrons. Unlike an RAF fighter squadron that would typically operate twelve aircraft at a time, the American squadrons tended to operate sixteen. In his book *The Silver Spitfire*, Neil describes his initial thoughts when first briefed on the size of the 100th Fighter Wing:

Neil's first Republic P-47C Thunderbolt.

The numbers involved quite took my breath away. Clearly there was going to be much more to my job than I had expected, as with a force of several hundred fighter aircraft in the wing, a lot of explaining and talking lay ahead of me. Flying, too, I hoped.

Neil was shown around the American facilities by a friendly young pilot, 23-year-old Major de Fehr, a West Point officer and now the wing's operations officer, after which his host took him flying in a Taylorcraft Cub. Their friendship, though, was to be very brief as de Fehr was about to leave for Italy to gain some combat experience. Neil never saw him again. The young American was killed within days of leaving Ibsley.

The following day Neil went for breakfast. It became immediately apparent to him just how different the lifestyle was between the Americans and the British. And when it came to food, there was plenty of everything on offer. 'What war?' again springs to mind. It was also during that same morning when Neil was first introduced to the commander of the wing, Colonel Homer L. Sanders, known as 'Tex', whom Neil describes as 'more resembling a Mexican gunslinger than a senior air force officer'.

With de Fehr on his way to Italy, and sadly about to have his life cut short, the new operations officer, Major Jim Haun, introduced

Neil to a recently delivered Republic P-47 Thunderbolt. It was the Headquarters Flight's first aircraft, and Neil was delighted when Haun suggested that he should take it up.

After flying the Spitfire, the P-47 seemed positively huge. The differences between the two fighters are too many to list but, for a start, its cockpit layout and instrumentation were all very different. However, after Haun's brief introduction to the aircraft, the American climbed down off the wing, leaving Neil to fly it for the first time. The flight went well. Neil later recalled:

> Of that first flight, I have little to report. The P-47 was like sitting in a rocking chair, easy to control, thoroughly amiable. I did not feel, though, that I was flying it; rather, it was flying me. If I was to go to war in this aircraft, then I would have to put in a great deal more practice.

Neil flew the P-47 several times in the coming days, such as on delivery flights of new aircraft to Ibsley, which included flying the improved 'D' model; the early arrivals at Ibsley had been older P-47Cs. But with either model, the P-47 would take some getting used to. To Neil there was 'too much electricity and too many switches'. He would later compare flying the P-47 to playing a Wurlitzer organ.

To gain more experience on the type, Neil would put the Thunderbolt through its paces in a serious way, particularly at high altitude. But one occasion nearly ended in disaster. While flying high over Salisbury Plain at nearly 35,000 feet, he spotted four aircraft against the cloud tops well below. Memories of 1940 came flooding back. Now he had the height advantage and so he decided to go down and have a look. Impulsively, he rolled the P-47 on its back and fell earthwards like a stone. The airspeed was building rapidly, and he was soon in a high-speed dive. He was going down extremely quickly, it was all very exciting, but he then started to sense that he might have a problem. What happened next is best summed up in Neil's own words:

> I felt the aircraft was running away with me and becoming beyond my control; concern rapidly turned into panic. By

this time, I could barely move the control column and when, with all my strength, I attempted to pull back and raise the nose, all I succeeded in doing was to push my aircraft further into its near vertical dive. At which stage, I felt the P-47 to be completely unmanageable and that, even at a height of something well over 20,000 feet, I was facing disaster.

The aircraft started to buffet and shake. Thoughts that it was about to suffer a structural failure flashed through Neil's mind. At such high speed and in a near vertical dive, there was no chance of opening the hood, let alone baling out. All Neil could do was to hang on. There was nothing else he could do. Then, for some unknown reason, the buffeting and shaking eased. He was still going down very fast, but he was slowly able to drag the nose of the aircraft up and finally he managed to level out.

By the time normal flight had been resumed, Neil was close to Boscombe Down. He knew from his time there earlier in the war that the airfield was home to the Aeroplane and Armament Experimental Establishment and so he decided to land there.

Having been courteously received, Neil explained what had happened, after which he was given an hour-long dissertation on flying at extreme altitude and speed. He learned that the latest fighters entering service were capable of such high speed that they were becoming affected by the sound barrier. Neil's first experience of high speed at high altitude had nearly cost him his life, and the memory of that day would remain with him for the rest of his life.

As well as the P-47, there were many other aircraft types at Ibsley and Neil was in a privileged position of being able to familiarise himself with them all. He had now been joined by the two other RAF officers that he had been told about at the start, to make up the team of three, the others being a squadron leader intelligence officer and a flight lieutenant equipment officer.

It was a very happy time for Neil. There was plenty of flying to be had and it had not taken him long to settle down and to acclimatise himself to all things American. He was most influenced by his colonel, Tex Sanders, the man he had initially likened to a Mexican gunslinger, whom he worked with most days, and Sanders's superior, Major General Elwood Quesada, the head of the XIXth TAC.

Sanders was a fearless and very capable pilot. He flew every type of aircraft in the wing, and while he might have given the impression of being a hard man, which he was, he also had a gentle and kindly side to his nature. Neil soon grew to like and admire him. Quesada, too, a man of similar age, was cast from the same mould.

Neil had infinitely more combat experience than those around him – the Battle of Britain, Malta, and having led a Spitfire squadron over occupied Europe – and so he did not need to prove himself, but he was particularly pleased to have made new friends and form fresh relationships, some of which would last more than sixty years. The Americans, in return, viewed him with great respect, tolerating his strange remarks from time to time, whether they agreed with him or not.

As more Americans arrived, Neil was busy giving lectures to successive groups of pilots on a wide variety of topics. As well as talking about air warfare during and since the Battle of Britain, and about the capabilities of the Luftwaffe, his presentations included talks on the geography and history of Britain, and its people, as a way of introducing the new arrivals to the country they were now living in, and he gave similar presentations on Europe. He was always in demand.

Being the only RAF pilot in the area, Neil was soon approached by an engineering officer from a maintenance unit based at the nearby airfield of Stoney Cross. The unit's task, he explained, was to recover and repair damaged aircraft that had come down in the area. Once fixed, an aircraft then needed to be given a test flight to determine whether it was fit to be returned to operational flying. Until recently, one of the RAF's pilots based at Ibsley would carry out these test flights but now that they had all gone, Neil was asked if he would kindly help.

Never one to turn down the opportunity to fly a different aircraft, Neil agreed. His first test flight was in a Lysander, a completely new experience for him. Word of his willingness to help soon spread.

Not only did he fly from Stoney Cross, but he also flew from other airfields as well. It was his first taste of test flying and he was flying over familiar countryside once more. It was all rather fun, albeit with several hairy moments along the way.

Neil was always doing something, whether it was flying one of the wing's many aircraft, or test-flying others, or giving lectures or travelling somewhere in his Morris Ten. It was now April 1944 and being in the south of England meant he could not fail to notice that the long-anticipated Allied landings in Europe were not far away. When flying along the coastline he could see harbours crammed with vessels of all types, and when moving around by road he would see armoured convoys and soldiers from all countries billeted along the Hampshire coast. He knew that it would not be much longer before the war entered its final phase.

Then, and seemingly out of nowhere, came news that the 100th Fighter Wing was to move to the Biggin Hill sector, with its squadrons to be spread across a bunch of airfields that Neil had never heard of. This was extremely welcome, not that his reason had anything to do with the Americans. During his brief time at Biggin Hill the year before, while in command of 41 Squadron, he had met an attractive, dark-haired WAAF. Being wartime, they had not kept in touch since, but Neil very much hoped that she would still be there.

Four days later, Neil left Ibsley in his Morris Ten bound for an airfield called Lashenden, which was near Ashford in Kent. With him were three passengers and as much kit as they could carry. The journey of well over a hundred miles along the south coast took them five hours to complete.

Although initially constructed as an advanced landing ground (ALG), Lashenden had recently been upgraded prior to the Americans moving in. But as there were no permanent buildings on the airfield, Neil and his colleagues were to be accommodated in a rustic old farmhouse situated in a quiet country lane. Their new home came complete with a large garden, an industrial greenhouse, and several outbuildings, and while it could never have been described as exotic, it was certainly decent enough.

Over the next few days, the wing's 300 aircraft – P-47s and North American P-51 Mustangs – arrived at the four ALGs the 100th had been allocated: Lashenden, Headcorn, High Halden and Staplehurst. It was from Staplehurst that Neil got his first flight in a Mustang, an aircraft of the 363rd Fighter Group:

> The aircraft was notably heavier than a Spit, but was a joy in the air, the engine smooth and seemingly better mounted than a Spitfire, and displaying a rock-steady, automatically controlled coolant temperature. Furthermore, all the flying controls were capable of being trimmed. Throughout, however, I was conscious of carrying a considerable load, which, of course, I was – the weight of about 300 gallons of fuel, as compared with that of a hundred or so in a Spitfire. This was certainly no light, fast-climbing fighter, but I liked it enormously, except for the hood as I was always keen to see any enemy behind me.

The first Mustangs arrived at Lashenden the following day. And there was even better news when Neil discovered that the attractive, dark-haired WAAF was still at Biggin Hill. He even took his senior American colleagues to Biggin on a familiarisation visit in the hope of seeing her. But not only was she not on shift that day, the visit did not initially go well. The Americans were not exactly made to feel welcome, even though Sanders commanded 300 fighters in the sector.

Embarrassed by the lack of hospitality of his own service, Neil made his feelings known to a comparatively elderly wing commander in the control and reporting section. It worked. The Americans were then given an hour-long guided tour of the operations centre. Even Sanders was impressed.

The attractive, dark-haired WAAF that Neil had hoped to see was 25-year-old Flight Officer Eileen Hampton, the daughter of an army officer and now the principal 'Ops B' officer at Biggin Hill. One of 250 personnel working in the operations centre, she sat to the right of the sector controller in the underground operations room and passed on his instructions to the squadrons and other units of the RAF's defence organization.

Although Neil had not managed to see Eileen that day, he did not have to wait too long to bump into her again at Biggin Hill. And, having managed to renew his acquaintance with her, he invited Eileen and one of her colleagues, Cynthia Oglethorpe, to Lashenden one day in mid-May to attend a social function hosted by one of the fighter groups.

Accommodation for the two ladies was arranged at Headcorn, and using one of Neil's American friends, the large and dynamic Major Robert A. Patterson, as his wingman, Eileen and Cynthia were hosted to a wonderful afternoon at Lashenden and then an unforgettable evening out. The following day, Neil drove the four of them out into the Kent countryside where they found a meadow and settled down to an afternoon in the sun. Neil best captures the moment in his own words:

> As we all lay on our backs with eyes closed, savouring the sun, we talked endlessly about trivial things, laughed at each other's harmless jokes, and vastly enjoyed an ambience in which there was seemingly no war, no stress or hurt, no flying accidents or death, no responsibilities or anything else, in fact. I believe that, sensing that we were all submerged in an atmosphere unusually warm and gentle and loving, I actually prayed that I might later be blessed with memories of that very special afternoon.

That very special afternoon was another defining moment in Neil's life. Later that month, he and Eileen escaped to the south-west for a few days of leave together: from Kent to Cornwall and back in his Morris Ten – an adventure in itself – and all in just a few days. It was the start of a wonderful relationship that would last over seventy years. Neil later wrote: 'Yes, life was fun! Life was absolutely super!'

By the end of May there were more than a thousand fighters, both RAF and USAAF, at a dozen or more airfields in the Biggin Hill sector alone. All the airfields were crammed full. The 100th

Flight Officer Eileen Hampton.

Fighter Wing had emerged from what, just weeks before, had seemed like chaos. At Staplehurst and Lashenden there were around 150 Mustangs of the 354th and 363rd Fighter Groups, while a similar number of Thunderbolts of the 358th and 362nd Fighter Groups filled Headcorn and High Halden.

It was now the final build-up to the Allied landings and so there were many official visits to the wing, all involving Neil to some extent or another. A day hardly seemed to pass without someone coming to look at the wing's preparations and amongst the high-profile visitors were General Dwight D. Eisenhower, the Supreme Commander of the Allied Expeditionary Forces in Europe, Lieutenant General George Patton, commander of the US Third Army, Major General 'Opie' Weyland, who had succeeded Quesada in command of the XIXth TAC, King Peter of Yugoslavia, and Viscount Trenchard, who went down extremely well with the Americans.

Sanders was always keen for Neil as the RAF liaison officer to be seen. He had fully immersed himself into his role and had even taken on a part-American appearance. He had little or no time for the RAF's new battledress, preferring instead to wear a light brown American windcheater jacket, which had shoulder straps on which he wore the gold-leaf insignia of a major. The reason for this was because most Americans struggled with the rank of squadron leader whereas its equivalent rank of major was fully understood everywhere he went. The combination of his American light brown jacket and blue RAF uniform trousers made him look rather odd, but he found this highly unauthorised rig-out was far more comfortable when flying. Besides, in truth, he was never much concerned about his appearance.

Although the Allied landings were clearly getting very close, Neil had no idea of what part he would be expected to play. Would he be attached to one of the groups and fly alongside his American colleagues in support of the landings, or would he be left on the ground or even sent off somewhere else? He simply did not know. The only way to find out was to raise the subject with Sanders, which he did.

The colonel was most understanding of Neil's eagerness to fly and even gave his support, his only words of caution being that it would be difficult for Neil to fly regularly, given that he had a job to do in the headquarters. Other than that, Neil took his comments as a green light.

Until that point, Neil's flying in the Mustang had been restricted to a few gentle excursions, and so he spent the following days learning as much as he could about the aircraft: its armament, its capabilities, its range and its endurance. Hours were spent talking with his colleagues and the ground crew to find out as much as he could about the aircraft, working on the principle that he would most likely be going to war in one within the next few days.

In the final days of May, Neil flew the Mustang several times, putting the aircraft through its paces and even visiting the coastal range to practice air-to-ground gunnery. He later wrote: 'Roll on the invasion! I was feeling in good heart. The P-51 was just about the best aircraft around in which to go to war.'

The long-awaited Allied landings began in the early hours of 6 June 1944, D-Day. After a year or more of build-up and expectation, it all came as a rather welcome relief.

For the 100th Fighter Wing based in Kent, the landing beaches in Normandy were some distance away and so there was initially little or no change to their daily routine. The pilots would have to be patient and wait until enemy airfields had been overrun before they would get the chance to cross the Channel. That could take days, weeks even. Nonetheless, D-Day was still a very busy day for the wing as the P-51s and P-47s went about their normal operational business.

Neil flew his Mustang twice on that historic day. With everything having been kept Top Secret, he knew nothing of the plan and had no idea where the landing beaches were. And so, his first flight that day was unmemorable. But by the time he flew his second in the afternoon, more information had filtered through and so he went in search of the beachheads.

It was a cloudy day and visibility was poor in places and so he stayed down at low level beneath the cloud base. From Beachy Head he set out across the Channel in the general direction of Le Havre, and soon spotted some ships heading in the same direction. Neil later recalled: 'I felt very buoyant. With a battery of six very potent 0.5-inch machine guns in my bright new P-51D, should I be lucky enough to meet any wandering Hun, I would really be able to give him what for, my goodness!'

As he approached the French coast at 1,500 feet he could see a wide expanse of dark smoke above a large huddle of ships, surrounded by a mass of smaller craft. He could also see bright flashes of gunfire in the distance. But as he was not in radio contact with any authority in the area, he decided against getting any closer. The last thing he wanted was to be considered as an unidentified aircraft approaching the area and then fall victim to a naval barrage of anti-aircraft fire. And as there were no enemy fighters to be seen, he turned for home, landing back at Lashenden after an uneventful, but unforgettable, hour in the air.

While D-Day had been a relatively uneventful one for Neil, the following day, 7 June, was anything but. Again, he flew twice and, again, the first flight was unmemorable. But having landed off his first sortie around midday, Neil was taken to one side by Sanders and introduced to a visiting general who was due to leave for the Normandy beachhead that afternoon in a Douglas C-47 Skytrain.

During the discussion that followed, Neil told the general what he had seen in the area and offered to escort the C-47 across the Channel. The general and Sanders agreed it was a good idea and so later that afternoon, Neil, in his P-51D, joined up with the C-47 over Lashenden and set course at 2,000 feet for the temporary landing ground at Saint-Pierre-du-Mont.

As they approached what was the American Omaha beachhead, the scene became nothing short of breathtaking, with masses of ships and craft, of all sizes, everywhere to be seen. Neil later said that he was 'almost hypnotised by the sight beneath him' and the prospect of an enemy attack had all but escaped his mind.

He then spotted a queue of C-47s flying in an orbit and waiting to land at a newly laid airstrip running parallel to the coastline and within yards of the water's edge. Having joined the orbiting queue alongside his own C-47, he watched the others, one by one, make their approach to land. What happened next is best described by Neil:

> On my fourth circuit, and for reasons I could never later explain, I decided to land. On a small advanced landing ground, later to be referred to as A-1, arguably the first to be constructed during the Allied invasion of Europe. What was I doing? Taking an unacceptable risk? As I was totally engrossed, the thought never crossed my mind.

He was not in radio contact with anyone and without a care in the world he was soon on the ground. He pulled over to one side of the landing strip, shut down and sat back to observe the scene. There were C-47s everywhere and enormous mounds of cargo, almost as far as he could see.

After a while he noticed someone waving his hands as if he was a policeman directing traffic. He watched him for a while longer and having decided that he was probably the person in charge, Neil decided to go over to him and explain who he was and why he had landed. As it turned out, the man waving his arms was just a stand-in because the man who had been in charge before had been shot dead by a sniper, roughly in the area where Neil had been waiting. With that, Neil realised the severity of the whole situation and within minutes he was back in the air once more.

It was a week before Neil dared tell anyone about his landing in France. Sanders eventually got to hear about it and raised the subject with him, insisting that he should have been told. 'Hell! You're probably the first guy in a fighter to land in France after D-Day,' he said, to which Neil respectfully pointed out that several fighter guys would have already landed in France since D-Day, the only difference being they had been shot down. This, Neil felt, did not make his landing to be anything of importance. Nothing more was ever said.

With the Allies breaking out of the Normandy beachhead, albeit slowly, attention turned to another more pressing problem in the south-east of England. There was now a new threat to London in the shape of the V1 flying bomb, known to the British public as the

Doodlebug, which was now appearing in increasing numbers. Being in Kent, the 100th Fighter Wing's airfields were in the line of fire and the Mustang was one of the few fighters capable of catching and shooting down the V1s.

The window of opportunity to intercept a flying bomb was very brief and so an interception had to be perfect if the fighter was going to have any chance of shooting one down. Neil got in on the act, although he never managed to shoot one down despite trying several times. He did get close on one occasion, as he later recalled:

> Having been fortunate enough again to intercept a Doodlebug low down, and some five or six miles into Kent, I followed it for some minutes at a speed of more than 450 mph, until I was certain I was alone and, at about 250 yards range, in a prime attacking position. Concentrating absolutely on my gunsight and my target, and controlling my speeding, bucking aircraft, I was about to open fire when I suddenly realised, to my dismay, that I was over a built-up area close to Sevenoaks, and that my success would probably result in the death of countless people below.

The irony was, of course, as Neil well knew, that the V1 would fly on and, perhaps, kill more helpless souls somewhere else. In his own words, he was later full of remorse and questioned what he should have done. It had been so difficult to decide at the time, and even now it is a painful dilemma for him to recall.

Being in Kent also meant that Neil could visit his parents, now living in Northwick Park in the north-western outskirts of London, the result of his father's further advancement with the railways. There was also time for Neil's relationship with Eileen to blossom. But then, at the beginning of July, came word that the 100th Fighter Wing was to move to France.

News of the wing's impending move to France caused much excitement at Lashenden. Everyone set about packing and making sure they were ready to go. Being part of the headquarters staff, Neil would be amongst the last to leave but, with his departure imminent, he proposed to Eileen – not in person, but over the telephone one night while she was on duty. She accepted, and the following night was spent celebrating in London. Three days later, during the morning of 6 July, Neil left for France.

He landed near the small coastal village of Cricqueville in Normandy, at a new landing ground designated A-2 (the 'A' denoting the landing ground was American and '2' because it was the second prepared). It was just inland from the Utah beachhead and although the landings had taken place exactly a month before, he had flown over a vast array of ships and craft just off the coast.

It all seemed rather surreal, but he was soon greeted by familiar faces and was taken on a tour of the local area. Driving around the countryside, Neil witnessed the harsh reality of what war was like on the ground. The fighting had long been over, but the area was still a mess. He later wrote:

> After some minutes, sickened by the sight and reek of so much death, I think we were all relieved when our driver turned our vehicle about and headed back towards our newly created headquarters site, all of us silent and with me thanking God that I was an airman and did not have to face violence in its starkest, most upsetting form, as did the poor wretched army chaps fighting for their lives on the ground.

The 100th Fighter Wing established its headquarters in a splendid old château at A-15 (Maupertus) near the village of Saint Pierre Église on the Cherbourg Peninsula. The airfield was also being used by the P-51s of the wing's 363rd Fighter Group but its other groups had long disappeared somewhere out into the Normandy countryside. It was a fluid situation and, at times, a confusing one with aircraft and units constantly on the move. It was a very different air war to the one that Neil had fought over southern England four years before.

For the headquarters staff, though, life soon settled into something of a routine, with morning briefings, which Neil contributed to, followed by meetings to discuss whatever needed discussing at the time. Neil did manage to fly, though. In addition to his Mustang, he also spent many hours piloting the headquarters' Cessna C-78 and Fairchild C-61, ferrying people and equipment backwards and forwards across the Channel.

When he did get airborne in the Mustang, he would fly over the Normandy region to see what was happening on the ground. He remembers flying over Caen and seeing the devastation, which reminded him of his father's stories of Passchendaele all those years before. Although he was flying around an active battle area, he had little fear of being jumped by the Luftwaffe. They, it seemed, had all but disappeared, which was rather odd, sad even, for Neil, who clearly remembered the Luftwaffe of old with its extremely effective fighter force.

As the Allies advanced further into Europe, the wing's head-quarters moved again, this time to the city of Rennes in eastern Brittany. The Germans were still holding out in the fortified Atlantic naval centres of Brest, Lorient and St Nazaire, and so the decision was made to bypass these German strongholds rather than to assault them on the ground. It was a case of waiting for the Germans to surrender, although in some places this would not happen until the end of the war.

The airfield at Rennes had only recently been liberated by the American Third Army and so it was still in a very poor state when Neil arrived. The P-47s of the 362nd Fighter Group were already there, although there was no sign of the P-51s of the 363rd. Again, there seemed to be utter confusion. Fighters came and went, to where no one seemed to know. Neil later wrote:

> I found myself wearily shaking my head. This was a chaotic situation. Units and aircraft kept turning up out of nowhere, and then just as quickly disappearing. Someone important probably knew what was happening and was issuing the orders, but I was certainly kept in the dark. And I was a member of the so-called controlling headquarters staff, for heaven's sake!

This time there was to be no splendid château, just a tent shared with his long-term and closest friends, Lieutenant Colonel Alvin Hill and Major 'Bodey' Bodenheim. From Rennes, Neil was able to fly freely over the battleground as the Allies enjoyed the luxury of air superiority across the region. He could see the dramatic effects of air power, particularly against the German Panzers. He remembers it all being very different to what he had seen on the newsreels four years before, when the Panzers had rolled into France and the Low Countries. But he also remembers seeing American columns at a halt because they had pushed ahead too quickly and too far, outstripping their own supply lines, and could not help thinking how lucky all those stranded figures on the ground were that the Luftwaffe was now too far away to cause them any harm. It could so easily have been rather different.

It was now the middle of August. Sanders had found another château for his headquarters staff to live in, and life was ticking along all rather pleasantly, but Neil was beginning to wonder how he could do more. The wing's Mustangs had all disappeared and flying the only P-51 at Rennes meant that he could hardly attach himself to the P-47s. Besides, he had regularly flown around the area and along the coast, and it had become evident that the war was now being fought elsewhere.

Then, late one morning, as he was going out to fly his P-51, Neil noticed a Spitfire parked up nearby. It was a Mark IX carrying the squadron code '3W-K', indicating it was from an Allied squadron rather than an RAF one. Other than that, there was no one near it. After making some enquiries, he soon discovered that the Spitfire had recently landed at Rennes, but the engine was in a bad way and so its pilot had been picked up by another aircraft. Now, the Spitfire was just standing there, and no one seemed to want it back.

The full story of what happened to the Spitfire is covered in Neil's book *The Silver Spitfire*, but, in short, the American mechanics sorted out its engine problem and Neil took it flying. Then, when the 100th Fighter Wing headquarters was ordered to move forward to the town of Le Mans, there was a discussion about what should happen to the

Spitfire. It was still at Rennes and no one had been in touch as to getting it back. There was no paperwork in the cockpit, and so no one knew anything about it, or its past. But rather than leave the Spitfire behind, the decision was made to take it with the wing to Le Mans, and that Neil was to fly it there. Neil quickly scribbled a note and left it at the control hut at Rennes. The note simply read: 'To whom it may concern. Have taken Spitfire 3W-K to Le Mans. Pick it up there.'

Having signed the note, Neil then flew the Spitfire to Le Mans. But even at Le Mans, there were still no enquiries as to 3W-K's whereabouts. Although its engine had been fixed to a certain degree, it was not performing sufficiently for the Spitfire to be used operationally. The wing's mechanics had done all they could, but their knowledge of the Merlin engine was limited. As it stood, the Spitfire was of no great use to anyone and so Neil decided to take it back to England and use his former contacts there to try and get the engine overhauled. Which he did, and after spending a couple of days at Ford, Neil took the Spitfire back to Le Mans.

A month passed, but still no one came for the Spitfire. It was now clear that no one wanted it back. So Neil decided to keep it. He was due some leave and to avoid attracting further attention to his Spitfire, he took it back to Ford and asked to have the camouflage and squadron markings removed, leaving only the roundels on what was otherwise a silver Spitfire.

When it was pointed out to Neil that some might consider he was pinching the aircraft, his answer was that he had not pinched anything. When the Spitfire had been dumped at Rennes it was unserviceable and had it been left behind when the wing moved to Le Mans it would surely have been vandalised or at least robbed of its parts. No, Neil explained, he had not pinched it. He had simply saved the Spitfire.

Neil returned to Le Mans two weeks later only to find the 100th Fighter Wing had moved out while he had been away. He arrived at an empty airfield and with no idea of where everyone had gone. After making numerous enquiries, he was advised to fly on to Villacoublay, near Paris, where, he was told, the Ninth Air Force HQ had been established. And when he arrived at Villacoublay, he made further enquiries before eventually finding out that his wing's HQ had now been set up at A-64 at St Dizier.

As it was already late in the day, Neil spent the night at the Palace of Versailles, not in luxury but sleeping rough on the marble floor. The following day he flew on to St Dizier where his arrival created much interest, not just because he was back, but because of his silver Spitfire.

It was now late September and the wing's P-51s and P-47s had mostly disappeared to operate further forward in the ground-attack role. As luck would have it, though, Eileen had just arrived in France with a group of WAAFs amidst much media interest as reportedly the first British female contingent to arrive in the country since the landings had taken place. They were to work in a sector operations room near Amiens.

Things had become easy and agreeable. The war was in its final phase and victory was in sight. For many, life was a cocktail of flying and fun. Other than seeing Eileen whenever he could, the weeks that followed were spent ferrying passengers backwards and forwards across the Channel in the wing's twin-engine Douglas C-53 Skytrooper or flying the Spitfire.

Since finding the Spitfire, Neil had not once flown a P-51. But the Spit could not be re-armed as the Americans did not hold the right ammunition. Neil later wrote: 'I was, in short, a warrior without weapons and, for the first time ever, I was beginning to feel superfluous and that I was wasting my time.'

In truth, Neil was now surplus to requirements and his wonderful time with the Americans was about to end. He had been with them for almost a year, but they no longer needed an RAF liaison officer. Although he was recommended for a higher award, his meritorious service with the 100th Fighter Wing would later be recognised by the award of a Bronze Star. When the time came to move on, there was no official posting or transfer. In fact, Neil had not heard anything officially from the RAF all year. He simply went to Sanders and asked if he could leave so that he could return to his own service. Sanders agreed and, after saying farewell to his American friends, Neil jumped in his Spitfire and flew back to England, landing at Northolt on the north-west side of London from where he could easily get home. It was 18 November 1944. All he had to do now was find another job. And of course he had to get rid of the Spitfire.

Chapter Twelve

Victory at Last

After arriving back in England, Neil took a few days of leave. Having been away with the Americans for so long and having had no official posting or correspondence from the RAF, he was unsure of what he should do next. He needed to let someone know that he was back and so he thought the personnel section at Headquarters Fighter Command at Bentley Priory was the obvious place to start.

He soon found out there had been significant changes while he had been away and as far as manning was concerned, the RAF was described to him as 'being in a state of flux'. Neil would later describe this period after his time with the Americans as 'utterly confusing'. It had quickly become apparent that he was a forgotten man. Nothing was seemingly on offer and, now short of ideas, he got in touch with his former group captain at Kirton-in-Lindsey, John Hawtrey.

Keen to help, Hawtrey wrote to a colleague at No. 83 Group and for a while it looked like Neil might become wing commander flying at an airfield near Antwerp. He even went out to Belgium for an interview, but the only memorable thing that came of the idea was a near miss from a V2 rocket, which hit the perimeter of the airfield just a thousand yards from where Neil was standing at the time.

His silver Spitfire, meanwhile, was still at Northolt. It had already been a month since Neil arrived back in England and still no one showed any interest in it. He decided to fly it across the Channel to visit Eileen, but disaster struck as he was taxiing it across the rain-sodden grass airfield at Amiens. Before he could do anything about it, the Spitfire was suddenly standing on its nose. It seems that a filled-in bomb crater had suddenly opened up because of the rain.

The problem now, of course, was that the Spitfire needed to be repaired, which in turn led to the question again being raised as to where it had come from. It was to be another of those grovelling conversations between Neil and his wing commander engineer colleague at Ford, the outcome being that Neil returned to England, courtesy of an Avro Anson, while the Spitfire was to be fixed in France. Then, after a few days back home, Neil arranged to return to Amiens, this time in an Oxford courtesy of the communications flight at Biggin Hill, so that he could spend Christmas with Eileen.

After returning to England once more, Neil was finally told to report back to Bentley Priory. It was now early January 1945 and, at last, there was a job for him. He was to be one of the RAF instructors at a new tri-service establishment called the School of Air Support, based at Old Sarum in Wiltshire. The school had originally been set up after the First World War as the School of Army Co-operation, to encourage senior army and air force officers to work together better. Since then it had become the School of Land/Air Warfare and now, as a tri-service establishment under its new title, the school's remit had been broadened to include amphibious operations.

Neil drove down to Old Sarum in his Morris Ten. It was a crisp, cold day when he arrived, and he found the set-up a joy to behold. The officers' mess was a delightful place and there were several aircraft of varying types parked near a hangar.

He was officially welcomed to the school by Group Captain Peter Donkin, a reconnaissance pilot from New Zealand, who commanded the Offensive Support Wing. During their chat, Donkin explained that Neil would be part of the Air Support Wing and was required to give lectures on a variety of subjects, as well as organising the air displays and flying demonstrations for the various courses. Also, Neil was told, there might be a visit to the Far East in the offing so that he could broaden his knowledge of operations out there.

Next up was a chat with the school's commandant, Air Vice-Marshal Leslie Brown, a South African affectionately known to his staff as 'Bingo' Brown, who had previously commanded No. 84 Group. With their conversation seemingly going well, Neil took a chance and threw in the idea of getting the silver Spitfire on the school's books. But Brown would not give the plan his support, explaining the school already had two Spitfires and so a third 'would be altogether too much of a good thing'.

There was plenty to do in preparation for the arrival of the school's first students, and much to learn. Neil was told to arrange a driver and some transport, and then to get around and find out as much as possible to broaden his knowledge on all the topics that he would be giving lectures on.

For the next month he travelled all over the country, learning as he went and collecting bits and pieces for his lectures along the way. He was also allowed to fly the school's aircraft, his most popular choices being a Spitfire XII, which he was well familiar with from his days commanding 41 Squadron, and a Grumman Hellcat fighter from the Royal Navy. He even found time to recover the silver Spitfire from Amiens and then deposit it back amongst the other aircraft types at Northolt. And, better still, he flew a captured Messerschmitt Bf 109 during a visit to the Air Fighting Development Unit at Wittering. It was a special moment in his flying career:

> I remember the cockpit being a bit small for even my normal-sized rump, but the aircraft was very nippy and pleasant to fly, although the thumping great 39-litre Daimler-Benz engine up front was somewhat rougher than the Merlin or even the Griffon engines in our Spitfires.

The first students were about to arrive at Old Sarum when Neil was suddenly given the news that he was off to Burma as part of a group of four, led by Brown's deputy, Brigadier 'Pip' Hicks. Although the possibility of a trip out to the Far East had been mentioned when he first arrived at the school, nothing more had been said since and so the news came as something of a surprise, particularly when he was told that he would be leaving within a few days and that he could expect to be gone for at least a month.

The long trip out to Burma, and back, was made in an RAF Douglas DC-3 Dakota. During his time away Neil visited many places, one notable visit being to Eastern Air Command, a combined British/American headquarters near Calcutta on the eastern side of India, to learn about the command's methods of operations. It was also an opportunity for Neil to meet up with his good friend and former colleague from 249 Squadron, 'Nick' Nicolson, who had won Fighter Command's only VC earlier in the war and was now a wing commander staff officer in EAC. Neil still remembers the meeting well:

> He was still his charming, noisy, garrulous self, and we enjoyed a riotous weekend together, with him telling outrageously untrue stories to his American colleagues about me being so successful a Battle of Britain fighter pilot. We ate stomach-searing curries, drank a lot of wine, put dead snakes in each other's beds, and generally behaved like a couple of adolescent delinquents.

Sadly, it was to be the last time the two would see each other. Nicolson was killed just days later when flying as a supernumerary crew member on an RAF B-24 Liberator, which crashed in the Bay of Bengal. Neil later described his friend Nick as 'his endlessly loquacious mate, and a most likeable, even-tempered and capable officer – a very bright star, which suddenly went out'.

While out in the Far East, Neil managed to fly the Hurricane II on a couple of bombing sorties with the Indian Air Force. These were flown from Akyab, an airfield in the Arakan on the west coast of Burma, so that Neil could see for himself just how the army and air force worked together during their fight against the Japanese. The sorties proved in the main to be uneventful, but the targets were, to his untrained eye, almost impossible to see. They had been attacking a Japanese headquarters hidden in a series of jungle ravines. Neil later wrote:

> Over the targets, I just followed my leader. From about 5,000 feet above jungle level, we each dived steeply into

each ravine before releasing our bombs at the lowest possible height, and then climbed at full power up the side of the steep jungle-clad cliff-faces praying that we had enough speed to totter over the top, the trees meanwhile seemed always to be reaching out to snatch at us as we limped by. I never did see my targets or the effects of my bombs, and I am sure the Japanese were not in the least inconvenienced by my bombing efforts.

Being an area of jungle-covered hills, with its narrow coastal strip of rice fields and mangrove swamps, and the monsoon, this was not at all a comfortable place to fly over in a single-engine fighter. It was not an environment Neil particularly enjoyed. Nonetheless, his two sorties had provided him with invaluable experience, on which he would base some of his lectures at the school.

Neil arrived back at Old Sarum in mid-April. Three weeks later, the war in Europe was over. Then, on Sunday 3 June 1945, just a month before Neil's twenty-fifth birthday, he and Eileen got married, the service being held in the attractive parish church of St Mary-the-Virgin, at Kenton in Middlesex. The next two weeks were spent on honeymoon in the small coastal village of Sennen Cove in Cornwall. Neil was not eligible for service married accommodation – married quarters were for those in more privileged positions – and so newly-weds like the Neils were left to find their own homes.

With the war in Europe over, Eileen was in the process of leaving the WAAF and so they moved into rented accommodation in the New Forest. Neil stayed at Old Sarum as an instructor until the end of the year. He enjoyed lecturing, and was very good at it, but as soon as the war in the Far East was over he knew that it would not be long before it was time for him to move on once more. He was keen to stay in the post-war RAF, he was certain of that, and wanted to return to flying as soon as possible, but there was much confusion when it came to postings in the immediate aftermath of the war and so he had no idea what the future might be.

Neil thought it would be best to find something for himself before someone else decided for him, and something that would provide

Wedding day, 3 June 1945.

him with some stability until everything settled down. He was a good pilot, he knew that, and he had already flown several different aircraft types, particularly during his time with the Americans the year before, even though he was still only twenty-five. He had enjoyed flying them all. He had also enjoyed his brief time air testing previously damaged aircraft while he had been at Ibsley to help the maintenance unit nearby, and he felt that he had a keen interest in, and natural ability for, that sort of flying. And so Neil applied to be a test pilot.

Given his background it is not surprising that he was successful in his application. Neil was initially selected for a course that was due to start in just a matter of weeks, but his commandant, Bingo Brown, was not keen for him to leave the school quite so soon. Neil explains:

> Bingo Brown, in fact, tried to talk me, and my wife for that matter, out of becoming a test pilot altogether, feeling that it would not be the best move for my career. But, with all that was going on in the maelstrom of the post-war era, when those intending to stay in the RAF were grabbing all the best jobs for themselves, I just wanted to get away and into a flying post before someone else determined what I was to do next.

As for the silver Spitfire, the saga had continued. Various ideas of how to dispose of it quietly had led to nothing and so he continued to fly the aircraft until it eventually ended up at Worthy Down. Then finally, through a friend of a friend, Neil arranged to have it picked up and flown out to Germany and it was last known to be in the hands of the Poles. What happened to it after that became a story of great interest following an article written by Neil in 1982 for the popular aviation magazine *Aeroplane Monthly*, which received letters of interest from all over. The rest is best told in Neil's book *The Silver Spitfire*.

Chapter Thirteen

Testing Times

At the end of the Second World War, there were three main air-testing establishments in Britain: the Aeroplane and Armament Experimental Establishment at Boscombe Down, where aircraft and equipment intended for service use were tested; the Royal Aircraft Establishment at Farnborough, which carried out all experimental work on aircraft and equipment; and the Marine Aircraft Experimental Establishment at Felixstowe, where there was still considerable interest in flying boats and other maritime craft.

Air testing had come a long way in a short period of time. One of the biggest developments had been the establishment of the Empire Test Pilots' School in 1943 at Boscombe Down after the deaths of many pilots during the testing of new aircraft about to enter military service. Initially called the Test Pilots' Training Flight and then the Test Pilots' Training School, it was the first school in the world dedicated to teaching test flying and came under the A&AEE organisation. The school was set up to provide suitably trained pilots for testing duties in aeronautical research and development establishments within the military services and industry. Its title soon changed again, this time to the Empire Test Pilots' School, as it is still known today. Then, after the war, the ETPS was moved to Cranfield in Bedfordshire, due to the rapid expansion of the A&AEE at Boscombe Down. This was increasingly disrupting the students' training so it had been decided that the school would be better off elsewhere.

Cranfield was a pre-war airfield and had ample administrative, domestic and maintenance facilities, with classrooms, large hangars and comfortable messes. Rationing was still in force and so every effort would have to be made to make the food as good as possible, but other than that Cranfield was considered ideal for the training of test pilots. By the end of the year preparations were complete for the school to receive its first students.

Neil arrived at Cranfield at the beginning of January 1946 to join No. 4 Course, the first course to be run from the school's new home. He had been fortunate to find somewhere nearby for Eileen to live. She had now moved up to Bedfordshire and was living in a pub in Cranfield. And there was even better news. The couple were expecting their first child. Everything was going incredibly well.

The thirty-four students on the course were mostly RAF but there were also seven pilots from the Royal Navy's Fleet Air Arm and one Canadian. They had all been assessed as 'above average' pilots and had a varying number of flying hours depending on their background, although for most all their flying had been carried out on just a handful of aircraft types and generally in one role, such as on fighters or bombers. Some were decorated fighter aces like himself, one being Neville Duke, then a flight lieutenant, with a DSO and three DFCs, who would later go on to become the holder of the world air speed record.

The move to Cranfield had prompted a much-needed change in the school's fleet with a naturally greater accent on jet aircraft. Gloster Meteors and de Havilland Vampires had been added to the inventory, although the Oxford and North American Harvard continued to be the staple advanced trainers. Avro Lancasters and Spitfires were also indispensable but there was a greater influx of naval types, including the Fairey Firefly and a Seafire 46, quite the most fearsome version of the Spitfire yet to fly.

Altogether the school had thirty-three aircraft of seventeen different types. Such a diverse array of aircraft types would give the students a wide range of experience and idiosyncrasies with which to cope, which was one of the main purposes of the course. The future test pilots would learn to become critics of an aircraft by analysing its performance and capabilities on the ground before flying it and assessing its handling qualities in the air – anything from a small single-engine aircraft to a four-engine heavy bomber to the most modern jet fighter.

There were many lectures to endure, involving mathematics and physics, and topics such as aerodynamics and engine theory. Because the students were expected to fly many different aircraft types while on the course, the Harvard was used to convert those with bomber or maritime experience onto the school's fighters, while the Oxford was used to covert the fighter pilots, such as Neil, onto multi-engine types. It says much about the calibre of student selected, and of the quality of tuition provided, that there would be no serious accidents during the course. There were also many long reports to write as well as several exams. In fact, much of the first three months of the course was spent in the classroom. And for every hour flown in the air there were three or four hours spent preparing for the flight and after that writing the report.

Jet aircraft were still very new and so there was a great deal for the students to learn. The school's Meteors were powered by the early Derwent III engine, and there were many lectures on the principles of the new jet engine. These were often given by the school's commandant, Group Captain Hugh 'Willie' Wilson, a legend in the test-pilot world, having been the RAF's chief test pilot for captured enemy aircraft during the war and the first man to exceed 600 mph in flight, which he achieved in a Meteor. As with many young pilots of his era, Neil found the whole jet engine thing fascinating. He described the lectures as being 'both mind-boggling and mysterious'.

Having been fed all sorts of facts, figures, information, horror stories and just about everything else, the students were finally given the opportunity to take to the air in the Meteor:

> Cowed almost into submission by such lurid mis-information, we took to the air in these fearsome aircraft, only to find they were very much like other types of aircraft, only faster, smoother, and very much quieter! Thinking back, I do not remember encountering any technical or

other difficulties on those first Meteors. However, I do recall that, in terms of handling, those early Mark 3s were the most miserable aircraft I had ever flown, with controls so leaden and stick forces so great that a pilot needed an extra set of muscles to make even the most straightforward circuit and landing.

There was no dual instruction on the Meteor. The students were simply told and shown how the aircraft worked, and off they went. Neil flew four hours on the type during the course and although it might have been a difficult introduction to the Meteor, he would later grow to love the aircraft.

In May, after five months of intensive training, the course suddenly ended. Twenty-one of the students were hurriedly passed out of what was now being termed No. 4 (Short) Course and posted to their new units, having learnt the rudiments of performance testing but little more. The others, including Neil, were retained at Cranfield as students for the new long course about to be introduced, which was to start in the next few weeks and last nine months. However, because of the training they had already completed on the short course, the thirteen students selected were not required to join the other members of No. 5 Course until the second term, due to start in September.

Neil would spend his time waiting to join the long course taking some leave and flying as much as he could to put into practice what he had been taught so far. He had, so far, flown a total of just over thirty hours on ten different types at Cranfield: Tiger Moth, Harvard, Spitfire, Firefly, Oxford, Mosquito, Dakota, Lancaster, Meteor and Hawker Tempest. It was in a Tempest II that Neil flew his first test flight in earnest on 2 July. Unfortunately, though, it was to be an occasion he would remember for the wrong reason. Neil explains:

> Having started up, I taxied out across the grass towards the take-off point. I had just braked to a stop to run up my engine when, out of the cloud directly in front of me, a Meteor appeared, tumbling, and spinning to destruction, to crash in a chaos of smoke and debris, less than a mile

from where I sat. Needless to say, I was stunned, horrified, and suddenly very quirky in the stomach. What a start, for heaven's sake!

Neil had just witnessed the death of a Polish test pilot, Squadron Leader Antoni Majcherczyk, a former bomber pilot who had been carrying out spinning trials in a Meteor 3. Neil had only been talking to him an hour or so before.

Sadly, Majcherczyk's death would not be the last he would witness during his time as a test pilot, far from it. But he knew that he had to be professional and carry on. There was nothing he nor anyone else could do to help the young Pole, except keep on with the work they believed in. So Neil took off and continued his own flight in the Tempest, which did go as planned.

The following day, Eileen gave birth to their son, Terence, and Neil went on leave. There had been talk of him being posted to the Flight Division of the Royal Aircraft Establishment at Farnborough, known as the 'Aero Flight', but Neil really wanted to go to Boscombe Down; he much preferred the area. Also, he had now officially been told that his application to remain in the post-war RAF had been successful, although the permanent commission he had been granted was with the substantive rank of flight lieutenant with his seniority backdated only as far as September 1945.

This was quite normal for those staying in the RAF after the war. Wartime rank was rarely carried over, and so there was a brief period when Neil had to drop back a rank, but given that he had served as a squadron leader for so long during the war it was only a short-term measure and he was soon allowed to put up the rank of squadron leader once more, albeit it was officially only acting rank at that time and he would have to wait a while longer before it became substantive.

It was soon time for Neil and his short-course colleagues to join the twenty-two members already established on No. 5 Course. These included students from overseas air forces – from Canada, America, Australia, China, Holland and Greece – as well as civilian pilots from aircraft manufacturers. Also, the school's instructional staff had been strengthened by the addition of two qualified flying instructors, two navigators and two flight engineers. All were qualified on the four-engine Lancaster, and its successor the Avro Lincoln, so that the students flying these types would benefit from having an experienced crew to work alongside them, whereas previously the students had been left to muddle along as best they could. Flying tutors were also appointed, all squadron leaders and with recent test-flying experience at Boscombe Down. This tutorial system would prove particularly successful, not least for the foreign students.

Even though Neil was only required to complete the last six months of the long course, it inevitably meant more learning and more analysing. But at least there was more flying as well, although this was severely disrupted by the most devastating winter for many years. With plenty of snow and strong winds causing drifts several feet high, the weather was so bad, in fact, that all flying at Cranfield ceased for several days, while several RAF stations elsewhere were closed.

The final month of the course was spent touring major aircraft companies around the country, by which time Neil had flown a similar number of hours, and on the same types, as he had on the short course. He had made several new friends along the way and having overseas students on the course had been fun, despite the occasional language problems and cultural differences due to the mix of nationalities. Overall, though, the last few months had not been the most memorable for Neil. When summarising his days at ETPS learning to be a test pilot, he recalls:

> I cannot honestly say that either course did very much for me, the first being totally disorganised because of the move, and the second not very much better. The only bright spot in an otherwise protracted period of classroom learning and amateurish test flying, was the erudition of our little Welsh tutor and boffin, Maclaren Humphreys, whose knowledge of aerodynamics was awe-inspiring and whose patience and teaching were quite beyond reproach.

It was now March 1947 and with his training as a test pilot over, Neil went straight to Boscombe Down. The A&AEE then had 176 aircraft on charge, almost randomly parked around the airfield due to the lack of hangar space for them all. With his background, Neil joined 'A' Squadron, broadly speaking the fighter element, under the command of Wing Commander Johnny Baldwin, another highly decorated wartime fighter ace.

The squadron had more than twenty aircraft, including Meteor 3s, some new Meteor 4s, and a Vampire. There were also some later marks of Spitfire, including a Mark XIX for a special high-altitude radar task and a Mark 22 which was being evaluated as a potential ground-attack aircraft, as well as Tempests, a de Havilland Rapide, known in the military as the Dominie and used for communications purposes, and a rather strange looking Auster prototype.

Rather interestingly, though, Neil's first flight at A&AEE was in a two-seat Spitfire. He had arrived at the hangar that morning to find the bright yellow Spitfire with the civil registration of G-AIDN parked outside. It turned out that Vickers-Armstrongs had saved a few Mark VIIIs and Mark XIXs and had now converted them as trainers for the overseas market. Neil was rather intrigued and so he flew the aircraft from both front and rear cockpits, down to Tangmere and back with one of his former ETPS course colleagues, Flight Lieutenant Ian Crozier.

Neil had thought that would be the last he would see or hear of the aircraft, but more than forty years later he was delighted to learn that the same Spitfire was still flying in America. It was pleasing to know that it had survived the scrapheap, unlike so many others. He had the misfortune to witness the demise of several Mark VIIIs during a visit to High Ercall, where he had earlier introduced the Mark XII into service while in command of 41 Squadron. He clearly remembers watching in silence as a man with a blowtorch went up and down the flight line cutting each aircraft in two.

It was a busy first month for Neil at Boscombe Down as he was introduced to the RAF's new jet fighter, the Vampire, and for the next three years he would spend seemingly half of his life in one. It was the RAF's first jet fighter to be powered by a single engine, the de Havilland Goblin turbojet producing just over 3,000 lb of thrust, and, as with the introduction of any new aircraft type into service, it was continuously being modified and its weaponry and stores improved. Neil later described the Vampire as a 'squat, rather ugly-looking aircraft' and although it was extremely easy and pleasant to fly, he found its performance to be well down on that of the Meteor 4.

However, an experimental version of the Vampire, powered by a significantly more powerful Rolls-Royce Nene engine of around 5,000 lb thrust, was delivered to Boscombe Down for evaluation. This was TG280, a far nippier aircraft and capable of reaching more than 50,000 feet. Neil first flew TG280 that summer and soon became involved in high-altitude trials for the development of pressurised cockpits, which frequently involved flying above 40,000 feet. He recalls:

> At such a breathless height there would be no apparent movement and almost complete silence. Then, when I was least expecting it, the pressure cabin relief valve would give out a hearty 'PAHHH', which never failed to make me almost jump out of my skin.

An unofficial and unsuccessful attempt had already been made to get the Vampire up to what would then have been a world record height of more than 56,000 feet. Neil remembers the Vampire well, although he always thought it a shame that it did not have just that little bit extra. It later did, by which time it had become the Venom.

One of the lesser known aircraft to be flown by Neil during his time as a test pilot was the MB5 fighter. Now better known for manufacturing ejection seats, the Martin-Baker aircraft company produced a short series of innovative fighter prototypes during the Second World War, with the MB5 being the ultimate development aircraft:

> With an underslung radiator and wide, robust undercarriage, it was somewhat reminiscent of the North American P-51D

Mustang, but differed in that it had shortish, high-lift clipped wings and a big six-bladed contra-rotating airscrew. With a Griffon 60-series engine, its performance was like that of the Spitfire Mark 22. I liked it a lot, as it flew beautifully, and one could see out of it, which is more than could be said of some of the earlier Spits. Moreover, all the panels, of which there were many, could be removed with a small coin, making it a particularly attractive proposition for servicing and maintenance in the field.

Unfortunately, though, despite the fact that the test pilots and engineers seemed to like it, the MB5 would never go into production. Like other similar types, it simply came at the wrong time and was overtaken by the advent of the jet. The MB5 disappeared almost as quickly as it had arrived.

Being so close to the government's research facility at Porton Down, where the testing of chemical weapons was being carried out, meant Boscombe Down's test pilots were, at times, involved with the laying down of smoke and other more toxic horrors over the Porton range. These flights required the weather and wind conditions to be just right and were normally carried out in a Tempest II. Great care was always taken for obvious reasons, but Neil had a scare one day during start-up.

The Tempest required an electrically operated cartridge starter to get its big Bristol Centaurus 18-cylinder radial engine going. Having primed the engine and set the throttle, Neil fired the starter cartridge and watched the airscrew, expecting it to fire into life. But nothing happened except for the sound of a rather unusual crack.

The first sense of there being something wrong was when Neil saw his two groundcrew running away. He then became aware of something potentially unpleasant billowing under the wing, and so Neil was soon off too, not an easy thing to do when strapped into a cockpit high up off the ground. Fearing a disaster, the station alarm sounded for the next half an hour until the situation was declared safe. It turned out to be a simple electrical fault on the aircraft and

The Martin-Baker MB5 prototype, one of the lesser known aircraft
flown by Neil as a test pilot.

there was no danger of a chemical incident, but the memory of that
day has never gone away.

If supporting trials at Porton Down was one of the more hazardous
tasks of being a test pilot, then one of the more fun tasks at Boscombe
Down, although no less dangerous, was to establish the position
error correction factor for the airspeed indicator of each aircraft
being evaluated. This was because most evaluations required absolute
precision flying, and so it was essential to determine that the speed of
the aircraft was correct.

In simple terms, the airspeed indicator shows the speed of the
aircraft by using a pitot head, mounted on the aircraft at a position
least affected by disturbed airflow, such as ahead of the wing or in
the nose. The pitot measures the difference between the dynamic
pressure (due to the speed of the aircraft) and the static pressure. The
air pressure at the static port is conveyed to the airspeed indicator and
the aircraft's altimeter but differs at altitude. In an ideal static system,
the air pressure fed to the altimeter and airspeed indicator is equal to
the pressure of the air at the altitude at which the aircraft is flying.

And because air pressure can easily be measured on the ground, the test pilot's task was to fly the aircraft throughout its speed range as close to the ground as possible so that the boffins, armed with their equipment in the air traffic control tower, could take appropriate measurements. Neil recalls:

> Even the Meteors and Vampires of the late 1940s could reach speeds of up to 550 mph in level flight at less than 50 feet above the ground. Such tests were usually carried out in the evenings when air turbulence was less severe and there was no other flying activity in the area – aircraft zipping across the middle of the airfield at 500-plus mph could clearly not be tolerated during normal flying hours. Moreover, at those speeds and at that height very accurate flying and great concentration was demanded of the pilot.

Amongst the many other tasks Neil carried out from Boscombe Down was a series of gunnery and bombing sorties in the Spitfire Mark 22 over the firing range at Lyme Bay in Dorsetshire. But it was not only the A&AEE's Spitfires that he flew. Occasionally, the test pilots were invited to nearby Chilbolton, used by Vickers-Armstrongs, to fly some of the later marks of Spitfire that were still at the airfield. The company was concentrating more on the advent of the jet fighter and had effectively ended its interest in the Spitfire, and so there was plenty of flying to be had. Amongst the variants available to be flown were Mark 21s, 22s and 24s, mostly with five-bladed airscrews although some had six-bladed contra-rotating props. Neil loved the look of the later marks of Spit, although he found them not so pleasant to fly:

> In my opinion, those late Spitfires were the most beautiful aircraft ever designed; with their enormous spinners, teardrop hoods, cutaway fuselage and enlarged tails, they looked absolutely right. Unfortunately, I found them less attractive to fly. Considerably heavier than the original

Spitfire, with their Griffon 60-series engines, they had much more than twice the power and a maximum performance approaching 500 mph at altitude. I could never get used to the harshness of the grumbling Griffon.

In addition to the later marks of Spit, Neil also flew the Griffon-powered Supermarine Spiteful, the planned successor to the Spitfire, and its naval counterpart, the Seafang. Aircraft designers had long realised that the characteristics of the Spitfire's wing would ultimately limit its performance at very high speed, and so this eventually led to development of the Spiteful XIV and its order into production (there were no earlier marks, the designation simply carried on from the original Spitfire XIV conversion).

As things turned out, though, the advent of jet propulsion and the development of the jet fighter resulted in the order being cancelled, and so very few Spitefuls were ever built. But it was not clear at the time whether jet fighters would ever be able to operate successfully from naval carriers and so it was decided to develop a naval version of the aircraft, the Seafang, with folding wingtips, an arrester hook and two three-bladed contra-rotating propellers.

However, with the Vampire having already demonstrated that it could operate from a carrier, and with the subsequent development of the Sea Vampire jet fighter, there was soon no longer a requirement for the Seafang. Nonetheless, the Spiteful and Seafang had both been interesting aircraft to fly. They differed from the Spitfire in that they were designed with laminar-flow straight wings, incorporating powered ailerons. Neil remembers flying the Seafang F.32, with its six-bladed contra-rotating airscrew, and considered it to have been a most impressive aircraft in the air.

With the Spiteful having been rejected by the RAF, Supermarine designed a jet aircraft around the Rolls-Royce Nene engine, but using the Spiteful's wings and undercarriage. Initially referred to as the Jet Spiteful, the aircraft soon became known as the Attacker. The prototype, TS409, which Neil also flew that year, arrived on 'A' Squadron for evaluation, although it was soon moved across to

'C' Squadron, the naval element at Boscombe Down, as the Attacker was destined to be the Royal Navy's first jet fighter.

Neil remembers the Attacker as being about as fast as the Meteor 4, but rather heavier in the air, and the Nene engine was known to make an unusual sound, which was put down to something odd happening in the air intakes either side of the cockpit. The sad end to the story of the Attacker, though, happened some months later when Neil was the acting superintendent of flying. He was out on the airfield when he heard the chilling sound of an aircraft overhead, travelling very fast but clearly out of control. Looking up, he recognised the aircraft to be an Attacker, TS413 as it happened, the first naval prototype, which was heading downwards like a dart before it then impacted the ground with a devastating explosion not far from the airfield boundary.

Neil was first on the scene, but there was nothing he could do. All that was left was a smoking crater. It was another horrific moment in his life, particularly so because the pilot, Lieutenant Commander Tobias 'Spike' King-Joyce, was a former course colleague of Neil's from the ETPS. Neil remembers him as a delightful, dark-haired and burly Southern Irishman. King-Joyce had been undertaking handling trials. He had been operating at high speed at around 6,000 feet when the tail section broke up. Without an ejection seat, he had been unable to abandon the aircraft. Neil recalls: 'Later there was talk of rudder overbalance, the adverse effect of carrying a new ventral tank, and much else besides, all of which sounded very strange to those of us who had flown the aircraft and witnessed the accident.'

Because he was required to fly in all kinds of weather, as well as teach and supervise others flying in poor weather conditions, Neil took time out of the busy test-flying schedule to attend the Empire Flying School at Hullavington near Chippenham in Wiltshire, to receive specialist training in bad-weather flying.

The school was primarily responsible for maintaining the standards of flying instruction at the many flying schools across the world. Neil attended No. 18 (Instrument Weather) Course, which lasted ten weeks and involved many hours of practising and perfecting instrument-flying techniques and procedures. These exercises were flown in the single-engine Harvard (thirty-one exercises, a total of twenty-eight flying hours) and the twin-engine Oxford (twenty-two exercises, twenty-five hours), although Neil also flew a handful of sorties in a Spitfire, a Meteor and a Bristol Buckmaster.

In the same way that the Spitfire was coming to the end of its service life, so too was the Mosquito, although it would be retained on some squadrons for a while longer as a night fighter. Neil was not particularly fond of the Mosquito. Its success had led to many variations and with extra equipment it had, over time, become a much heavier aircraft to fly.

Among the several Mosquitos belonging to 'A' Squadron, two remain vividly in Neil's mind. One, a PR.34, was at Boscombe Down for a special radar task rather than for flight testing. This involved a fair amount of high-altitude flying and so many hours were spent in the freezing cold because of the aircraft's inadequate heating. The other was an NF.38, the last night-fighter variant, which was fitted with all the latest radar equipment.

He found that everything was fine in the Mossie provided that both engines were behaving, but should an engine fail on take-off, for example, it was not a nice place to be. He would also glance across to the lower right-hand corner of the cockpit and wonder how he might get out of the aircraft through the small nose escape hatch should it ever become necessary, while wearing his bulky parachute, and then avoid the whirling airscrew beyond; getting stuck in the hole or being decapitated by the propeller seemed very real possibilities.

It was in a Mosquito that another of Neil's former course colleagues nearly died. Peter Lawrence, the chief test pilot of the Blackburn Aircraft company, had allowed his engines to overspeed and exceed 3,600 rpm. Neil still remembers the high-pitched wail, which could be heard on the ground for miles around. But although he had been lucky that day, Lawrence would sadly lose his life a few years later after joining the Gloster Aircraft Company when he was killed while test-flying a prototype Javelin.

Peter Lawrence was one of many of Neil's former course colleagues at ETPS to lose their life while test-flying; ten were killed within five years of completing the test-pilot course. Another was Peter Garner, Westland's assistant chief test pilot, who was killed flying the prototype single-seat W.34 Wyvern TF.1, a carrier-based multi-role strike aircraft, when the propeller bearings failed in flight. Garner had been attempting a forced-landing in a field just short of the airfield.

Then there was Boulton Paul's chief test pilot, Robert Lindsay Neale, remembered by Neil as a pleasant and urbane gentleman, who was killed flying a Balliol T.2 advanced two-seat military trainer, which was to replace some of the Harvards in service with the RAF. During 'A' Squadron's evaluation of the Balliol, a frequent observation had been that the front windscreen appeared to bend at high speed. After the company had reassured the pilots that everything had checked out to be in order, the trials continued, but there were always some nagging doubts. Finally, as the Balliol was nearing the end of its evaluation schedule, Neale and a colleague were flying the aircraft when it went out of control, and at high speed the canopy reportedly collapsed, killing both crew members on board.

Another death of a former course colleague to be witnessed by Neil was that of Squadron Leader Philip Evans, a test pilot with 'B' Squadron, who was testing a four-engine Handley Page Hastings C.1 with two others on board. Neil was returning to Boscombe Down in a Vampire at the time. The weather was good, and he could see several aircraft in the circuit above the airfield. Neil then noticed one larger aircraft, which he then identified as the Hastings, doing some rather unusual things. He recalls:

> The aircraft would claw its way into a stall-turn, the nose would then fall away into a dive, followed by a swooping pull-out and climb, the Hastings all the time getting closer to the ground. Finally, it failed to recover from its last agonising swoop and crashed in a chaos of fragments and dust on Beacon Hill, yards to the north of the airfield.

It transpired that an underslung belly pannier being carried on the aircraft had torn off and hit the tail, causing the aircraft to become uncontrollable and crash. Sadly, the list of others to lose their life went on.

Occasionally, Neil flew with the heavies of 'B' Squadron. This usually came about if the squadron requested an opinion from someone who was not necessarily familiar with an aircraft type. The process worked the same way for the heavy pilots to join 'A' Squadron for an evaluation but, for some reason, those on 'B' seemed less inclined to accept an invitation.

On one occasion, Neil was asked by 'B' Squadron to evaluate the Bristol Brigand, designed as a twin-engine anti-shipping torpedo-bomber and the planned successor to the Beaufighter. The end of the war had meant that Coastal Command no longer needed a coastal anti-shipping aircraft and so it was decided to convert the Brigand to become a light bomber, destined for overseas.

During his evaluation, Neil found the aircraft had a stability issue and tended to wander around the sky, a characteristic not at all to his liking. His subsequent report turned out to be what those on 'B' Squadron had expected, and his opinion merely confirmed that of others. Neil later learned that a Brigand had crashed earlier during the trials, killing the pilot, after the aircraft had become uncontrollable in flight. Neil had been away at the time and so he had not heard about the incident, and no one had thought of mentioning it to him before his flight. He was not impressed.

In addition to the transition from piston-powered flight to the jet engine, the late 1940s were also dominated by the quest for high-speed, high-altitude flight. This era brought a whole range of challenges for designers, not least the aircraft-handling and structural problems associated with such extreme conditions of flight. On the aircraft-handling side, for example, power-assisted controls were virtually unknown at the time, and so the flying control surfaces – ailerons, elevators and rudder – had to be carefully balanced aerodynamically, to enable the pilot to operate them manually with a reasonable degree of ease throughout the entire speed range of the aircraft.

Aircraft were now capable of reaching altitudes of 50,000 feet and above, at which heights and temperatures both men and materiel had not been designed to operate. Ideas of how to keep the pilot alive at such extreme altitudes and temperatures were still very much in the infant stage. The pressurised cockpit, for example, which maintained the pressure inside the cockpit at a safe level, was still in the early stages of design, as were anti-icing and heating systems. However, in the case of an emergency, such as the loss of the canopy, the poor pilot was offered no protection against the elements at all.

In addition to the problem of extremely cold temperatures, which could be as low as –65 °C, the oxygen content at high altitude is so limited that the human body cannot function. The pilot's chance of surviving an emergency at high altitude was almost zero.

Considerable work was being done to rectify this problem at the RAF's recently established Institute of Aviation Medicine at Farnborough in collaboration with their American counterparts at Wright-Patterson Air Force Base in Dayton, Ohio. In July 1948, a small team of three, including Neil, went out to the United States to experiment with a capstan pressure suit, designed by the two nations to compensate for an explosive decompression at very high altitude. In the event of a decompression the suit would activate automatically and so provide the pilot with an internal oxygen supply and external pressure on the body in balanced amounts, allowing him to survive while descending to a safer height.

With Neil being the only pilot in the team, he was to be the guinea pig for the trial, while the two other members were both from Farnborough: Squadron Leader Harry Roxburgh, an eminent chemist, physiologist, and doctor of medicine, and a Mr London, an engineer and expert in small-valve technology.

Their work in America lasted twelve weeks, during which Neil was fitted with a moulded headpiece, which incorporated a sealed visor and some rather complicated valves. He remembers the whole contraption being rather bulky, restricting and unpleasantly claustrophobic. He also had a special nylon suit made, which was initially worn next to the skin and, like the helmet, was incredibly uncomfortable to wear. Neil recalls what he had to go through during the various trials:

The capstan pressure suit, which Neil trialled at Wright-Patterson
Air Force Base, USA, in 1948.

The many experiments carried out in the pressure chambers
at Wright-Patterson were both instructive and fraught.
The delicate and sensitive valves were by no means fool-
proof at first. Being explosively decompressed to the
equivalent of 80,000–100,000 feet, with no guarantee
that the equipment was going to work when you got there,
produced some heart-stopping moments. Moreover, as the
natural function of breathing was reversed, which meant
having to exhale forcibly, there were occasions when mild
panic resulted in moments of stress.

With the tests over, Neil returned to England to spend some time
with his family; their second son, Patrick, had been born just as he
was leaving for the United States. In conjunction with the doctors,

Neil's two new pressurised suits were then modified and improved, although he was never able to test them in the air because the required cockpit equipment had not been perfected by the time his tour at Boscombe Down was at an end. He was, however, due to demonstrate the new suit to HM King George VI, only for the demonstration to be cancelled the day before because the king was unwell.

Neil returned to Boscombe Down in October to be told that he was to conduct the evaluation of two aircraft in competition to replace the Tiger Moth as the RAF's next *ab initio* trainer. One was the Fairey Primer and the other was the de Havilland Canada DHC-1 Chipmunk. It was clearly not a popular evaluation as far as his fellow test pilots were concerned but, having just had three months in America, Neil was given the task.

Two prototypes of each type were made available for the evaluation. Neil had already flown one of the Chipmunk prototypes, CF-D10-X, soon after he had arrived at A&AEE, when the two aircraft were first brought across to Britain still bearing their Canadian civil registrations. This aircraft had since been registered as G-AKDN, while the other Chipmunk was G-AJVD. As for the two Primers, one was still carrying its experimental number G-6-5 while the other had the civil registration of G-ALBL.

Neil flew each aircraft several times. On one day in November, for example, he flew four sorties to evaluate their take-off and landing characteristics. Neil recalls:

> It soon became evident that the Chipmunk was the more solid and workmanlike design, although each type flew well enough and in terms of performance and handling, the two were fairly evenly matched. There were, however, other considerations, such as ease of maintenance and other peripheral factors. Consequently, without much debate, the Chipmunk was selected.

Designated the Chipmunk T.10, this tandem two-seat single-engine primary trainer served the RAF with distinction for nearly fifty years. Some forty years after he had first flown the Chipmunk at Boscombe Down, Neil was reunited with the same aircraft, G-AKDN, by then privately owned.

Nowadays, combat aircraft break the sound barrier with ease, but back in the late 1940s the apprehensions of flying at such speeds were very real. Without going too far into the theory of aerodynamics in flight, shock waves develop when an aircraft (or any projectile) approaches the speed of sound, which at sea level occurs around 760 mph (but less at altitude), with an enormous increase in drag. Quite simply, if the aircraft's thrust is sufficient to overcome the increased drag encountered during transonic flight then the speed of sound will be exceeded.

However, during Neil's time as a test pilot at Boscombe Down the thrust of aircraft in service was never sufficient to break through the sound barrier, even when in a dive. And so, when flying at very high speed, shock waves would break away from parts of the aircraft where the airstream had accelerated to sonic speed, such as curved surfaces, causing all sorts of trim changes and sometimes some very unpleasant buffeting and shaking. The Meteor 4, for example, which Neil tested regularly, would exhibit strong changes of trim at high speed and became quite nasty with buffeting and shaking. This could, and did, lead to loss of control. As Neil says: 'It was not very nice!'

These flights took a lot of nerve. The pilot needed to use his controls and tail trimmer with great care, because when action was taken to recover the aircraft he could grossly overtax the wings and fuselage. Such were the risks of high-speed flight at the time that a policy was introduced whereby all experimental work exploring flight beyond the speed of sound was to be carried out in wind tunnels using models.

This policy simply reinforced Neil's belief that transonic flight was a fraught and deadly business, although he also believes that this decision, albeit well-meaning, simply resulted in the initiative being passed to the Americans and Russians, both of whom would move ahead of Britain in the development of high-speed flight.

Another of the less pleasant tasks of a test pilot was spinning. Fighter aircraft had to be put into spins, left and right, for two complete rotations before recovery action was initiated. For those aircraft destined to be trainers, the number was increased to a minimum of eight rotations. Neil recalls:

> Those eight spins – and often more – seemed endless and meant many tedious climbs and much whirling about and height being lost. Given that it had to be done, I preferred spinning fighters to trainers – at least it was over fairly quickly.

It was hoped that a spin would not develop into a series of flat gyrations, at which point the rudder, the vital control in any recovery, would be blanketed by the tail and rendered useless. And it was for this reason that prior to any spinning trial being conducted a parachute was fitted in the tail which, when deployed, had the effect of dragging up the rear of the aircraft to allow the rudder some air.

Sometimes, as with the Vampire, no two aircraft of the same type seemed to spin in quite the same way. This could be for several reasons. Even something as simple as the aircraft having been manufactured slightly differently during production could make a difference.

In addition to the normal spinning tests on the Vampire, Neil was also asked to investigate spinning off a turn and to broadcast his remarks as it happened. But flying in a Vampire F.1, TG275, Neil could not get the aircraft to do what he wanted. Several times he tried to put the aircraft into a spin off a tight turn, but all TG275 did was simply shudder and fall away. Eventually, though, but only after using as much force as he could muscle, he managed to get the aircraft to spin. However, after a couple of lightning flick-rolls the Vampire always ended up on an even keel. Furthermore, the gyrations were so swift that Neil could never squeeze out a word while the earth and sky flashed around his ears. Finally, he gave up and simply reported that the Vampire was almost impossible to spin off a turn and that anyone who managed to do so deserved everything he got.

Aircraft undergoing trials at the A&AEE that might one day be destined for service overseas required testing under tropical conditions. The Tropical Trials Unit was then based at Khartoum in the

Sudan where temperatures were guaranteed to be high, typically around 48 °C, and where the air content had an appropriate amount of sand.

Neil went to Khartoum in the summer of 1949 as part of the evaluation of the Avro Athena, which was in competition with the Boulton Paul Balliol to replace the Harvard as the RAF's new advanced trainer.

The day started early, around 6 a.m., so that the work could be over by the heat of midday, although occasionally it meant continuing into the afternoon if really high temperatures were required for the trial. Neil remembers all too well the Athena's tropical evaluation:

> Strangely, despite the often-unpleasant flying conditions, I have the happiest recollections of testing the Athena at Khartoum. Modern amenities were as scarce as a hen's teeth; there were few refrigerators or cooling devices throughout the base, so that working conditions were little short of intolerable. Life was especially trying for any test pilot obliged to endure ninety minutes sitting on the ground in an enclosed 'glasshouse' cockpit. In the air, engines were frequently tested to the full on such trials, which had coolant and oil temperatures off the clock and the Merlin engine positively panting.

The evaluation then moved on to the next stage, which was carried out at Eastleigh in Nairobi, Kenya. Although the airfield was almost on the Equator, it was at an altitude of 5,000 feet and so, like Khartoum, it proved to be a challenging environment for aero engines, albeit for differing reasons.

The journey from Khartoum to Nairobi took almost eight hours in the Athena via refuelling stops at Malaki, a remote landing strip bordering the Nile, Juba in southern Sudan, and Kisumu, near Lake Victoria in Uganda. Neil would later write:

> With endless wastes of desert, the wandering Nile and vast areas of swampland and tropical vegetation drifting

beneath, those were fascinating flights with some of the wonders of the world on display. On top of those, some of the worst weather in the world could boil up in a single morning into frightening cumulo-nimbus cloud barriers more than 40,000 feet high, emphasising the fact that tropical Africa was not a country to be trifled with when flying a lone, single-engine Athena!

Neil found life in Kenya to be quite civilised. He would later describe the vast yellow plains around Eastleigh as being 'a wonderland of nature seen to best advantage from the cockpit, and contrasted spectacularly with the stark, snow-capped beauty of Mount Kilimanjaro in the distance'.

With all testing complete, it was time to fly the Athena back to England, via Khartoum. The journey involved nine stop-offs and took more than twenty-six hours, leaving Neil with two everlasting memories: firstly, the sight of hundreds of tanks, vehicles and crashed aircraft, all abandoned in the desert, even though the war in North Africa had been over six years, and, secondly, landing at Istres in the south of France in a raging 70-mph Mistral wind, which he remembers making the landing run very short!

Evaluating the Athena was just about the last thing Neil did as a test pilot and his month-long trip overseas had been a great way to finish his tour. However, it is best left for Neil to sum up his thoughts about test flying in his own words:

> Far from being the death-or-glory existence so beloved of the Hollywood fiction industry, test flying was, and remains, a fairly routine business, carrying out an endless series of handling and performance sorties at differing heights and with the aircraft at various permutations of load and configuration.

While Neil modestly describes test flying as routine business, the fact remains it was also a very dangerous business to be in. During his time at Boscombe Down there were fifty-one major incidents, resulting in serious damage to both aircraft and pilots. Neil has the final word:

> It always seemed to us at the sharp end, so to speak, that those directly in control of our affairs should not only be qualified themselves but be thoroughly conversant with the precise nature of our work and what we were trying to achieve. Alas, it was seldom the case, official posting policy remaining strangely ambivalent in that respect. In those immediate post-war years, admittedly a period of change and uncertainty in the RAF, square pegs were thrust into round holes for reasons of expediency or through the exercise of influence. Sadly, it resulted in resentment and more than a few unnecessary problems. One way and another, test flying in those exciting times claimed many splendid lives. Looking back, I often feel that our efforts were not that much appreciated.

Chapter Fourteen

208 Squadron

With his time as a test pilot over, Neil arrived at Bentley Priory in January 1950 to take up his next appointment at Headquarters Fighter Command. He was pleased to have settled his family into a house at Flamstead, just to the north of Hemel Hempstead, and with Eileen expecting their third child there was much to look forward to.

Neil was posted to the Air Staff to work for Wing Commander Training, George Brown, under the overall command of the Senior Air Staff Officer, Air Vice-Marshal David Atcherley. As Training C, Neil was to be responsible for all instrument-flying training across Fighter Command.

It was now the early days of the Cold War and there existed a very real threat of attack against the United Kingdom from the Soviet Union's long-range bombers. All-weather flying was therefore an essential part of the RAF's capability. If accidents were to be avoided when flying in poor weather, particularly amongst student pilots, it was essential they were trained and supervised properly. An instrument rating, known as a green card, was introduced, which allowed qualified pilots to fly to certain weather minima, while other levels allowed student pilots to fly in poor weather conditions, taking into account their relative inexperience.

Even though he was in a staff appointment on a so-called ground tour, Neil would still get the opportunity to fly to keep current and maintain his flying proficiency. He flew four times in the first few weeks, twice in a Meteor and once in an Oxford, and on the fourth occasion he flew to Tangmere as co-pilot in a de Havilland Devon with Air Marshal Sir Basil Embry, his Air Officer Commander-in-Chief, as captain.

Although Neil had been posted to Fighter Command to be its specialist in instrument-flying training, it was not long after he arrived at Bentley Priory when he was given the additional task of organising an event then called the 'Royal Air Force Display.' This high-profile public-relations event was to be held at Farnborough in July and would provide an opportunity to raise money for the RAF Benevolent Fund.

Organising an event as big as this took a huge amount of work and just about all of Neil's time. He was even able to use it to his advantage and during the final month leading up to the event he flew fifteen times, in six different types, either to or from Farnborough as part of the final preparations. This included another trip in the Devon with his AOC-in-C when Neil took Embry down to Farnborough to see how things were going for himself.

Royal Air Force Display took place over two days, 7–8 July 1950, and was attended by anyone and everyone, including the royal family, senior politicians and the highest-ranking military officers, including many from overseas. All the RAF's latest aircraft were there on display for the public to see, alongside many of the aircraft that had become household names during the war, as well as veteran aircraft from the First World War.

With Neil giving the commentary – he looked the part and sounded the part – the public were treated to a magnificent flying display that could only be dreamt of today. Amongst the attractions were a demonstration of formation flying by four Harvard trainers from the Central Flying School; formation aerobatics by a team of four Meteors of 263 Squadron; more formation aerobatics by three Vampires from 54 Squadron; aerobatics by two Chipmunks from the Central Flying School; and individual aerobatic displays by a Vampire of 247 Squadron, a Meteor from No. 203 Advanced Flying School, and a Spitfire XVI of 17 Squadron. There was also a flypast of four veteran aircraft – a 1909 Blériot, a 1911 Deperdussin, a 1912 Blackburn, and a Sopwith Pup from 1916 – and a so-called Helicopter

Dignitaries at the huge Royal Air Force Display, 7 July 1950.

Circus from the Airborne Forces Experimental Establishment. There was a demonstration of airfield defence, showing a squadron scramble of twelve Meteor F.4s from 66 and 92 Squadrons to counter a simulated raid by an 'enemy force', made up of Mosquitos and de Havilland Hornets from seven different squadrons. And then there were flying demonstrations from four types of new jet aircraft representative of modern design trends: an experimental aircraft for trials with swept wings called the Hawker P.1052; a de Havilland Venom fighter-bomber; a Vickers-Armstrongs 510, an experimental prototype that led to the Supermarine Swift jet fighter; and the English Electric Canberra bomber.

At the end of the day, there were two mass flypasts involving aircraft and crews from several nations. The first was by aircraft of Coastal, Transport and Bomber Commands – Short Sunderlands, Dakotas, Hastings and Lincolns – followed by Boeing B-29 Superfortresses of the United States Air Force. Also included in the first flypast were a Lincoln of the Royal Australian Air Force, a Canadair North

Star from the Royal Canadian Air Force, a Dakota of the Indian Air Force, and two of the aircraft from Transport Command were flown by crews from the Royal New Zealand Air Force and the South African Air Force. The second flypast, which brought an end to the event, was a parade of fighters: Spitfires, Hornets, Vampires and Meteors. Included in the fighter flypast were jet fighters from Belgium and France, and two Hawker Furies of what was then the Royal Pakistan Air Force.

Not only was it all such a great spectacle in the air, the public could also visit the main hangar to see special exhibits illustrating various aspects of RAF activities and successes, including some of the outstanding peacetime achievements of the RAF, ranging from high speed flight during the inter-war years and its success in the Schneider Trophy, to the crossing of the Atlantic, to the work of Transport Command during the recent Berlin Air Lift of 1948–9. There were also demonstrations in fighter control, flight simulation, night-vision training, gunnery training, engine design, photography, the RAF's medical services, and aircraft servicing and maintenance. Meanwhile, in the smaller hangars there were more demonstrations highlighting the attraction of the RAF apprenticeship scheme and, for the younger generation, the Air Training Corps. Events throughout the day also included performances by various massed bands; a gliding demonstration by the ATC; a 3-inch mortar demonstration by the RAF Regiment; an aerobatics display flown by two Boulton Paul Balliol aircraft, which performed any normal aerobatic manoeuvre asked for by the spectators using a roving microphone passed through the enclosures; a massed physical training display; displays by RAF police dogs; and drill by the RAF Regiment. During the lunch-time interval, two photo-reconnaissance aircraft – a Spitfire XIX and a Mosquito XXXIV, took photographs of sections of the crowd that were later displayed in the Exhibition Hangar.

On the first day there was also the Cooper Trophy Race, an annual competition for the twenty Royal Auxiliary Air Force fighter squadrons, run over two laps of a closed circuit; a total distance of seventy-two miles. Eliminating heats had been held earlier in the summer and so eight squadrons competed in the final, with three representative types of aircraft – Spitfire, Meteor, and Vampire – handicapped according to performance. On the second day the RAuxAF carried out an event called Air Drill, the flying equivalent of precision movements carried out on a parade ground, demonstrating a high degree of discipline and flying skill. The aircraft taking part in this event were Vampires from two Auxiliary squadrons and Spitfires from three others.

It was a huge event, involving an enormous amount of work, and it had come at a busy time in Neil's life. His third son, Ian, was born in September and in the New Year came his substantive promotion to the rank of squadron leader.

Although his time at Bentley Priory was considered a ground tour, Neil somehow managed to fly seventy times during his work there. He even flew a Hurricane again, on 28 September 1951 for the record, from the nearby airfield at Bovingdon in Hertfordshire. The aircraft was LF363, a Mark IIC, which had been used by various station flights since the end of the Second World War. This aircraft is believed to have been the last Hurricane to enter service with the RAF and would soon become an original member of the Historic Aircraft Flight, now known as the Battle of Britain Memorial Flight, and LF363 is still thrilling crowds some seventy-odd years after its service debut.

Neil had done well as a staff officer and he was clearly showing the potential to reach air rank, and so he was selected to attend Staff College at Bracknell the following year. It was good news, although it would mean another move for the Neil family, this time to Camberley.

Staff College was, and remains, an essential part of an officer's career development. At the end of the Second World War it had been decided there was a need for two RAF staff colleges. The RAF's first staff college had been established at Andover just after the First World War, and now a second was established at Bracknell in Berkshire. Each college developed its own characteristics, but their fundamental attitudes were still rooted in the pre-war Andover tradition. By January 1952, when Neil arrived at Bracknell to join No. 42 Course, there was no specific reason as to why a student would be selected for one staff college rather than the other. Although the British Army and Royal Navy had their own staff colleges, at Camberley and Greenwich respectively, there were still a handful of Army and Navy students on the RAF's course, as well as some from overseas, bringing the total number of students on Neil's course to nearly a hundred.

They all gathered on the opening day to listen attentively to the welcome address by the Commandant, Air Vice-Marshal Alan 'Peter' Gillmore. At first glance, the slightly built and bald commandant may not have had the physical presence of some senior officers, but he was a ready and entertaining speaker, a clear and decisive man, who instantly came across with great personal charm and kindness.

Staff College not only helped Neil broaden his knowledge of the RAF, but it also gave him a better understanding of national defence as a whole. While lectures formed a considerable portion of the teaching, the bulk of the instruction was given in syndicates, taking into consideration the varying backgrounds and experience of the students, and there were many exercises to be completed. The course content was much as expected for the development of a senior officer, focusing on written and oral communications, as well as presentations on the organisation of the RAF and its personnel. There were also lectures on the importance of mobility for the RAF, which included supply and movements, and the maintenance of equipment, and there were lectures on all aspects of warfare, including naval and land warfare, which included the history of smaller conflicts.

These lectures brought into discussion the political and economic environments, including the introduction of international law, and there were briefings on the North Atlantic Treaty Organisation. The world had changed significantly in the seven years since the end of the Second World War. Although Britain, the United States, France and the Soviet Union had then been allies against the Axis powers, disagreements over many issues, particularly the shape of post-war Europe, had existed both during and after the war. NATO had come into existence in 1949 when its member states agreed to mutual defence in response to an attack by any external nation or organisation. For its first few years, NATO was little more than a political association but the conflict in Korea, which had started in 1950 and was still ongoing during Neil's time at Staff College, galvanised the member states and led to a more integrated military structure. The Cold War that had started in the immediate aftermath of the Second World War would dominate the years ahead and shape politics, coalitions, propaganda, technology, and, of course, the development of military equipment and weapons – both conventional and, very soon for Britain, nuclear.

Fortunately, the long days were broken up by occasional opportunities to fly, and thirteen more entries were made in Neil's log book during his time on the course, mostly a mix of trips in the Anson and Percival Proctor, although he did also manage to fly once in a Spitfire.

The course finished just in time for Christmas and with Staff College successfully completed, there was talk of Neil being posted to Headquarters No. 205 Group at Fayid in Egypt. But Neil was not so keen and argued against the idea. He had done a staff tour prior to attending Staff College and did not want another quite so soon. Neil won the battle and got his way. He was to be given a flying appointment instead, although he was still off to Egypt.

Neil was posted to Abu Sueir in the Canal Zone. Initially, he was considered for the OC Flying post, but this was a wing commander appointment and promotion would have to wait. The good news, though, was that he was to take over command of 208 Squadron instead. Neil recalls:

> Although I had not volunteered for an overseas tour, particularly Egypt because I knew from the outset that it would mean time away from the family, I was not against the idea either. And so, taking everything into account, I didn't mind the thought of going out to the Middle East, particularly because it meant commanding another great squadron. Besides, I had been out to that part of the world before and felt that I knew the region quite well.

Originally called 8 Naval Squadron and part of the Royal Naval Air Service during the First World War, 208 Squadron had spent all its operational life overseas. After the Second World it had remained a fighter-reconnaissance squadron in the Middle East, based in Italy, Cyprus and Palestine, but more recently it had moved back to Egypt where 208 had spent the inter-war years. It was now operating the Meteor FR.9.

There had been many changes to the RAF's structure in the Middle East since the end of the Second World War, largely brought about because of political developments in the region, but also by the post-war evolution of British defence policy. With the war over, it was inevitable that the British would one day leave Egypt, but there was a reluctance to give up present bases, primarily because of the security of the Suez Canal as well as the fear that a British withdrawal would leave the way open for Russian influence to grow in the Middle East.

One major change had seen Headquarters RAF Mediterranean and Middle East, then based in Egypt's Canal Zone and split between Ismailia and Abu Sueir, re-designated as Headquarters Middle East Air Force. The organisation of the new MEAF had initially remained unaffected by the change of title. However, the status quo was not maintained for long. This had nothing to do with the inadequacy of the command structure in place, but it was all to do with political developments in the region.

The British military presence in the Suez Canal Zone had long been a source of irritation to Egypt, and as the political pressure for the departure of British forces mounted, Ismailia and Abu Sueir were becoming increasingly unsuitable and insecure as locations for a large headquarters with its static population of administrative personnel and their families, not to mention the large number of local employees of, perhaps, rather questionable loyalty.

The 1950s would see a continued series of minor, and a few major, crises in this turbulent part of the Middle East, primarily because of the growth of Arab Nationalism. British forces, particularly the RAF, were either on almost permanent standby or actively engaged on operations. The Egyptian Revolution of July 1952, which involved

3,000 Egyptian troops and 200 officers, not only succeeded in over-throwing King Farouk but, amongst other things, was intended to bring about an end to the British occupation of Egypt. Then, with the declaration of the Republic of Egypt, General Mohammed Naguib simultaneously became the first President of Egypt, the Prime Minister and Chairman of the newly formed Revolution Command Council, and set up a government mostly composed of army officers. It was against this backdrop that Neil arrived at Abu Sueir in May 1953 to take up his new command.

Located around ten miles to the west of Ismailia and just over seventy miles to the north-east of Cairo, the airfield of Abu Sueir had been strategically placed to guard the Suez Canal. During the Second World War it was a key British and American airfield of the North African campaign, and today it is a major base of the Egyptian Air Force, but when Neil arrived it belonged to the RAF. Under the command of Wing Commander Pat Hanafin, Abu Sueir was the largest airfield in the Canal Zone and, in addition to being home to 208 Squadron, it was also the location of the rear headquarters of MEAF.

Neil took command of 208 Squadron just as the celebrations to mark the coronation of HM Queen Elizabeth II were about to take place, and so his first month was spent overseeing flying displays at the RAF stations in the Canal Zone. The squadron's aerobatic display team of four aircraft first thrilled the onlookers before joining up with the rest of the squadron for a mass flypast at the official air show at RAF Deversoir.

The squadron's Meteor FR.9 was an armed reconnaissance version of the much-produced F.8 fighter. Powered by two Rolls-Royce Derwent turbo jets and armed with four 20-mm Hispano cannons, the FR.9 was essentially an F.8 airframe fitted with a new nose section, nearly a foot longer, to accommodate an F.24 camera mounted obliquely on either side or as a forward-facing camera. Performance-wise, the FR.9 was capable of 600 mph at 10,000 feet, had a rate of climb of 7,000 feet per minute, a service ceiling of 43,000 feet and an operating range of 600 miles, although it would always be limited in range and endurance when operating in the tactical reconnaissance role.

Although Neil's introduction to the Meteor a few years before, while he was a student at the ETPS, had been disappointing, he soon learned to love the aircraft:

> The squadron's Mark 9 fighter-reconnaissance variant was a delight to fly, and a thoroughly reliable aircraft in which to wander round the Mediterranean and the deserts of Egypt, Arabia and far beyond. There had clearly been much work done since its early years just after the Second World War when I first flew the Meteor.

There was a pleasant and informal feel about life at Abu Sueir. Many considered it to be the best posting in the Middle East. One difficulty, though, was a lack of accommodation for married personnel. No married quarters were built on overseas airfields during the Second World War, and so the post-war marriage explosion had left the services with something of a problem. Although married accommodation was provided with some urgency in the immediate aftermath of the war, there was never enough to meet the demand and many married personnel had no choice but to serve overseas unaccompanied.

Tour lengths varied for all sorts of reasons, but, typically, an unaccompanied serviceman would spend a year in Egypt. Those who were entitled to what limited married accommodation there was at Abu Sueir, such as senior officers in the headquarters, generally completed two years in theatre. Being a squadron commander, Neil's tour length was two and a half years and even for him married accommodation would rely solely on availability. He explains:

> Because there was no married accommodation available for me, I had to leave my wife and young boys back in England living in a surplus married quarter at West Malling in Kent. And so, I was accommodated in the officers' mess, although the living quarters were in huts. But there was hope that married accommodation might become available

later in my tour so that my family could come out to join
me, but, even if it that was to happen, it was not going to be
for at least a year.

Neil would get the occasional opportunity to return home to see
his family, such as when taking annual leave, but apart from that,
he would spend the first year and a half of his tour at Abu Sueir
unaccompanied.

With summer fast approaching, the daytime temperature was
already 32 °C and it would soon be soaring through 38 °C every day.
It was important for new personnel arriving in Egypt to become
acclimatised to the conditions as quickly as possible. Because of the
heat, the working day started early, for most around 7 a.m., but it
also finished early, normally by 2 p.m. But there was always a high
risk of sunburn, heatstroke, and heat exhaustion, particularly during
the early part of the tour, so salt tablets were available for those who
needed them. Neil's fair skin meant he had to be extremely careful
when exposed to the sun, and so he would spend most of the time in
the shade or covered up.

Not only did Neil have to adjust to the heat of Egypt, but he also
had to adjust to flying conditions in the Middle East. The standard
of the airfields and landing grounds in the region varied enormously,
ranging from high-class major operating airfields to every conceivable
kind of runway surface, length and gradient. Improvements to the
airfields tended to lag some way behind the development of aircraft,
and so the wear and tear on aircraft based in the Middle East – such
as on the engines, undercarriage systems and tyres – was far greater
than what might have been expected back in Britain. Otherwise, the
weather was clearly very good and so flying at high altitude was a
delight:

> In the reconnaissance role, we operated at all altitudes,
> mostly in pairs, and over a vast area that stretched as far as
> Libya and Tunisia to the west, down as far as South Africa,
> over much of the Mediterranean to the north, and across to
> Iraq in the east. With long-range fuel tanks we could fly for

more than two hours. Much time was spent tracking the Egyptian Army, particularly over Sinai, although we were not permitted to fly over Israel.

The squadron's reconnaissance role meant that a great deal of time was spent working with the army and so Neil felt it important for 208 to get the right people. He explains:

> We were always affiliated with one of the Guards regiments, and so 208 was mostly an all-officer squadron as far as the pilots were concerned, with the majority of the first tourist junior officer pilots having been trained at Cranwell. I told them when they first arrived to make the most of this opportunity and to get around as often as they could and to see as much of this exciting part of the world as possible.

The weather was unbearably hot during the height of summer and so the intense heat, and the glare, took some getting used to. If an aircraft had been left standing in the sun for hours on end, it was not unusual for the temperature inside the cockpit to reach a staggering 65 °C. Makeshift canvas covers were erected to keep the cockpits in the shade as much as possible, effectively reducing the cockpit temperature by around 10 °C, but it was still an extremely sweaty and uncomfortable start to a sortie. And because of the heat and dusty conditions, Neil had to get used to the standard of working dress on the flight line where shorts, sandals and sunglasses were the norm.

Commanding a squadron in peacetime Egypt was proving to be a different challenge altogether to what Neil had previously experienced commanding a squadron in wartime Britain:

> As the officer commanding, I had to exercise discipline in a different way to what I had been used to before, but the squadron, and Abu Sueir for that matter, was full of delightful people. Officers and airmen were thrown together in quite difficult conditions, but it forged strong relationships between pilots and ground crew, and between officers and airmen.

Away from work, there were some excellent facilities on camp for all ranks: a swimming pool; sports pitches, with regular sporting events between the service establishments based in the Canal Zone; a NAAFI, which provided recreational and shopping facilities; the YMCA, the oldest and largest youth charity in the world, which regularly held a dance; the Malcolm Club, one of a number of so-named recreational facilities on British bases overseas named after Wing Commander Hugh Malcolm, VC, which provided additional amenities to those provided by the NAAFI; and a cinema called the Astra, with films changing several times a week.

The cinema was also used to host various touring productions, such as those put on by Combined Services Entertainment, the live entertainment part of the armed forces, or by visiting bands, as well as for putting on other local shows. These were always popular events. All the facilities, in fact, were popular and most of the time the venues were full. Otherwise, reading and letter-writing took up much leisure time. For those with families at Abu Sueir, there was a school on camp for the children. There was also an education centre where station personnel could take a wide range of courses to add to their qualifications.

Away from the camp, the village of Abu Sueir was right outside the gate. It did not take long to learn enough Arabic words to get by. Going slightly further afield there was the town of Ismailia, or 'Ish' as it was known, a popular destination for shopping, particularly on market day. There was also a railway station there from where onward journeys could be made. The camp ran a regular bus service to and from the town. The rather pleasant journey followed a tree-lined road running parallel to what was known as the Sweet Water Canal, now the Ismailia Canal, originally dug to facilitate the construction of the Suez Canal, but which has since provided fresh water to the otherwise arid area.

On the southern side of Ismailia is Lake Timsah, always a popular destination for people wanting to swim or simply lounge in the sun. Even further south, and next to the RAF's airfield at Fayid, the Great Bitter Lake was another popular resort for personnel based at Abu

Sueir, particularly the Blue Lagoon on the edge of the lake, which the Suez Canal joined on part of its course, and the beach from where bathers could watch ships passing through the canal.

Because of the anti-British feeling in Egypt at the time, it was rarely possible to venture outside the Canal Zone. Egypt's capital Cairo, for example, was considered out of bounds. Closer to Abu Sueir, though, the locals were mostly pro-British. After all, many worked on the camp and so their livelihoods depended on the British being there. Nonetheless, when travelling on duty by road, such as to RAF Fayid or to the Army garrison at Moascar, near Ismailia, the journey was usually made in a small convoy of three or four Land Rovers with armed guards. Even then, there were still occasions when vehicles were known to come under small arms fire.

Despite the security situation at the time, Neil made the most of his time in Egypt. Seeing the land from the ground and when in the air gave him a wonderful opportunity to explore further his interest in biblical history. On the downside, though, the deteriorating political situation in the region meant that politicians and senior officers were regular visitors to Abu Sueir. All required hosting, often by Neil.

By the end of the year there was a real concern that the Egyptian Army might carry out an attack on Abu Sueir. There had been a series of large-scale manoeuvres in the area and so 208 Squadron was busy flying daily tactical reconnaissance sorties to monitor the situation around the major British camps. Then, in April 1954, Colonel Gamal Abdal Nasser, one of the leaders of the July 1952 revolution, succeeded Naguib as prime minister and leader of the RCC. Nasser's priority was to expel the British as quickly as possible and in July an agreement was reached, which would see British forces leave Egypt within two years.

Despite such a mandate, life for Neil and 208 Squadron carried on much as normal, although plans were already in place to move the HQ MEAF from the Canal Zone to Cyprus by the end of the year. This was good news for Neil because it meant that more married accommodation would become available and, soon after, his family left England by sea to join him at Abu Sueir.

208 Squadron was also off to Cyprus, but only for four weeks to conduct its annual armament practice camp at Nicosia. Thirteen aircraft deployed, and the intense flying programme included air-to-air firing against a banner, followed by air-to-air firing against a twenty-five-foot glider and, finally, air-to-ground gunnery.

Each pilot had twelve shoots on the banner, which was towed by another Meteor at 10,000 feet. Up to four aircraft could be on the banner at any one time, with pilots taking it in turn to fire, their ammunition being tipped with different colours to determine each pilot's score. The technique required the firing aircraft to close in on the banner until within range and then for the pilot to fly steadily, with only minor adjustments, to achieve a maximum effectiveness of fire.

The second phase involving the glider, again towed by another Meteor, was carried out at 20,000 feet, making the attack more realistic, although it was more difficult to carry out a good high quarter attack. The final phase, the air-to-ground gunnery, involved firing in a thirty-degree dive against a ten-feet square target, with each pilot allocated four shoots. The first two shoots lasted ten minutes, allowing the pilot to make as many attacks as he could in the allotted time, while only two attacks were allowed in the final two shoots.

A squadron can only be good at two roles if both are practised regularly. The majority of 208's daily taskings were carrying out reconnaissance duties and so the squadron was extremely proficient at that. But, as far as being a good fighter squadron was concerned, there were never enough hours available for Neil's pilots to become good fighter pilots. Learning to put rounds into a banner that was being towed behind an aircraft flying a predictable pattern at a known height and speed was far more academic than re-creating reality. Neil had his worries:

> If I am being completely honest, we were not very good at
> shooting down things. Air-to-air gunnery training, such as
> the annual armament practice camp, was fine, but we did

not practise our fighter role often enough and so the new
arrivals had very little training in their role as fighter pilots.

208 Squadron returned to Abu Sueir to find the HQ MEAF
move to Cyprus was complete and that they were now to be joined
by 13 Squadron, a long-range photographic-reconnaissance squadron
equipped with the Meteor PR.10. The two squadrons would operate
side-by-side from Abu Sueir for the next year.

With his family having safely arrived in Egypt, the final months
of Neil's tour at Abu Sueir flew by and were full of wonderful times.
His family absolutely loved being in Egypt, and particularly enjoyed
the glorious weather. After so much time apart, it felt good for them
all to be together again.

Neil's tour in command was all but at an end when he received
news that 208 Squadron was to receive a standard in recognition of
its meritorious service rendered to the sovereign and the country.

In the same way that a Regimental Colour has historical importance for the British Army, a Squadron Standard carries the same
importance for the RAF. It is the ceremonial flag of the squadron
and is only used on special occasions, such as on formal parades and
at dinners. They were first instituted by King George VI in April
1943 to mark the twenty-fifth anniversary of the RAF, with the basic
requirement for a squadron to receive a standard being the completion
of twenty-five years of service.

Although he was due to hand over command of the squadron
just prior to the standard being presented, Neil was keen to be
involved in this historic event and so he managed to prolong his time
in command to take part. The presentation of a standard generally
follows a set formal pattern, including a dedication ceremony, and
so when Neil first announced that 208 Squadron was to receive a
standard it generated a great deal of activity on the parade ground, in
the hangar and in the air in preparation for this unique event.

Many hours were spent practising flying in perfect formation
ready for the big day, while for the ground personnel more time
was spent on the parade square working on their drill than doing

Presentation of the 208 Squadron Standard, 18 November 1955,
with Neil (*right*) looking on.

anything else. Two RAF Regiment non-commissioned officers were
brought in to bring the squadron's drill up to standard. Aircraft were
cleaned and polished, re-sprayed silver even, with the nose of each
aircraft painted either red for 'A' Flight or blue for 'B' Flight, while
Neil's aircraft was given a white nose.

Reveille was early on the morning of 18 November 1955, the day the standard was to be presented to the squadron. It was a misty start to the day and just before 9 a.m. the airmen were formed up in two flights, ready for Neil to address his squadron before marching on to the square. Summarising what he said that day, Neil recalls: 'The presentation of the Squadron Standard was a historic and glorious event. I told everyone that the occasion was something they would remember for the rest of their lives. It was a very proud moment.'

Appropriately, the presenting officer was Air Vice-Marshal Sir Geoffrey Bromet who had been 208 Squadron's first commanding officer when it formed in 1916. Other official guests included Major Christopher Draper, a First World War flying ace and the squadron's second commanding officer. He had since become known as 'The Mad Major' after becoming a stunt pilot and actor, as well as being involved in espionage work during the inter-war years. Also attending the ceremony was Air Marshal Sir Claude Pelly, the C-in-C MEAF, and the AOC No. 205 Group, Air Vice-Marshal Denis Barnett.

Following a quick formal inspection, the assistant Chaplain-in-Chief MEAF consecrated the standard before Sir Geoffrey Bromet presented it to the colour party led by Flying Officer Laurence Jones (later Air Marshal Sir Laurence Jones). The standard was then paraded for the first time, after which the squadron gave a flying display, which included an air-to-ground attack by four aircraft using live ammunition on a target in the middle of the airfield. There was then a synchronised formation display of aerobatics by two teams of four, and a solo aerobatic display. Finally, the eight aircraft all joined up for a flypast culminating in a roll and a loop.

A cocktail party followed the display and that evening there was a formal dinner in the officers' mess, which included many amusing speeches, including one by Draper who delighted the audience when he told them about the time he flew under the London bridges of the River Thames. Finally, the following evening, there was an all-ranks party during which Neil addressed his squadron for the last time. It was the culmination of much hard work and brought a close to a truly memorable occasion.

It had been a historic end to Neil's highly successful tour in command of 208 Squadron, for which he would soon receive official recognition in the New Year's Honours List with the award of the Air Force Cross for his 'outstanding work' with the squadron.

After handing over 208 Squadron to his successor, Neil and his family left Egypt. But they were not the only ones leaving. The British withdrawal from the Canal Zone was imminent.

Chapter Fifteen

Moving On

It was a rather long flight home from Egypt. The four-engine Handley Page Hermes was comfortable enough, but for Neil and Eileen with three young boys – now aged nine, seven, and five – it was never going to be an easy journey to make. The chartered flight from Fayid took them via Malta to pick up more service personnel and their families, before finally landing at Blackbushe Airport in Hampshire. But, at least for Eileen and the boys their journey home was far quicker than the one out by sea had been. Now safely back in England, and with some wonderful and everlasting memories of their time together in Egypt, it was time to enjoy a family Christmas.

After nearly two months of disembarkation leave, Neil was ready to take up his next appointment. It was February 1956. Now wearing the rank of wing commander, although it would not be substantive for another year, he was returning to his old stomping ground of Essex where he had served during the Battle of Britain.

Fighter Command was then split into operational sectors. Neil was initially destined for No. 11 Group's Southern Sector as Wing Commander Operations, but his posting was changed, even before he had arrived, to the Metropolitan Sector, which was responsible for the air defence of the Greater London area and its surrounds.

As one of two wing commander senior controllers, Neil was to work in the sector operations centre (SOC) located at a little-known place called Kelvedon Hatch, near Ongar. But first, though, he was off to Hampshire for ten days to attend the fighter controllers' control and reporting course at Middle Wallop.

With his course successfully over, Neil took up his new post at Kelvedon Hatch. Resembling a quiet chalet bungalow deep in the heart of the Essex countryside rather than a secret military operations centre, Kelvedon Hatch had been built four years earlier as part of a programme called ROTOR, the nation's improved and hardened air defence network. It was one of six SOCs established nationally to control the UK's air defence. None of the SOCs had radar and so they had to rely on information provided by the various radar stations situated around the country.

The bungalow was only the entrance and guardroom to the bunker and masked the fact that a three-story concrete structure lay beneath. Once inside the building, a door led to a long tunnel, forty yards or more in length, leading down into the bunker. Access to the operations room, more than a hundred feet beneath the ground, was through a set of blast doors.

The bunker had been designed to withstand a near miss by a nuclear weapon. It had its own water supply, generators and filtered air. Those who worked at Kelvedon Hatch were administered, accommodated and fed at North Weald, and so every day two buses transported the sixty or so personnel the ten miles between the two sites. For Neil, though, his family had moved into a rather large, and very nice, service house in Ongar, previously allocated to officers of rank more senior than him, and so it was only a short drive for him to and from the bunker.

The Metropolitan Sector controlled six airfields – Biggin Hill, Duxford, North Weald, Waterbeach, Wattisham and West Malling. It was an exciting era for those in Fighter Command. New jet fighters and improved variants were being introduced into operational service on a regular basis. At Waterbeach, for example, its two resident squadrons, 56 and 63, were both in a period of change. In the past year 56 Squadron had gone from operating the Meteor F.8 to introducing the Swift into service. But the squadron had briefly reverted to the Meteor following the withdrawal of the Swift after a series of technical problems and accidents and was now in the process of introducing the Hawker Hunter into operational service as the

RAF's main fighter to replace the Meteor. 63 Squadron, meanwhile, was exchanging its Meteor F.8s for the improved Hunter F.6. And if all that was not enough for those at Waterbeach to contend with, 253 Squadron was in the process of re-forming with de Havilland Venom NF.2 night-fighters to complete its day and night fighter wing.

It was a similar story at Biggin Hill and Wattisham, where Hunters had replaced Meteors, while at West Malling there were three squadrons of Meteor NF.12 and NF.14 night-fighters. Meteor night-fighters had also been introduced at Duxford, alongside Hunters, while the only squadrons to retain the Meteor F.8 were the sector's five Auxiliary squadrons – two at Biggin, two at North Weald and one at West Malling.

To maintain his flying currency, Neil was allocated sixty hours each year. He regularly flew the Anson, mostly from Wattisham or West Malling to several of the group's stations, and he also flew the Meteor many times. And during his second year in post he added the Hunter F.6 to his log book, flying the aircraft several times from nearby North Weald. With its clean lines and swept wing, an up-rated engine, leading-edge wing extensions, and an all-moving tail plane, the single-seat Hunter F.6 was the RAF's best performing fighter of its day and the most iconic jet fighter of the time.

Next stop on Neil's career path, in 1958, was a year-long course at the RAF Flying College at Manby in Lincolnshire. The college had been formed after the Second World War, absorbing the work of its predecessor, the Empire Air Armament School, and having combined certain aspects of work carried out at the Empire Flying School at Hullavington and the Empire Air Navigation School at Shawbury, so that the new college's studies and doctrine could be more closely integrated.

The RAF Flying College soon became the place for all senior air-crew officers to go, not only from the RAF but from other air forces across the world as well, to further their careers. They received lectures and presentations on all key flying-related matters, for example on topics such as flying supervision and authorisation and they were trained in more sophisticated techniques for their specific roles.

During the time Neil was at Manby the Commandant was the former Battle of Britain ace and world air-speed record holder, Air Commodore Teddy Donaldson, soon to retire from the RAF. There was so much to learn from people like Donaldson and others such as his deputy, Group Captain John Davis, a highly experienced navigator who earlier in his career was at the centre of researching techniques of aerial navigation, such as navigating in Arctic regions and blind landings.

It was a good course for everyone. In addition to the lectures, presentations and visits, there was plenty of flying on many different aircraft types. Neil recalls:

> It was at Manby where we were taught how to conduct ourselves as senior officers. It was a very considerable course and involved plenty of flying on various aircraft types. In addition to flying in aircraft types familiar to me, such as the Hunter, there were other less familiar types as well, such as the four-engine Lincoln and the new Canberra bomber. And it was in one of the college's Canberras that I reached the highest altitude that I had ever flown – 53,000 feet.

As the course approached its end, it looked as though Neil was destined for a station commander post in RAF Germany, a new command, but for whatever reason the idea never came to fruition. Then, out of nowhere, came news that he was off to America instead.

In February 1959, Neil travelled out to America alone to take up his next appointment as secretary to the chairman of the British Joint Services Mission at the British Embassy in Washington, DC:

> It was impractical for my family to go too. I had little notification of the posting and my three sons were all settled at boarding school. It didn't seem at all sensible to take them out of the education system at home and introduce them into the American system. And so, for now, Eileen remained in England, still at the family home in Ongar. Our plan was for her to bring the boys out to

America during the school holidays, and we hoped that she would later be able to join me in America, at least for the last year of the tour.

The origins of the British Joint Services Mission go back to the early months of the Second World War when a series of Anglo-American talks held in London led to service missions being established in America. These missions were to provide closer links between the various British and American government departments concerned with the war effort, and to bring about closer military co-operation between the two nations. After the Americans entered the war, the missions expanded rapidly, with a nucleus mission established in Washington, which, amongst other things, provided advice to the British Ambassador in the United States on strategic and other important military matters. These missions peaked during 1944 with a thousand British military personnel, plus a similar number of civilian staff, spread over some fifty locations in North America.

The end of the war had brought a reduction in staff and activities. Individual missions were abolished, and their responsibilities were absorbed into what soon became known as the British Joint Services Mission in Washington, with its chief at the time Neil arrived being Admiral Sir Michael Denny who reported directly to the newly created Ministry of Defence back in London.

Neil moved into a lovely house in Langley Forest, Virginia, in the western suburb of Washington and adjacent to the Potomac River. From there it was just a short and pleasant drive along the George Washington Parkway, following the river into the city centre and to work. Because the British Embassy was in the process of being redeveloped at the time, Denny's office was at the Pentagon and so Neil would spend his first months in America working from the US Navy building nearby, where the rest of the tri-service team were lodged.

There were three main parts to Neil's work. Firstly, Denny was the UK's Military Representative to NATO and so much of Neil's time was spent working on NATO matters. Secondly, the fact that the British Joint Services Mission was directly responsible to the rapidly expanding MoD in London meant that Neil became involved in almost all defence-related matters between the UK and USA, such as combined overseas operations, contingency planning, bilateral defence co-operation, inter-operability, and matters such as overseas defence trade. The third aspect to Neil's work was dealing with the Foreign Office on confidential intelligence and security matters involving the two countries, for which he was given the highest security vetting possible. Neil was a busy man. He later said: 'Everything passed through my office and so I was given three secretaries to help me with the different areas of responsibility. I probably knew more than anyone else on the British military staff in Washington at that time.'

Denny was a highly respected naval officer who had served through both world wars. He was a former Third Sea Lord and Controller of the Royal Navy, and Commander-in-Chief Home Fleet. Neil remembers his first job in Washington with him:

> I accompanied Admiral Denny to New York as he was due to carry out an inspection there. We flew up there in our own private aircraft and were greeted at the bottom of the steps by some generals of the US Army. We were then given the full VIP red carpet treatment and then whisked away in an enormous limousine. It was all very grand.

Neil had arrived in America as Denny's three years in Washington were coming to the end; he was about to retire. As the Chairman of the British Joint Services Mission was a rotational appointment between the services, it was next the turn of the RAF to fill the post.

Denny's successor was Air Chief Marshal Sir George Mills, a former head of Bomber Command and now starting his last tour in the RAF, with Group Captain Peter Ottewill appointed as his Executive Assistant. The changeover came at about the time refurbishment of the British Embassy was complete, and so Neil was pleased to move into his new office, which he shared with a Guards officer, Colonel Tony Duncan. The Embassy was also home to the Air Attaché, Air

Vice-Marshal Walter Sheen, and his staff. It was a delightful place to work. There was always plenty going on and Bertie Mills, as he was known, was a wonderful man to work for.

Every month Neil travelled to New York to attend the monthly meetings of the Military Staff Committee, a subsidiary body of the United Nations Security Council, responsible for planning UN military operations and assisting in the regulation of armaments. These meetings brought Neil into close contact with military representatives of other nations, notably the Russians and the Nationalist Chinese, as they, along with the USA, UK, and France, were permanent members of the Security Council. With the position of Chairman of the MSC rotating monthly, these occasions provided Neil with some everlasting memories of good times and some funny moments.

Neil's work took him all over the United States, to every state, in fact, except Alaska. His many tasks included escorting the senior military officers from the internationally renowned Imperial Defence College in London during their month-long overseas visit to the United States. They were all destined for the highest positions in their respective organisations and the overseas visit came during August and September, immediately after the summer term during which they had been introduced to international issues from a strategic perspective. While some of the course went to Europe and others to the Middle East, around thirty students travelled to the United States to improve their knowledge of US defence and matters of security, and to gain a better understanding of the international relationships between the USA and other nations.

Neil enjoyed hosting these visits as he was given a free rein to organise what he thought to be best. The itinerary stretched from Washington and New York on the east coast to San Francisco and Los Angeles on the west coast, with stop-offs at many points in between, such as a visit to the US Air Force Academy in Colorado Springs, the American equivalent to the RAF College Cranwell. He would start the programme in Virginia with visits to Jamestown and Williamsburg so that the students could gain an appreciation and understanding of the early British presence in America, and then work westwards from there, with air travel being provided by the US Air Force. It was a great time.

The year following Neil's arrival in America was dominated by the American presidential election, which ultimately resulted in John F. Kennedy narrowly defeating Richard Nixon, the then-incumbent Vice-President, making Kennedy the youngest person elected to the office. By now, Eileen had joined Neil in America. She had even managed to get some work. Her perfect English accent and charm meant she was much in demand, and she was soon running a hospitality team in Washington as part of the American political scene, responsible for hosting senators and other members of congress from all over the United States.

Living in the beautiful Virginian countryside and working in Washington was a wonderful way of life for the Neils. They both thoroughly enjoyed all that life in America had to offer, particularly when their boys were able to join them during the school holidays. As a family, they made the most of every opportunity they had to travel together all over the United States, as taking time off during the long summer holidays was never a problem. It seemed like the whole of the country was away from work at that time of year. From their home in Langley Forest, they could explore Virginia and its neighbouring states of Maryland and Pennsylvania to the north, through West Virginia to Ohio out to the west, and through the vast state of Virginia down to North Carolina when heading south. It was a wonderful place to live and such a marvellous experience for the Neil family.

The biggest event in Washington, DC, during Neil's time there was the inauguration of John F. Kennedy as the thirty-fifth President of the United States, which took place on 20 January 1961. It was a day Neil would remember for the rest of his life:

> Eileen and I could have attended, but the weather during that period was awful. It was the height of a very cold winter and there had been chaos on the streets of Washington

during the days leading up to the inauguration, not only because of the weather but also because many police officers were taking time off before the big event. And so, for a start, the traffic situation was terrible. Also, the temperature had plummeted to -7°C and around eight inches of snow had fallen overnight, causing further transportation and logistical problems on the day. Everyone seemed to want to be in Washington for the occasion, but the combination of the bad weather and increased security arrangements made it all but impossible to move around. Cars were left abandoned in the snow and so we decided to stay in and watch the event unfold on television from the warmth of our home.

Although the weather on the day of the inauguration was better than it had been leading up to the event in that the sky was mostly clear, the amount of snow that had fallen during the previous days meant the inaugural parade was almost cancelled. Thousands of people and many snow-clearing vehicles were involved in making sure that the inauguration could go ahead. And even then, for those who did witness it, the inauguration day was anything but smooth and it provided some unforgettable moments for Neil:

> The Americans often struggle with formality and one problem on the day was that the bad weather seemed to cause the timing to suffer, making things run late, and so thousands of people were left standing around waiting on Capitol Hill on what was a freezing cold day.

The situation had not been helped by a snowstorm at Washington airport, which had reduced visibility to the point that aircraft could not land and so some dignitaries could not even get to the event. Neil continues:

> When the ceremony did get under way, a lectern caught fire during the invocation due to a faulty heater, and the Vice-President, Lyndon Johnson, fumbled his words. There was

also the moment when the 86-year-old poet Robert Frost, who had written a new poem for the occasion, was unable to read it out once he was on the presidential podium and so he decided to recite another poem from memory instead. And then there was the inaugural address, which, although uplifting, lasted for almost a quarter of an hour. The inaugural parade went on for hours and, again, meant thousands were left standing around for what seemed like an eternity in the freezing cold. Eileen and I just watched the television with some amusement. The whole thing was unforgettable.

The title of British Joint Services Mission had now been changed in favour of a new collective name British Defence Staffs. However, the change in title made little or no difference to Neil's work as its purpose was simply to serve the military interests of the British government in the United States, with Mills being the British Ambassador's senior adviser on matters of defence as well as maintaining his responsibility as the UK's Military Representative to NATO.

On the matter of security, one incident has remained permanently lodged in Neil's memory from his time in Washington. Some confidential government planning papers had been misplaced some-where in the British Embassy and it was Neil's job to inform Mills of the bad news.

As the British Defence Staffs in Washington were directly responsible to the MoD, there followed a discussion as to whether the loss of papers should be reported back to London or not. The Chief of the Defence Staff in London at the time was Admiral of the Fleet Earl Mountbatten of Burma, but the post of CDS was still a relatively new one. It was always an interesting discussion when it came to decide what should be dealt with and managed in Washington, and what should be reported back to London. Mills was an exceptionally strong character and, in the end, decided against telling London that the papers had disappeared. He was about to retire from the RAF and, besides, the loss of such important papers would cause an embarrassing situation for Mountbatten. Nothing more was said, but the papers were never seen again.

The last part of Neil's time in Washington was dominated by events in Cuba. Just three months after Kennedy's inauguration, the Cuban leader, Fidel Castro, declared Cuba a socialist republic after a force of fifteen hundred American-trained Cuban exiles landed at the Bay of Pigs with the aim of instigating an uprising amongst the Cuban people and deposing Castro. The invasion was quelled by Cuba's military forces, and Kennedy was left to negotiate the release of the survivors. But the incident had left Castro feeling threatened by a possible American invasion and so he built up his military forces, with the backing of the Soviet Union.

The United States, meanwhile, feared that any alliance between Cuba and the Soviet Union would result in the expansion of communism in Latin America. In early 1962, the USA imposed an economic embargo against Cuba and later a joint US Congressional resolution authorised the use of military force against Cuba should American interests in the region become threatened. There had already been a major American military exercise in the Caribbean that focused on the invasion of an island to overthrow a political leader, and the Cuban government saw this resolution as further evidence that the US was planning to invade. Consequently, Castro and the Soviet Premier, Nikita Khrushchev, agreed to place strategic nuclear missiles in Cuba.

The stage was set for a full confrontation between the USA and the Soviet Union, which would have a dramatic impact on the rest of the world. Western military doctrine at the time was based on the strategy of massive retaliation, but after days of negotiations between the world's two superpowers, and some uncomfortable incidents in the waters off Cuba, the threat of all-out nuclear confrontation was averted.

The thirteen-day Cuban Missile Crisis of October 1962 marked the darkest period of the Cold War, but Neil's tour in Washington had ended while the situation in Cuba was still escalating. By the time things came to a head, he and Eileen were already back in London.

Neil was now working at the Air Ministry and had become part of the commuter gang, making the daily journey into the centre of London from his married quarter in Stanmore. He was one of four wing commanders working for the Director of Joint Plans, then Air Commodore Deryck Stapleton, with Neil's geographic area of responsibility being the Middle East.

It was an appointment for which Neil was well suited. He already knew the region well from his time in command of 208 Squadron in Egypt, although it had been more than six years since he had left the Middle East. Furthermore, he had arrived in London during a period of change. The Air Ministry was in the process of merging with the Admiralty, the War Office, and the Ministry of Aviation, to become one modern department and near enough the MoD that can be recognised today, although it would be a few more years before the final piece of the jigsaw, the Ministry of Aviation Supply, merged into the new MoD organisation.

Mountbatten was still Chief of the Defence Staff and, having arrived in his new post, Neil was called to his office for a briefing. Neil still remembers what he was told:

> In a period of financial savings and changing policies, there had been several organisational changes and reductions in manning and equipment overseas, including the Middle East. With the MoD still finding its feet, it was important to find the right balance between how much we managed from London and how much we left to those in theatre. Although it might have been relatively easy to try and do so, we did not want to interfere in matters that were probably best dealt with by those in the Middle East.

Much, of course, had happened since Neil was last in the Middle East. Many of the problems that had been emerging then had now become issues of huge political importance, such as Britain maintaining a military presence in the Arabian Peninsula. One of Britain's primary reasons – if not the primary reason – for keeping bases in the Arabian Peninsula after the Second World War was to safeguard the oil supplies that lay around the Persian Gulf. Arab hostility towards Britain in the Middle East, notably in Egypt, Iraq and Saudi Arabia, had put these supplies at risk, and so there was a need to strengthen Britain's ties with other Arab oil-producing states, such as Kuwait, as well as safeguarding the routes by which oil reached the UK in view of the unreliability of the Suez Canal.

Not long before Neil arrived in post, Britain had supported the newly independent state of Kuwait against territorial claims by its neighbour Iraq. There had also been a civil war in Yemen, which overlapped with a campaign of terrorism being waged by Arab nationalists within the Federation of South Arabia, and so the centre of gravity in the region had now shifted from the eastern Mediterranean to Aden.

Neil had arrived in London at a time when the building programme in Aden, particularly at the RAF airfield of Khormaksar, was making good progress. He travelled out to the region by Bristol Britannia so that he could see for himself just how things were developing. He had been to Khormaksar before, during his time in command of 208 Squadron, to conduct an inquiry into the loss of a Vampire jet aircraft, but things had moved on since then. Facilities were now sufficient to allow the operation of many aircraft types and to establish a wing headquarters to support the two Hunter squadrons – 8 Squadron and 208 Squadron, Neil's previous command – of the Khormaksar Wing. Khormaksar would soon become the RAF's biggest overseas station and the largest staging post between Britain and Singapore. Meanwhile Britain was also spreading its influence deeper into the Arabian Peninsula to control inter-tribal rivalries and unrest.

The Aden Emergency that followed was an insurgency against British forces. It began in 1963, reached boiling point the following year, and would last for three more years beyond that. As Neil entered his final year in London, the RAF's presence in Aden was at its maximum strength, with nine squadrons and two flights operating nearly a hundred aircraft of eleven different types.

For a while now Neil had been suffering with a bad back, probably the result of years of cramming his six feet-plus body into small cockpits, and so it was time for him to go into the RAF hospital at Ely in Cambridgeshire to have it sorted. There then followed four months of rehabilitation at Headley Court in Surrey. It was, just about, the last thing that happened to him in the RAF.

Although his career had gone well up to now, Neil had for some while been thinking about leaving. The main reason was simply the lack of time he had spent with his family, particularly with his three sons – now aged seventeen, fifteen, and thirteen – all of whom had been boarding at Felsted School in Great Dunmow for many years. With no idea of what the RAF had in store for him, he now had to think about his own future and that of his family.

Neil was now in his forties and a wing commander. He knew that he was not best suited to staff tours. He was, after all, a fighter pilot. Yet there were so many plusses to think about. He had been fortunate to be retained in the post-war RAF and had been selected for Staff College. During his career so far, he had been lucky enough to command two squadrons and had twice served overseas since the end of the war. His previous tour, particularly, had been very special. It had not only reaffirmed his close affinity with the Americans, but it had also given him an insight into what life might be like living in the United States.

Taking all things into account, and having discussed the future with Eileen, Neil concluded that it was time to leave. Looking back, he recalls:

> On the ground, I was never an instant thinker. I preferred to dwell on things and so life in a headquarters or at the MoD was probably not best for me. Besides, our family life had become disjointed, with the boys away at boarding school. I also knew there were times that I had probably taken the wrong course of action during my post-war career. My time spent as a test pilot, for example, and then my tours over-seas, in Egypt and America, had all seemingly taken me out of the main stream for promotion. And so, I had no idea what the future might hold if I stayed. I simply knew that it was time to leave.

Thus, in the summer of 1964, after more than twenty-five years of serving his country with courage, loyalty and distinction, and having flown more than a hundred different aircraft types, and with nearly 3,000 flying hours, Neil's time in the RAF was at an end. Only those who have served so long, and who had fought so gallantly during the Second World War, can have any idea of how that must have felt. But it was now time for Neil to move on.

Chapter Sixteen

The Author

The combination of having worked with Americans during the Second World War and his recent experience of living in America had shaped Neil's life to the extent that he wanted to live in the United States once he had left the RAF. He had moved in great circles while in Washington and he hoped, and thought, that he would be able to use his many contacts to forge a second career in America.

Given his flying background, particularly as a test pilot, and with his experience of working in the British Embassy in Washington and at the MoD in London, there was every reason to think that he would be snapped up by the Americans. Accordingly, in search of work, Neil travelled out to America alone, leaving Eileen at their new family home in Moreton, near Ongar in Essex. As Neil says, there really was no alternative. His sons were at a crucial stage of their education and so, again, it would have been a major disruption to them to have moved the family out to America at that time.

Neil had some good friends in Boston, Massachusetts, and so that is where he went. But his hopes of being snapped up by the Americans just simply did not happen:

> I had good friends everywhere and so I was invited over to America as their guest. Unfortunately, I soon found out that working in the defence industry or working with the universities was not going to be an option simply because, as a British civilian, I would never get the security clearances required to fill such posts. Everything I once had in the way

of clearances, both in America and in Britain, had lapsed once I had left the RAF. I was not put off, though, as I still had some rather grand ideas of what I wanted to do next, one idea being that I wanted to join National Geographic because of my fascination with biblical history. And so, I wanted to write about that.

The reality was, however, that no matter how hard he tried, Neil could not get a job. Furthermore, he soon realised that his open invite 'to stay as long as he wanted' was not quite what he had imagined:

> If I had offered someone to stay with me for as long as they wanted, then I would mean exactly that. But, to my American friends, it was almost like inviting me to stay for as long as I wanted, but then after a couple of nights or so making me feel like it was time for me to move on. I felt like I was being tolerated, but nothing more.

All kinds of people offered to help Neil find a job but, again, the reality was they never seemed to quite manage it. He felt like he was considered as competition by some of them. Neil even wrote to his former boss, Bertie Mills, asking if he could use some of his American contacts to help find him something, but nothing came from it.

He found somewhere to live in the suburbs of Boston, but six months passed without any sign of work, and it was soon time for him to return home. He had all but given up hope, but then, out of nowhere, came an opportunity.

Neil had joined the British Officers' Club of New England, a private club dating back to 1921, which caters to the social needs of past and present officers of Britain's armed forces. While at the club Neil had met a couple of British men who were in the process of setting up a large shoemaking business in the United States and, after explaining their plans to him, they offered Neil the opportunity to run the company's interests in the USA as a company director.

Neil is the first to admit he knew little or nothing about shoes, but it was work. After going back to Essex for a few days to see his family and to prepare for the next chapter in his life, Neil returned to Boston to head up the new organisation, Scientific Leather Measurement Inc. It was not long before the company's interests spread from Boston to Chicago, and his work took him all over the country, living in hotels, as he visited all the major shoemaking companies in the United States.

Although he would never particularly enjoy his time working in the shoe industry, either while he was in America or later in his life, things seemed to be going well. In fact, as far as his job in America was concerned, things went very well for the next year or more, but Neil was desperately missing his family. He rarely saw them, which had been one of the main reasons why he had left the RAF, and now the same was happening again. Furthermore, it had become increasingly apparent to him that he was part of a company now facing financial difficulties.

Neil decided to look for work elsewhere rather than invest his own money into the company, and in the end, he returned home to England. He had made some good contacts in the shoe industry, which led him to the long established Norvic Shoe Group, based in Norwich, which soon offered Neil the opportunity to become a director.

Having accepted the position, the Neil family moved to the south Norfolk village of Brooke. With responsibility for the group's overseas division, Neil's work took him to many different countries across the world, mostly to Rhodesia (as it then was), South Africa, Australia, New Zealand, and back to America. Once again, all seemed to be going well. He and Eileen very much enjoyed living in the quiet Norfolk countryside, while their boys had finished their education and were now moving on with their own lives, but within just a couple of years things again started to look bleak.

Britain's shoe industry had thrived during the wartime years when production had geared up to make footwear for the armed forces, but in the peacetime years the industry had struggled to regain commercial viability. By the early 1970s, the competition from foreign shoe companies was growing stronger and soon the British market was dominated by imports from overseas. The British shoe industry was in difficulties, and the Norvic Shoe Group was part of that decline. Gradually its assets were sold off and soon the group would disappear, leaving Neil, once again, without a job.

Finding himself out of work yet again, for the third time in a matter of years, Neil was convinced he did not want to work for someone else again and so he decided to set up a business on his own. He had always enjoyed the world of art and so he established himself at a gallery at Buxton Mill, just to the north of Norwich, with his son Patrick, a talented artist. Father and son worked together running the art business, selling drawings and paintings, as well as mounting and framing pictures, and putting on many art exhibitions during the 1970s. His other two sons, meanwhile, Terence and Ian, had followed in Neil's footsteps to become pilots in the armed forces.

The years at Buxton Mill that followed were most pleasant and enjoyable. As a businessman, Neil was held in high regard and was much respected by his professional colleagues. For ten years he was the secretary of the Great Yarmouth Chamber of Commerce. But the decade was marred by the loss of Neil's parents, his mother first and then his father three years later in 1977. Given how close he had been to them, and considering all that his parents had been through, particularly during the war, it was very sad. Neil's parents had adored him, and he had adored them. That is very clear to see.

After his parents died, Neil had the sad task of going through their possessions spanning sixty years of married life. It was then that he came across a box containing all the letters that he had written to his parents during the war, all in chronological order and still in their original envelopes, along with other bits of correspondence from him that they had kept over the years. Altogether there were more than 600 items.

Having retired in the 1980s, Neil and Eileen moved into their new family home, which they had built just a few miles away in the quiet hamlet of Thwaite St Mary on the Norfolk/Suffolk border. It really is a beautifully quiet and idyllic part of the East Anglian countryside. It was then that Neil decided to pursue his interest in writing. From a very early age it was evident that he had an ability to write. Indeed, he was just five years old when he received his first recognition for a piece of written work at school, and his countless letters home during the war years were creative, articulate and, at times, quite graphic.

Writing about his own wartime experiences would give Neil a way of reflecting on all that had happened to him during the Second World War. He had received unconditional support from his parents during those hard years, but it was only after they had died that he started to reflect upon the scale of what happened and on their contribution. He had written articles about his experiences as a wartime fighter pilot before, which had been snapped up by eager editors for various aviation magazines, but now the publisher William Kimber approached Neil to write a book about his early flying with the RAF.

The period of interest spanned the three years from Neil's first flight after joining the RAFVR in 1938 up to, and including, his service in Malta. Given all that he had been through during that time, particularly during the Battle of Britain and then the Siege of Malta, it did not take long to work out that Neil's memories would be too large for any single book. And so it was decided that the material would be broken down into three, with the first book being entitled *Gun Button to Fire*, with the next two books, under separate titles, to be published later. Unfortunately, William Kimber went out of business before these arrangements could be finalised, and so the second and third books would have to be done elsewhere. But *Gun Button to Fire* went ahead as planned and was first published in 1987.

The book's title simply refers to the last vital action performed by a Hurricane pilot before he went into combat. To trigger the eight Browning machine guns, he pressed a button on the spade grip of the control column, which could only be activated when he twisted the knurled surrounds to the button from the 'SAFE' position to 'FIRE'.

Gun Button to Fire covers the eight hectic, but memorable, months from May until December 1940 when Neil was serving with 249 Squadron during the Battle of Britain. Using the letters written to his parents during that period as the basis for the book, together with other records, both personal and otherwise, Neil tells his story in much detail. Indeed, it was the letters that often reminded him of events in his life that had long been forgotten.

While Neil's accounts of his time during the Battle of Britain might, at times, seem rather graphic to some, he has always maintained that it was the aircraft he was determined to bring down, not the pilot or crew. It was never a personal thing, but it was war. More than that, it was the Battle of Britain. The country stood alone against Nazi tyranny and so it is important that nearly eighty years on, judgment is not casually passed. The book is also light-hearted at times, which Neil explains in his foreword:

> It may be thought that I write too light-heartedly about a period of great tragedy, sacrifice and unhappiness. But war is a young man's business and youth sees great humour in almost everything – even destruction and death.

When reading *Gun Button to Fire*, or any of his books for that matter, it is immediately obvious that Neil is a gifted author. Not only is the book a dramatic account and an inspiring read, but it is superbly written. It fully captures the spirit and feelings of the RAF fighter pilot, as well as his fears, at that time. It rightly earned marvellous reviews. Sir John Grandy, for example, Neil's squadron commander during 1940, described it as 'The best book on the Battle of Britain'. It is a wonderful compliment.

Following the success of *Gun Button to Fire*, Neil's next book *Onward to Malta* appeared in 1992. This covers the next part of the story when he went with 249 Squadron to the Mediterranean. Unsurprisingly, this second book is every bit as good as Neil's first and is written in the same straightforward conversational style. His vivid account picks up instantly from where the previous book had ended, dealing first with his squadron's activities from North Weald during early 1941. The reader is then taken on the long journey to Malta, hearing about what it was like to fly off a carrier in the dangerous waters of the Mediterranean for the first time to make the long and hazardous flight to the island. Neil then describes in detail the harsh conditions of living on the island of Malta during the siege, and what it was like to fly in the air battle being fought in the sky above, before ending with his hazardous voyage to Egypt at the end of his tour on the island. Throughout the book he recalls his good friends of 249 Squadron, many of whom he had fought alongside during the Battle of Britain only the year before, with humour and sadness and with the greatest of respect. It is another book of the highest quality and another must-read.

With the original *Gun Button to Fire* having been published in 1987, and *Onward to Malta* in 1992, the final book of the trilogy entitled *A Fighter in my Sights* was published in 2001. This book, like the second, is now quite rare, with *A Fighter in my Sights* containing most of the original text from *Gun Button to Fire* but also including Neil's account of his pre-war flying with the RAFVR and then his flying training during the early months of hostilities.

It is hardly surprising that all three books have sold well and are still much in demand. Years later, as the number of veterans from the Battle of Britain and Siege of Malta were dwindling away, Neil thought it appropriate that the original three books should be offered once more to the public under the single, separate title *Scramble*, which was first published in 2015.

Neil's wonderfully creative writing skills ensure the book stands way above similar titles written by wartime veterans and provides a marvellous record of his experiences during those tumultuous years from when he joined the RAFVR until he returned from Malta. In his author's notes, he refers to the reducing number of those who fought in the Battle of Britain:

> Sadly, but inevitably, we shall all soon drift into oblivion. For this reason, I feel it vital for our nation's history and future existence, that those boyhood companions of mine who fought with me, sacrificed their lives or were crippled mentally as well as physically by their ordeals, should be remembered fondly with pride and gratitude and granted the greatest honour and respect.

In his introduction to *Scramble*, the highly respected British military author and broadcaster James Holland describes the book as 'such an enthralling and compelling read'. He goes on to describe it as 'a vivid and superbly written account by one of the great heroes of the Battle of Britain'. Holland is, without doubt, right and as himself a best-selling author of books that include *Battle of Britain* and *Fortress Malta*, he should know.

Neil's trilogy of books are not his only published works, far from it. In 1990 he wrote *From the Cockpit: Spitfire*. Apart from his very brief introduction to the Spitfire in May 1940, before he had even experienced combat, Neil had flown Hurricanes during the early years of the war. This book therefore focuses on the two marks that he flew while commanding 41 Squadron during 1942/43, the Mark V and the Mark XII.

As well as giving the reader a thoroughly detailed description of the two marks of Spitfire he had flown operationally, the book is marvellously illustrated, not only with images of the marks specifically covered in the book. The book also provides some interesting features, such as what it was like to fly on night defensive operations on the west coast of Britain during November 1942, and his memories of the squadron, its role and his pilots during that period of the war.

Next up in Neil's titles was *The Silver Spitfire*, first published in 2013. This book covers his experiences while assigned to the Americans as an RAF liaison officer with the 100th Fighter Wing during 1944. It not only covers his time with the Americans in detail, but it also captures some of his personal life that year, most notably when he met Eileen, his wife to be.

The book takes its name from the abandoned Spitfire in France, which Neil later commandeered as his own personal aircraft. In his author's notes, Neil, then in his nineties, explained the dilemma he had when first asked to write the book. He had written a light-hearted account about the abandoned Spitfire before, but that was some thirty years earlier. Being such an unusual story, it soon spread worldwide with the reaction of the reader being almost one of disbelief. Taken at face value, the thought of someone belonging to such a disciplined

Signing a copy of his book *The Silver Spitfire*.

organisation as the RAF taking possession of a front-line fighter and then using it for his own personal purposes, without being discovered and held to account, was difficult to take in. He was therefore unsure whether he should write the book or not, as he explains in his own words:

First, as a 91-year-old author, I was not altogether in favour of any arrangement which would result in me being sentenced to two years' hard labour writing a book! Second, it would involve me in an arduous memory exercise, trying to recall a host of unrecorded facts relating to events and incidents that occurred seventy years before. And finally, almost all of the people about whom I would be writing would now be dead and therefore unable either to confirm or to challenge my assertions.

Written in Neil's naturally easy-to-read style, fictional almost, *The Silver Spitfire* provides yet another gripping story in which he delves into the minds and attitudes of his American colleagues serving in wartime Britain. Furthermore, having had the privilege to fly two of America's principal fighters of 1944, the P-47 Thunderbolt and the P-51 Mustang, Neil gives a rare insight into what they were like to fly from a British fighter pilot's point of view, and makes comparisons with the RAF fighters that he had previously flown.

Neil finds himself amongst a rare group of extremely talented authors. He has spent most of his retirement thinking and writing about his wartime experiences, and when reading any of these books it is easy to see why he has also chosen to write several 'faction' stories in recent years. He naturally adopted this method of writing as he believed it to be the best means of more truly reflecting the excitement and horrors of the times without having to get too involved in the statistics and facts when writing about aircraft performance and air campaigns. Instead, he dwells more on the effect on those young people who were caught up in the exuberance and thrills of battle but who also encountered the many stressful and heart-rending aspects of war; many of them, of course, did not live to see the victory that they had fought so gallantly for.

What makes Neil's collection of short stories particularly relevant is that they are all based on his own experiences and people that he served with during the Second World War. They are all soundly grounded on fact and deal with events that did take place, although the endings have been dramatised to enable Neil to illustrate more clearly the horrors of the war and the effect it had on many young men and women who were directly involved. They clearly illustrate their youthful emotions, their courage, hopes and failings, as well as their loves, heartaches and tragedies.

These short stories are presented under three titles: *Flight into Darkness* (with four stories – 'Flight into Darkness', 'A Welcome in the Hillsides', 'A Question of Responsibility' and 'A Richer Dust') was published in 2006; *Questions of Guilt* (three stories – 'Questions of Guilt', 'An Escape to Tragedy' and 'The Story of Jamie Bell') was published in 2008; and *Acts of Fate* (three stories – 'Acts of Fate', 'Jonathan Kerr' and 'An Unusual Period of Rest') is the most recent, published in 2017.

Given his success with these short stories, Neil also wrote *Portrait of an Airman*, published in 2017. Again faction, and based on his own experience during the war, the story is of a 22-year-old RAF pilot who is invited back to his old school to talk about his adventures in the Battle of Britain. He soon strikes up an unlikely friendship with his old French teacher and despite their considerable age difference, they grow ever closer as the war takes its toll on them both. Surrounded by danger, jealousy and heartache, they find themselves pushed emotionally to their limits, and beyond. It is a dramatic story of love, courage and sacrifice amid the tumult and trauma of war.

Neil has deserved every success with his books. The combination of his wonderfully creative and exceptionally rare writing skills, and the most vivid accounts of his past experiences, make them all a must-read. Neil is, without doubt, a most gifted author and amongst the best. Long may his books continue.

Chapter Seventeen

On Reflection

Sitting in silence at his home in the quiet, peaceful and idyllic south Norfolk countryside, Tom reflects on the past and all that has happened to him throughout his quite extraordinary life.

Memories of his childhood years are happy ones. His loving parents had given him the best possible start in life. But, unlike the current generation of teenagers who enjoy a life of freedom, often with little responsibility, Tom had to grow up fast. He and his young colleagues in Fighter Command, men later to be immortalised as the Few, collectively carried responsibility for the nation's survival during its darkest hour while individually fighting for their own lives.

Now, nearly eighty years on, Tom not only reflects on his experiences of war but also on the many peacetime years since – his time in the post-war RAF, the years of work that followed, his retirement, and, of course, his wonderful family. But it is the part he played in the Battle of Britain that has made Tom Neil a name synonymous with the nation's finest hour.

In time of war, a country needs its heroes. Tom was one of those heroes, although he is far too modest to admit it himself, and he is the first to say that he enjoyed more than his fair share of luck. He was never shot down, but he did spend a lot of time ducking and weaving, and he quickly developed a sensitivity, knowing where to look and when to guard against being attacked from behind. He had that extra sense needed to survive.

History seems to judge fighter pilots by the number of enemy aircraft they shot down. But those same fighter pilots know better than anyone that to judge them by a number, like a cricketer putting runs on the scoreboard, is wrong. Many brave young fighter pilots defended the nation during the summer of 1940 without ever shooting down another aircraft. And many of those gallant young men paid the ultimate price, while others spent the rest of their lives troubled by horrific injuries. Besides, what about those who flew with Bomber Command, or Coastal Command, or Transport Command? Or those who served with the Royal Navy or the British Army or were civilians on the Home Front. They were no less brave.

But, if a 'score' must be attached to the achievements of a fighter pilot, then Tom is often asked how many he shot down. The answer, of course, is never that simple. Furthermore, sources vary, even after many years of research by historians and aviation enthusiasts. For example, the excellent book *Aces High*, by Christopher Shores and Clive Williams, credits Tom with twelve destroyed, four shared, plus others 'probable' or damaged. Others, such as James Holland, credit him with the destruction of no less than fourteen enemy aircraft, while Tom feels the real figure is closer to seventeen. With aircraft seemingly everywhere, and often with cloud in the sky, or when fighting over the sea, it was impossible to determine the fate of an enemy aircraft, or for its demise to be witnessed by others. There was simply not the time in the heat of battle just to sit there and watch.

Whatever the actual figure is, though, there is no doubting that Tom's total is high. To put his achievement into some context, less than five per cent of RAF fighter pilots were credited with shooting down five aircraft or more during the Second World War to become a so-called ace. Those who went on to shoot down ten aircraft or more fell into an elite club. And of that elite club, Tom has long been Britain's highest-scoring living ace.

In the decades that have passed since the end of the Second World War more has been discovered about the events back then. There is also, of course, the benefit of hindsight. It is unsurprising, therefore, that over the years Tom has been openly critical of many factors relating to the Battle of Britain, such as the lack of suitable training prior to a new pilot joining a fighter squadron, which undoubtedly

With young relatives of Air Chief Marshal Sir Keith Park.

resulted in the deaths of many good men. He has also been critical of No. 12 Group and its so-called 'Big Wing' tactics, which led to the peevish tiff between its commander Air Vice-Marshal Trafford Leigh-Mallory and his No. 11 Group counterpart Keith Park, and of the legendary Douglas Bader, then a squadron leader, for his influence within No. 12 Group at that time, although, as Tom makes perfectly clear, Bader's personal courage can never be in doubt.

Tom has also publicly aired his views on the performance of the RAF's fighters during the early years of the war, particularly the inadequacy of the Hurricane when up against the Luftwaffe's principal fighter the Messerschmitt Bf 109. And when Fighter Command first went on the offensive, with fighter sweeps across the Channel, he has questioned some of the tactics used. These missions were carried out by squadrons based throughout the southern counties of England, allegedly to encourage the offensive spirit, but they were also carried out for political reasons. He would later describe these missions as ridiculous forays that resulted in the deaths of countless gallant and experienced pilots who were sacrificed with very little to show for their efforts.

Too many of his good friends and colleagues were lost in this way, which was not helped by a clear lack of co-ordination between the squadrons of Fighter Command at that time. During one fighter sweep to northern France in January 1941, for example, two of his squadron's Hurricanes were bounced by marauding 109s. It later turned out that another squadron had been operating in the same area with the intent of stirring up trouble to get the 109s airborne. Whilst this was fine in terms of the other squadron's aim, it was completely unknown to the pilots from 249 Squadron.

The inadequate performance of the Hurricane was again evident during Tom's time in Malta and so he has questioned those charged with the re-supply of fighters to the besieged island and wonders why the decision was not made to deploy Spitfires to the island until 1942, by which time it was very nearly too late.

Tom has fond and emotional memories of those he fought along-side with 249 Squadron. It was, after all, the defining period of his life. Of the twenty or so pilots that originally formed the squadron in May 1940, Tom is, he believes, the only one still alive. But even though he knew some of them for only a short period of time, they all remain etched vividly in his memory. He still remembers their voices, their laughter and their jokes, and all those alcohol-fuelled destructive games in the mess. These days it might all be considered rather juvenile behaviour, but then again most were not much older than teenage boys.

John Grandy, his first CO, went on to become the only Chief of the Air Staff to have flown in the Battle of Britain. Tom met up with him many times after the war and would often visit him during the final years of his life. By Grandy's own admission, he was never one of the best fighter pilots, but he was a person of considerable charm and an extremely capable administrator, and so it is not surprising that he went on to enjoy a long and very successful post-war career in the RAF, rising to the supreme rank of Marshal of the Royal Air Force. Sir John Grandy died in 2004 at the age of ninety.

Ronald Kellett, Tom's first flight commander, was another Tom kept in touch with during the last years of his life. The two men had bumped into each other later in the war, but they did not see each other again for fifty years or so. Then, after the publication of Tom's book *Gun Button to Fire*, Kellett contacted him, asking to meet up and chat about old times. They did. Kellett was living alone by then and Tom remembers how he had mellowed a bit – but not very much! Kellett died in 1998 at the age of eighty-nine. He was another to have served his country well.

And then there was Butch Barton, who Tom considers to be one of the best RAF fighter pilots of the Second World War. Barton might not have looked or sounded like a hero, and, according to Tom, had little dress sense and awful hand writing, but he was always calm and fearless in the air as well as being a determined, self-effacing leader. Barton remained in the post-war RAF before retiring from the service in 1959 and spent his later years living a quiet life back home in Canada. Tom had hoped to visit him some years ago, but it never happened. Age had caught up with them both. Barton died in 2010 aged ninety-four. His ashes were scattered on his favourite lake in British Columbia on the morning of 15 September, Battle of Britain Day.

John Beazley, who had joined 249 Squadron around the same time as Tom, remained a great friend for seventy years before his death in 2011 at the age of ninety-four. Pat Wells, the South African, and brave as a lion in the air, was also a good friend of Tom's until he died in 2002 aged eighty-five.

Tom had become a focal point for 249's veterans and their families. He kept in touch with the widow of James Nicolson, Fighter Command's only VC of the war, and was approached by Denis Parnall's family to help cast light on his death all those years ago. Tom also met up with the family of Keith Lofts several years after Lofts had been killed in 1951 flying a Vampire jet. Tom readily confesses that he had not found it easy to get on with Lofts during their time together on 249, finding him slightly different to the rest, but when he was given the opportunity to read many letters written by Lofts during the war he realised just how patriotic, thoughtful and sensitive he had been, as well as being totally devoted to the task.

Tom admits to having misjudged him, leaving him humbled and feeling a need to apologise.

And then there was Richard Smithson's family too. Smithson had left 249 at the end of 1940 and was sadly killed the following year. When a distant nephew wrote to Tom trying to find out more about Smithson, he was pleased to help. The brave, smiling, disciplined Smithson had risen from the ranks and was a splendid companion who met all his responsibilities courageously and in the most competent manner.

Long after the war was over, Tom also visited the family of George Barclay. The two had flown together many times during the Battle of Britain. Barclay did not go with 249 to Malta, but the two men did meet up again in 1942 after Barclay had returned to England. Having been shot down over France, he had made the long and difficult journey home with the help of the French Resistance and then via Spain. At the time Tom met up with him again, Barclay was about to go to North Africa where, soon after, he was killed. It was an extremely sad end for such a gifted young man. Many years later, Tom was invited by Barclay's father to the family home in Hertfordshire to read a mass of letters and diaries written by George with a view to having them published. They were published, in 1976, in a book entitled *Battle of Britain Pilot: The Self-Portrait of an RAF Fighter Pilot and Escaper.*

Then there was Bryan Meaker who had been killed during the Battle of Britain. Nearly fifty years later a memorial was placed on the spot where he had fallen to his death. He would never be forgotten. Killed on the same day, and within hours of Meaker's death, was the South African Percy Burton who had been recommended for the Victoria Cross. Tom met his sister later in life during a visit to South Africa. She was, by then, a tiny old lady aged ninety-two, but still very active. Sadly, she would die soon after their meeting, but Tom has always remembered the loyal and splendid family.

Tom also met up with his good wartime friend Ossie Crossey when in Malta during the 1970s and 1980s before Crossey's death. Crossey never let Tom down during their time on 249 together. Some years earlier, during the 1950s, Tom even met up with the old adjutant of 249, Ewart Lohmeyer. Always remembered, Lohmeyer's contribution to the squadron's success was enormous. There were others, too, who had served as non-commissioned officer pilots during the Battle of Britain. Tom would often bump into them at reunions, the most notable being John Beard and Tich Palliser. The list goes on.

When reflecting on his time in command of 41 Squadron during 1942–3, Tom can see how challenging his tour had been. After months of no enemy activity with No. 9 Group, there had then been the difficulty of introducing a new Spitfire variant into operational service, the Mark XII, which was plagued with engine problems and drop-tank issues. There were also dangers because of its clipped-wing design, not in terms of aerodynamic performance but because it gave the Mark XII an unfamiliar shape, resulting in several incidents over southern England when a Spitfire XII was nearly shot down by friendly fire.

Tom acknowledges that at the age of just twenty-two, he had been too young to be in command of a squadron. It was never going to be easy having to explain to families, like the family of young Thomas Scott, how their son or brother had come to be killed, not by enemy action, but in a tragic flying accident. There was far more to commanding a squadron than simply being a good fighter pilot. Tom makes a valid point.

In truth, the seemingly never-ending technical problems of the Spitfire XII meant it struggled to meet its role. And when it came to him resuming operations across the Channel it appeared that nothing much had changed during the past two years. Tom was never an advocate of flying ground-attack missions in an aircraft that had been designed as a fighter. Certainly, in his opinion, the Spitfire, no matter how good it was as a fighter, was not well suited to ground attacks. The view ahead and below from the cockpit was indifferent, and with its exposed radiator it was highly vulnerable to ground fire. Furthermore, its armament of cannons and machine guns was hardly effective against many targets, such as buildings, locomotives and armoured vehicles.

Amongst Tom's most horrific memories of war are when he witnessed its effects close up. In 1944, and after the Allies had landed in Normandy, he crossed the Channel to the 100th Fighter Wing's new headquarters just inland from the Utah beachhead. From there he ventured into the surrounding countryside only to be shocked by the sight of the sickening effects of war on the ground, and the ghastly reminders of death. Such memories would never go away.

As the years moved on, it became increasingly apparent to Tom that the comparatively short but memorable time he had spent with the Americans during 1944 not only affected the rest of his service career, but it also influenced his future life. Knowing and understanding the Americans led to him happily spending more time with them in the years ahead, first as a test pilot when he visited Wright-Patterson Air Force Base in America and later while working in the British Embassy in Washington, DC.

For many years, Tom kept in touch with Tex Sanders, who went on to command the Ninth Air Force, and his good friend Alvin Hill, whom Tom saw several times during the post-war years. Tom and Eileen spent many pleasant times with Hill and his wife. It was a deep and enduring friendship. After both Hills had died at their home in Seattle, Washington, the Neils felt they had lost much more than just two good American friends.

Tom also kept in touch with his former American colleagues Robert A. Patterson and Jim Haun, who both lived long lives but who have now died. As for Sanders, Tom had also seen him several times in the post-war years, including once during his time as a test pilot at Boscombe Down. Sanders, then a general, went to the A&AEE as part of an official visit and once Tom's commandant had learned of their previous connection, Tom was told to look after Sanders for the day. As part of his tour of the establishment, Sanders was introduced to the Vampire. He even flew it that day. With just a minimal explanation of the cockpit, Sanders was off, which Neil thought a brave thing to do as the new jet fighters were not easy to fly. But Sanders landed safely around half an hour later – such was the never-ending courage of Tex Sanders!

Many years later, during a visit to the United States in the 1990s, Tom had hoped to go and see Sanders again at his home in New Mexico. Unfortunately, though, they were unable to meet up because of the travelling distance involved, but Tom did speak to Sanders on the phone. He was shocked and saddened, however, as he listened to the once powerful voice reduced to barely a whisper. Sanders died in 1998 at the age of ninety-four.

As far as Tom's post-war career in the RAF is concerned, he felt privileged to have been invited as a guest to the A&AEE at Boscombe Down many years after he had been a test pilot there in the aftermath of the war. Since then, of course, much had changed. The establishment, and indeed Boscombe Down, had developed into a dauntingly impressive place and he came away with a mental picture of bright new buildings and underground mysteries, and of high technology divisions. But, on that day, no aeroplanes.

After his visit, Tom left Boscombe Down with his head reeling from an acute attack of nostalgia. It was all quite different to his time there, although he considers his training to become a test pilot not the best. His short course had seemed rather disorganised because of the move to Cranfield, and the long course was not much better. Too much time was spent in the classroom and he would later describe the test-flying tuition as amateurish. But he did enjoy being at Boscombe Down and he liked the area. There might have been precious few facilities, but they did have plenty of aircraft to fly!

Although Tom remembers test-flying as being exciting at times, it was in the main, he says, routine business. But it was also very dangerous, and he was disappointed that those directly in control of the work being carried out by the test pilots were rarely qualified in, or conversant with the nature of, their work. One way or another, test-flying claimed many splendid lives and, looking back, Tom feels their efforts were not that much appreciated. In fact, he often thinks of his time as a test pilot as being four rather unhappy years.

Happier times, though, were the years spent in Egypt while in command of 208 Squadron. Abu Sueir was full of delightful people and his family absolutely loved living there. His tour, in fact, produced some of the happiest moments of his post-war career. The only thing he would like to have done later in his life, perhaps, was to have written about biblical history and his time in Egypt.

The decision to leave the RAF after twenty-five years could not have been an easy one. His career had gone well up until that point to reach the rank of wing commander, but he was already in his mid-forties and had no idea of what the service held in store for him should he stay. The chances of further flying were slim, and he knew that he was not best suited to staff work. Furthermore, there were long periods when he had seen precious little of his family, and his posting as a test pilot during the post-war years, followed by his overseas tours in Egypt and America, had taken him out of the main stream for promotion. Taking everything into account, the decision to leave the RAF and to move on had been the right one.

It is understandable why Tom had thought the family's future might lie in America, but it soon became abundantly clear that life in America outside the RAF was going to be very different to the time he had spent with the Americans during his service career. While things might not have worked out in the United States how he had hoped, and he had not particularly enjoyed working in the shoe industry, the world of shoes did eventually lead him to the quiet south Norfolk countryside where he has spent nearly fifty very happy years.

Retirement gave Tom the chance to pursue his interest in writing and from his family home in Thwaite St Mary he has written some wonderful books. His creative writing skills and vivid accounts of his past experiences make all his books a must-read. Even though he is now in his late nineties, he continues to produce books about things that happened all those years ago.

Always keen to meet up with old chums and to remember those who have departed, Tom has been an active member of associations and a regular, and popular, attendee at reunions and functions over the years, wherever they may have been held. Amongst the notable positions he has held are President of the 249 Squadron Association and Chairman of the Battle of Britain Fighter Association, which

At the National Memorial to the Few, Capel-le-Ferne, Kent.

was formed in 1958 with full membership only available to Allied aircrew entitled to the Battle of Britain clasp worn on the 1939–45 Star. As numbers have dwindled in more recent years, the role of the BBFA has moved more towards ensuring that what was achieved in 1940 is remembered long into the future. Tom is also a member of the 208 Squadron Association, while away from the many RAF associations he was a local councillor on the South Norfolk District Council during the 1980s.

There is nothing Tom would have changed about his life and, as he says, he has no regrets. But in August 2014 his world all but fell apart when his wife, Eileen, died a few days short of her ninety-sixth birthday. Described by everyone who had the pleasure to know her as every bit as charming as Tom, she was everything to him.

Tom describes Eileen as the most beautiful and talented woman he had ever known. When reflecting on when they had first met, he remembers the air force was Eileen's life and she had endured all the bombing while a plotter at Kenley during the Battle of Britain. They had only met briefly at Biggin Hill in 1942 and it was not until the following year, when Tom returned to Kent with the Americans, that he saw her again. They had soon agreed to marry but not until the end of the war. Eileen then had to cope with the upheaval of being a service wife, and even after Tom had left the RAF there was still moving around before the couple finally settled at their home in south Norfolk. They had, he has added up, thirty-five homes during their long and happy married life together. Eileen had always been so supportive and stood by Tom, no matter what. He cannot speak too highly of her. She did nothing but good. It was the epitome of love.

Tom has been blessed with three wonderful sons. He loves everything about them. It was unfortunate, Tom says, that there were long periods throughout his life when he was not able to be with them. He had not only missed them as children, but he had missed so many things as they were growing up. His sons now have their own wonderful families, and they all mean the world to Tom.

On 15 September 2015, to mark the seventy-fifth anniversary of the Battle of Britain, Tom took to the air again in a Spitfire, courtesy of the Boultbee Flight Academy at Goodwood Aerodrome in West Sussex, the site of the former Fighter Command airfield of RAF Westhampnett. The aircraft, SM520, was originally built as a single-seat Mark IX but has since been restored and converted to a two-seat Spitfire TR9 trainer and is owned by Steve Boultbee Brooks. It felt good to fly over the south coast of England again, where Tom had so gallantly fought seventy-five years before, after which he was able to spend some time with HRH Prince Harry. It was a truly wonderful day.

In 2016, at a ceremony held at the RAF Club in London, Tom was awarded the Légion d'Honneur, France's highest military honour, in recognition of his services in helping secure France's liberation during the Second World War. Then, in 2017, two of the Battle of Britain Memorial Flight's fighters – a Spitfire and a Hurricane – were painted with new code letters on either side to celebrate four Battle of Britain fighter pilots who were still alive at the time; it was a simple, yet emotive, way of the current generation thanking theirs for their sacrifices made. Chosen for the left-hand side of Hurricane LF363, the same aircraft that Tom had flown back in 1951, was GN-F, Tom's personal markings worn on two of his Hurricanes (P3616 and V7313) while serving with 249 Squadron during the Battle of Britain.

At the time of writing, Tom is just completing his ninety-eighth year. He looks extremely well and is never anything but the most charming and wonderful company. He is one of just a few survivors of a very special generation and he still has a presence that ensures that whenever he speaks people stop to listen.

Being one of just a handful of the Few still alive, Tom is still forever in demand – by the RAF, by television companies, by journalists, by historians, and, of course, by authors – particularly so this year, 2018, when Tom is centre stage at many events to mark the 100th anniversary of the RAF. A day rarely passes without Tom receiving letters or phone calls asking him to do something or asking him about someone. His legendary status as one of the Few is only rivalled by other heroes, such as holders of the Victoria Cross.

For many years now, as the Few have become fewer, Tom Neil has become the face of the Battle of Britain. He still tries to do as much as he can. Neither his age, nor the occasional operation, seems to get in his way. It is a privilege and honour to know him. He is one of the last of the Few.

Select Bibliography

Ashworth, Chris, *Action Stations: 5 – Military Airfields of the South-West* (Patrick Stephens, Wellingborough, 1982)

Barclay, George, *Battle of Britain Pilot* (Haynes, Yeovil, 2012)

Bowyer, Chaz, *For Valour: The Air V.C.s* (William Kimber, London, 1978)

Brew, Steve, *Blood, Sweat and Valour: 41 Squadron RAF 1942-1945* (Fonthill, Oxford, 2012)

Cull, Brian, *249 at War* (Grub Street, London, 1997)

Duke, Neville, *Test Pilot* (Grub Street, London, 1992)

Halfpenny, Bruce Barrymore, *Action Stations: 4 – Military Airfields of Yorkshire* (Patrick Stephens, Cambridge, 1982)

Halley, James J., *The Squadrons of the Royal Air Force & Commonwealth 1918–1988* (Air Britain, Tonbridge, 1988)

Haynes, Terry, *Abu Sueir Diary: A National Serviceman's Days in the Canal Zone* (Terry Haynes/Short Run Book Co., Maidenhead/Windsor, 2000)

Hough, Richard, and Denis Richards, *The Battle of Britain: The Jubilee History* (Guild Publishing, London, 1990)

Jacobs, Peter, *Aces of the Luftwaffe: The Jagdflieger in the Second World War* (Frontline, Barnsley, 2014)

——, *Airfields of 11 Group* (Pen & Sword, Barnsley, 2005)

——, *Fortress Island Malta: Defence and Re-Supply During the Siege* (Pen & Sword, Barnsley, 2016)

James, T. C. G., *The Battle of Britain – RAF Official Histories* (Frank Cass, London, 2000)

Lee, ACM Sir David, *Flight from the Middle East* (MOD Air Historical Branch, London, 1978)

Mason, Peter D., *Nicolson VC: The Full and Authorised Biography of James Brindley Nicolson* (Geerings, Ashford, 1991)

Neil, Thomas, *From the Cockpit: Spitfire* (Ian Allan, London, 1990)

——, *Gun Button to Fire* (Amberley, Stroud, 2010)

———, *Onward to Malta* (Airlife, Shrewsbury, 1992)

———, *Scramble* (Amberley, Stroud, 2016)

———, *The Silver Spitfire* (Weidenfeld & Nicolson, London, 2013)

Pitchfork, Graham, *Forever Vigilant: Naval 8/208 Squadron RAF, A Centenary of Service from 1916 to 2016* (Grub Street, London, 2016)

Ramsey, Winston G., *The Battle of Britain Then and Now – Fifth Edition* (After the Battle, London, 1989)

Rawlings, John, and Hilary Sedgwick, *Learn to Test, Test to Learn: History of the Empire Test Pilots' School* (Airlife, Shrewsbury, 1991)

Shores, Christopher, and Clive Williams, *Aces High* (Grub Street, London, 1994)

———, and Brian Cull, with Nicola Malizia, *Malta: The Hurricane Years 1940–41* (Grub Street, London, 1987)

Smith, David J., *Action Stations: 7 – Military Airfields of Scotland, the North-East and Northern Ireland* (Patrick Stephens, Cambridge, 1983)

Spick, Mike, *Luftwaffe Fighter Aces* (Greenhill, London, 1996)

Woodman, Richard, *Malta Convoys 1940–1943* (John Murray, London, 2000)

Wynn, Kenneth G., *Men of the Battle of Britain* (Gliddon, Norwich, 1989)

Official Documents

AIR 27/425: No. 41 Squadron Operations Record Book with Appendices, 1941–1943

AIR 27/425/41–62: No. 41 Squadron Summaries of Events, September 1942–July 1943

AIR 27/430: No. 41 Squadron Operations Record Book Appendices 1943

AIR 27/430/1–7: No. 41 Squadron, Operations Record Book Appendices, January–July 1943

AIR 27/1498: No. 249 Squadron Operations Record Book, 1 May 1940 – 31 December 1943

AIR 27/1498/1–21: No. 249 Squadron Summaries of Events, 1 May 1940 – 30 June 1942; and Records of Events, July 1940–April 1941

AIR 27/2622: No. 208 Squadron Operations Record Book, 1950–1955

AIR 50/96/101: Neil, Pilot Officer, 249 Squadron, Combat Reports (15 September 1940, 18 September 1940, 27 September 1940, 15 October 1940, 7 November 1940, 6 December 1940)

Index